PRACTICAL AND THEORETICAL ASPECTS OF PSYCHOANALYSIS

PRACTICAL AND THEORETICAL ASPECTS OF PSYCHOANALYSIS

Revised Edition

LAWRENCE S. KUBIE, M.D.

INTERNATIONAL UNIVERSITIES PRESS, INC.
New York

Library of Congress Catalog Card Number: 74-6433
ISBN: 0-8236-4181-3

Manufactured in the United States of America

CONTENTS

Section I

Chapter I
INTRODUCTORY

This book was first published in 1936 by W. W. Norton & Co. of New York City under the briefer title of *Practical Aspects of Psychoanalysis*. It is an indication of the growth that has occurred in the intervening years that the 1936 edition was dedicated to the future of the New York Psychoanalytic Institute (at that time a small organization barely five years old). The foreword pointed out that the book was written, "to help people recognize sound psychoanalytical procedure when they meet it and to introduce them to those institutes for the training of psychoanalysts which at present constitute their best protection against the charlatans in this field." It went on to say, "In part, therefore, this is a fighting book, in that one of its purposes in clarifying the meaning of psychoanalysis is to exterminate pseudo analysis by inadequately trained or irresponsible analysts, whether these are found within or without the official psychoanalytic fold." The book was often viewed as rigidly doctrinaire, but it must be pointed out that the above words called attention to the very fact that "inadequately trained and irresponsible analysts" could be found both within and without official circles. Clearly, criticism of the lack of adequate training should not have been confused with a rigid attack on any and all deviations from orthodox theory. In a personal note to the author, Freud called this a "very useful book."

In a brief editorial published in the *Journal of Nervous and Mental Disease* (1963),[1] I again emphasized my own ingrained and lifelong rejection of all orthodoxies. Among other things I pointed out that a true heterodoxy requires a continuous and watchful skepticism about one's own views as well as those of others. I expressed my regret that Freud, like most fallible human beings, could allow *himself* to be heterodox, but found it difficult to accept the heterodoxies of his colleagues and followers.

In 1950 a revised and enlarged edition of this book appeared under the title *Practical and Theoretical Aspects of Psychoanalysis*, published by International Universities Press of New York City. It is significant that in this edition I expressed some dissents from accepted dogmas. These troublesome reflections had been with me for a long time; here for the first time I explored them in writing. In keeping with this change, the dedication also was altered to read, "To analytic patients everywhere, to their families and medical advisors, and to my colleagues." It was not dedicated to any one institute, as the first edition had been, or to analysis, but to our patients.

[1] *Editorial note:* Throughout this book, dates within parentheses and unaccompanied by a name refer to publications by Kubie (see Reference list).

The second edition continued my earlier attempt to inform prospective patients, their families and friends, medical, psychiatric, and psychological advisors, and also the clergy about what it is like to go into psychoanalytic treatment; the role of the onlookers; how they can help or hinder; why they are usually kept at some distance from the treatment; how psychoanalysis is usually practiced and why it is practiced in this way; how long it may take and why it takes that long; why the duration and frequency of the sessions may vary; what it may cost, how this is calculated, and how to budget for it. Furthermore, because there have always been some people who called themselves psychoanalysts in spite of the fact that nothing in their training or experience gave them a right to do so, it tried to give prospective patients and their families and advisors some hints that would help them to distinguish between those practitioners who had in fact been analytically trained and those who pretended to be analysts. Such distinctions had nothing to do with the theories of divergent schools or their comparative values. It was, rather, an effort to correct through education some of the abuses prevalent at that time.

Even this effort had some unanticipated, unintended, and undesirable side effects. By sounding as though *any* deviation from a uniform pattern was undesirable (which was not my intent) the book again created an impression of rigidity, not as extreme as had been true of the first edition, but still troubling; and for this it was deservedly criticized. At the same time, we must face the fact that it is not always easy to distinguish between modifications based on clinical and scientific considerations and those which are opportunistic. I cannot claim that either of my two attempts at clarification was wholly successful.

Over the intervening years, I have written occasionally about many unresolved problems first discussed in the original book. Where it seems desirable, I will refer to those various publications so that readers who want to reconsider these problems by referring to earlier articles can review them in greater detail.

In the revised edition of 1950, I tried to soften some of the harshness and apparent rigidity of the original arguments and also to add a more inclusive consideration of theoretical concepts. This had become desirable largely because by that time people generally had grown more sophisticated about psychoanalysis so that students, prospective patients, and their families and physicians approached it with a clearer and fuller anticipatory understanding of its nature. This was true at least in our larger centers, although those who turned to psychoanalysis for help still continued to be a weighted sample not broadly representative of the population as a whole. Certainly they were never a true sample of the "backwoods."

There still is need for a meticulous explanation of the facts, buttressed by a more complete presentation of basic reasoning. These facts were introduced in 1950 partly through the addition of a few extra chapters and partly by expanding chapters from the 1936 edition.

The present revision carries this process further. There will be more discussion of related theoretical issues built around the core of the problems that concerned us between 1930 and 1950. In the thirties, among those who called themselves "analysts" and practiced what they called "analysis," were many who deviated from Freud's position and chose *of their own accord* new names for their techniques and theories. Over the years this has actually contributed to their survival as independent groups by calling attention to the fact that there are different kinds of analytic help available.

Without pretending to set up a new school or to be a psychoanalytic "Messiah" I have deviated slowly, steadily, and progressively from many colleagues in many ways. This was why, even before I retired from practice and left New York City in 1959, I had voluntarily ceased to teach at the New York Psychoanalytic Institute. I did not want to teach anything of which I was no longer certain. Nor did I want to add to the confusions of our students by imposing on them ideas which were still tentative and untried. It seemed kinder, wiser, and more honest to go through my own private soul-searching in silence. I therefore ceased teaching, although I continued to present papers at meetings of the New York Psychoanalytic Society and Institute as well as before other psychoanalytic societies and at meetings of the American Psychoanalytic Association.

Some "heterodox" colleagues still recall the rigidity that had marked the 1936 edition of this book. Some "orthodox" colleagues recall only my later misgivings. Consequently, one group has tended ever since to look upon me as too heterodox to speak to, while the others have tended to look upon me as too orthodox. Since I have never been one to have truck with any doxologies, not even the doxologies of those naive souls who saw themselves as great innovators (e.g., Horney, Rado, and Klein), this has on the whole amused me, although at times it has also made me feel somewhat lonely among my colleagues. I tried to express some of this in 1963, in the editorial already alluded to.

Furthermore, years of analytic practice led to an expanding experience as a consultant on the clinical experiences of other analysts (including men of long and broad experience). These forced me to realize that, *although for scientific and exploratory purposes the strict and constant conformity to basic or "orthodox" analytical principles and procedures had certain specific scientific values,* which have been discussed in many previous publications (1952c, 1956e), there is not one shred of evidence that either orthodoxy or heterodoxy solves more of our psychotherapeutic problems. There is no evidence, for example, that strict conformity increases the incidence of success, just as there is no evidence that nonconformity has increased the incidence of failure. I became convinced that it will continue to be impossible to make significant comparisons of the results of theoretical and technical modifications until we develop three things, to wit: (a) a new and more precise nosological system (1971b); (b) more precise criteria of change (1968a), whether for better or for worse—for improvement or for deterioration; and (c) more compelling indices of *when* to make such evaluations (1973a). These issues are at the core of a cluster of technical problems that still confront the analyst and demand humble, meticulous, objective study.

I therefore close this introduction with an observation applicable not only to psychoanalysis and its supporters, but also to its critics, as well as to all psychologies, including the simple, unschooled psychology of the layman. In a thousand ways every day without knowing it the layman expresses theories about psychology. Like M. Jourdain in Moliere's "Le Bourgeois Gentilhomme" who had been talking prose all of his life without knowing it, the average layman has been talking naively all his life in terms of psychological theory and even analytical theory, but without realizing it. He talks about being more or less afraid without being able to measure fear or what he means by more or less. He talks about being more or less angry or depressed without any measuring rod for anger or depression. He talks of being stronger or weaker with no measure or criteria of strength or weakness. He can measure crudely the *consequences* of fear, anger, depression, or elation, and in so doing has confused impressions of quantitative variations in the *consequences* of affective processes with measures of the *strength* of the affective process and drives themselves. This has led to confusion in theory and also in technique. Unfortunately, Freud himself, as well as Anna Freud, has been vulnerable to this same fallacy in all considerations of so-called energic, instinctual, libidinal processes. (This difficult issue was first discussed in several earlier papers [1947b, 1948a, 1956a].) Similarly, the layman, like his professional mentor, often confuses dogmatic thinking with explanatory concepts, as when he says that if a boy does not work it is *because* he is lazy. Even Freud makes this error. This misuse of purely descriptive epithets as explanations is found not only in the words of the man on the street, but also in the laboratory of the experimentalist, in the consulting room of the clinician, in the meetings of Psychoanalytic Associations, and in the clinical section of the American Psychological Association. We were all laymen before we could claim any technical psychological wisdom, and the struggle to shed the fallacies of lay psychologizing is long and difficult for all of us, especially for the analyst.

For this there is at least one obvious reason. All psychologies deal with transitory moments of human behavior, some sudden and some gradual, some isolated, and some repeated and recurrent. Each of these is a moment of interaction between man and his animate or inanimate environment, between man and man. But the moment of interaction passes and can never be recaptured or re-experienced or re-enacted precisely as it originally occurred, simply because the original event changed the participants. Furthermore, as I have already pointed out, our initial perceptions of these interactions, and our memories and reports of them are all fallible, and the fragments retrieved have to be represented by words—words that in turn are fallible representatives of events that cannot be recaptured and that, in retrospect, have become abstractions. It is precisely here that we are most vulnerable to fallacy: for these abstractions tend to become reified and are then dealt with as though they were objects, indeed, as though they themselves were the possessors of concentrated and variable powers, qualities, and aptitudes (in press). The mere recognition of these events and the description and naming of them give us no right to imagine that we have explained some aspects of human experience and human behavior, when at best we have only described them in borrowed metaphors. Thus, instead of speaking of *"the consciousness process"* we speak of *"Consciousness."* Instead of speaking of *"unconsciousness processes"* we speak of *"The Unconscious."* Instead of speaking of *"preconscious processing"* of data we speak of *"The Preconscious."* Psychoanalysis has paid a high price in conceptual errors for these logical and linguistic errors (1954d).

This edition is dedicated also to those colleagues and teachers who have taught me largely by the ferment, challenge, and stimulus of our disagreements. Next to what I have learned from my patients, these friendly, uncompromising, and thought-provoking disagreements with certain colleagues have been my best teachers, especially when paralleled by the heart-

11

warming fact that such disagreements have not cost me their friendship, or my admiration and affection for them, or my sense of indebtedness to them. I have already said that I have always been an heretic. It is natural, therefore, that I value most highly those colleagues with whom my heretical inclinations have so often led me into disagreements. A partial list of such colleagues and teachers must include the late Drs. Edward Glover, Ernst Kris, Bertram D. Lewin, David Rapaport, René Spitz, and Herman Nunberg; Grete Bibring, Phyllis Greenacre, and Sydney G. Margolin. The patients with whom and from whom I have learned so much are if anything even more important, yet, for obvious reasons must remain anonymous.

Chapter II
CORE CONCEPTS IN PSYCHOANALYSIS

Psychoanalysis is a specific technique for studying and influencing the form, distribution, and utilization of psychological processes. Its goal is to free the patient (or analysand) from enslavement to that obligatory repetitiveness which is at the heart of the neurotic process (1930, 1941b, 1968a). In short it aims to recapture for the patient the freedom for continuing and evolving change that from early childhood may have been impaired and progressively lost as the neurotic process moved gradually toward psychotic disorganization (1967c, 1974a).

The Domain and the Technical Objectives of Psychoanalysis

A scientific method is comprehensible only when one understands what it attempts to do in relation to some natural phenomena. Psychoanalysis is a complex instrument, and its subject matter and its aims cannot be summarized simply; but they can be subsumed under the following cumulative series of propositions:
(1) Human psychological processes consist of a rapid, continuous stream of what the old Wurzburg school of psychology called "imageless" thought.

(2) This stream, which Freud (1900, p. 541) later called "preconscious" and which William James referred to as "the fringe of consciousness," is active when we are awake or asleep—so long as we are alive and not in a profound coma.

(3) At the same time a fragmentary, weighted preconscious process of sampling of this continuous stream occurs.

(4) These samples are subject to conscious symbolic representation.

But it is this imageless or preconscious stream that is at the core of all human mental processes, whether we refer to it as the "fringe of consciousness" or as "preconscious" processing. By either, we mean the incessant stream of processing of all of the bits of data, past and present, that, whether we are awake or asleep, impinge upon the central nervous system through every sensory modality, and whether these arise from outside the body (exteroceptive) or from within the body itself (proprioceptive and enteroceptive). These afferent messages to the central nervous system are the result of changes in the body or in the world around sufficient in amplitude and in rate of change to register. They also include those bits of input arising from memory imprints, as projections of past experiences in anticipation of the future. All of these supply fresh bits of afferent input to the preconscious stream. Let me repeat that the fragmentary and weighted samples of this complex, imageless, rushing stream are at the core of all human mentation, once they have been represented by conscious symbols to make up the concurrent stream of conscious processing.

(5) At the same time, another concurrent stream of influences arises wherever the relationships are distorted or interrupted between the conscious symbols and those items of information the symbols are supposed to represent. When this occurs, the conscious symbolic process no longer represents them accurately for purposes of rumination, planning, and communication. These distortions in the relation of the symbols to their referents introduce interruptions, discontinuities, and dissociations into the stream of conscious symbolic representation to produce what are usually called "unconscious processes."

(6) Every moment of mental life is thus a conjoint product of preconscious processes and of concurrent conscious samples operating in varying degrees under the influence of unconscious distortions.

(7) Clearly, then, at every moment of life, those processes we label "unconscious" play an important if variable role in determining much of our behavior.

(8) Wherever these unconscious disruptions play a dominant role, the conscious and preconscious streams, and also resulting behavior itself, cannot be influenced materially without first altering the distorting influences of the underlying unconscious psychological processes.

(9) In order to do this it is necessary to find out what these are.

(10) This in turn requires the use of special techniques, among which the pioneer, and still one of the more important, is psychoanalysis.

(11) The purpose of this technique is to overcome the many internal obstacles interfering with the emergence of unconscious processes into awareness.

(12) At the same time the technique aims to modify the disturbing and sometimes destructive influence of unconscious processes, whether they remain unconscious or are brought into the open.

(13) Therefore, in therapy, in prevention of illness, and in education, the inclusive goal of psychoanalysis is to broaden the domain of conscious awareness and control in human life and to shrink that darker empire in which unconscious processes play the dominant role, so that the essential freedom to change and to continue to change, which has been lost or impaired in various phases of each individual's development, can be regained and, with it, the freedom to learn, to mature, and to grow (1968a, 1974a).

This summary embodies much controversial matter; but instead of entering into the pros and cons of these controversies, the summary itself will constitute the working hypothesis of this book.

Psychoanalysis, then, has as its goal the uncovering and modification of the distorting influence of "unconscious" psychological processes so as to diminish their relative importance. With a technique designed to achieve this purpose, psychoanalysis attempts to prevent and to relieve suffering whenever it is caused primarily by mental processes of which the patient is himself unaware. Psychoanalysis cannot be used to shield the patient from the accidents of life. Nor can it prevent diseases that are primarily organic in origin. In such situations the most it can do is to increase the patient's ability to cope with adversity and disease by lessening the destructive influence of stresses that originate in unconscious conflicts. Therapeutically its significance proves greatest where the unconscious forces are most important; and by and large its value is most restricted where purely environmental forces or bodily changes play a primary role in the process of illness.

Psychoanalysis began as a treatment for the neuroses, and primarily for but one type of neurosis. Gradually it has extended its domain, sometimes successfully, sometimes with difficulties. In the history of medicine, something similar has happened whenever a new medical technique has been discovered. Some degree of overexpansion is inevitable for a time. Whether it be a technique of investigation or of treatment, it is tried out hopefully on every old and unsolved problem. Like Leuwenhoek with his microscope, the psychoanalyst has been eager to examine every mental aberration that comes to hand.

The basic relationship of psychoanalysis to health in general will be more clearly understood when the concept of the neurotic process is described in Chapters IV and V.

The Name

In medicine every specific method of treatment or of investigation needs its own descriptive name. A tumor

may be treated by surgery, X Ray, radium, chemo-
therapeutic agents, or by other means. Without a
specific name for each method, much confusion would
result, both in scientific writings and in popular understanding. The same holds true for the various techniques and theoretical systems within the general
domain of psychiatry.

Certain of the early workers who deviated from
Freudian psychoanalysis recognized the soundness of
this principle and coined special designations for their
divergent methods—for instance, the "Analytical Psychology" of Jung, the "Individual Psychology" of Adler, or the "Phyloanalysis" of Burrows. Some more
recent innovators prefer to speak of themselves, and
with reason, not as *anti*-Freudian but as *neo*-Freudian;
and for their varied degrees of divergence in theory or
technique they continue to use the term "psychoanalysis." Just where to draw the line is difficult to say. It
would certainly not be wise to be arbitrarily dogmatic.
The general principle is clear, but its application is far
from easy. It is in everyone's interest so to limit the
term that it will characterize for laymen and physicians alike a recognizable set of basic hypotheses and a
related method for dealing with psychological problems. This enables everyone to understand what the
term means and it makes possible accurate comparisons of the relative efficacy of different methods.

At the same time, the term must be used broadly
enough to allow room for those changes and developments that come with experience and technical experi-

mentation. Otherwise there is danger of stagnation. How the present organization of psychoanalysis tries to avoid this danger will be explained below.

Dictum of the British Medical Association

In 1929, after a careful investigation by an impartial committee composed of physicians, surgeons, psychologists, psychiatrists, and analysts, the British Medical Association formulated the following definition and rules concerning the use of the term "psychoanalysis."

> There is in the medical and general public the tendency to use the term "psychoanalysis" in a very loose and wide sense. This term can legitimately be applied only to the method evolved by Freud and to the theories derived from use of this method. A psychoanalyst is therefore a person who uses Freud's technique, and anyone who does not use this technique should not, whatever other method he may employ, be called a psychoanalyst. In accordance with this definition and for the purpose of avoiding confusion, the term "psychoanalyst" is properly reserved for members of the International Psychoanalytic Association . . .
>
> Much confusion and misunderstanding relative to psychoanalysis has arisen from a failure to recognize and adopt the definition herein indicated. Thus, clearly, criticisms of psychoanalytical theory or practice should be confined to the teaching and methods of those who are psychoanalysts in the true sense of this term. This is not

always so, and the Committee has received a number of reports and statements adverse to psychoanalysis as a form of medical treatment which on inquiry are found to be based upon methods put into operation not by psychoanalysts, but by other practitioners who adopt or accept the name but lack the qualifications [*British Medical Journal*, 1929, p. 266].

This dictum, while it cleared the air of much confusion then current, is too restrictive for present-day thinking. How it has been modified and become more elastic over the years will become clear as we go on.

The Present Status

As the demand for psychoanalytic treatment grew rapidly, the statement of the British Medical Association helped to check the exploitation of human need by men who pretended to be psychoanalysts but who lacked analytic training. The year 1929, however, was a period of transition. There were not enough institutes to meet the demand for training. The institutes of that time were young and small and had not developed much individual prestige. Consequently, the only authoritative source of sanction was the International Psychoanalytic Association.

Here, a new danger arose. To look upon any scientific body, however wise, as a sole or final arbiter on any scientific issue creates the danger of premature standardization and excessive rigidity. During the late nineteen-thirties psychoanalysts began to decentralize the authority of the international body, a process hastened by the years of Nazi domination of Europe and by World War II. Some of the continental psychoanalytic societies and institutes were temporarily destroyed; some were decimated by emigration and deaths; some went underground. By the end of the war, the International Psychoanalytic Association consisted only of the Swiss, the British, and the Scandinavian societies, plus the societies that made up the American Psychoanalytic Association, some South American groups, a group in India and possibly one in Japan. After the war the old groups gradually formed again and new by-laws for the International Psychoanalytic Association were prepared. Under this instrument, the centralized control of training and of scientific issues, formerly exercised by the International, was eliminated; the sole remaining function of the International was to provide a forum for the exchange of scientific views and experience. All affiliated national societies or continental groupings of societies became arbiters of their own affairs. In this way, diversification of theory and technique could develop within a framework of tried and proven principles, and a healthy emancipation occurred in the practical definition of psychoanalysis and of psychoanalysts.

For the time being, however, in order to maintain high standards of training and to prevent the development of new confusions, it continues to be useful to define psychoanalysis as the professional activity of a group of men who have gone through a certain type of

21

training. This in turn is acknowledged by their election to membership in local psychoanalytic societies, which are affiliated with and recognized by the appropriate national or continental association. The decentralizing of authority described above makes it possible to use this as a practical working definition of psychoanalysis without serious danger of excessive rigidity and over-standardization. The popular notion of who is a psychoanalyst will always be the truest index of the level of popular understanding of the essential scientific aspects of psychoanalytic theory and technique. This understanding will grow as a result of education both within the medical profession as a whole and among the laity (Lewin and Ross, 1960). One of the purposes of a book such as the present one is to assist in that process of education.

Chapter III

WHAT CONSTITUTES
AN ENLIGHTENED ATTITUDE
TOWARD PSYCHOLOGICAL
AILMENTS

Until recently, people thought it was easy to be psychologically well and that one was either wholly well or wholly sick. The "mind" was a unit, all of a piece. If anything at all was wrong with it, then you were either an eccentric or "crazy" and in the latter case you should be put away in a special hospital. This would be necessary either because of the violence of your emotions or the "craziness" (i.e., the inaccuracy) of your ideas about the world. Gradually, however, the existence of a subtler but more frequent group of psychological disturbances was recognized. These came to be called the "psychoneuroses," or, alternatively and for short, the "neuroses." For a long time the neuroses had been held in contempt. They were thought to be the result of some defect occurring only in unfortunate individuals who were somehow inferior to the rest. The word "neurotic" became a colloquial epithet, implying weakness or inferiority, except in certan paradoxical exceptions where the hypothetical inferiority seemed by some redeeming alchemy to have been transmuted into genius.

To an extent, this attitude still persists even among physicians. An internist who would not think of saying that a patient with typhoid was "typhoidic," or that a patient with a cold was "coldic," does not hesitate to speak of the patient with a neurosis as "neurotic," implying, whether or not he realizes it, that there is something weak and inferior about the patient. There is clearly no logic in this; yet to replace condescension by respect in the world's attitude toward patients with neuroses is proving to be a slow process. The popular assumption that more women have neuroses than men is another expression of this condescending attitude. Statistics from private and clinic practice prove that the reverse is actually true. People are slowly coming to realize that there is such a thing as a universal neurotic potential out of which evolves a neurotic process that occurs in varying degrees in every living man, woman, and child, and that this process in turn sometimes crystallizes into the neurotic state. This neurotic process can, under appropriate circumstances, go on to psychotic disorganization (1951b, 1963c, 1967c, 1974b).

This admission comes slowly because man realizes that, once he accepts the universality of the potential and neurotic processes, he will have to face their manifestations and consequences in his own life. And once he acknowledges this, he will have to do something about it. The admission comes slowly also because a special aura of guilt attaches itself to all psychological disturbances. In the mythology of unconscious fantasies, mind-sickness is the ultimate punishment for sin. To admit that neuroses are universal is therefore to admit that we are all sinners, and sinners in a secret and shameful sense. There are thus powerful unconscious forces obstructing acceptance of the simple fact that the neurotic process is ubiquitous.

In the face of this obscurantism, the analyst must convince his fellow man that subtle and at times almost accidental factors determine whether this universal neurotic process will manifest itself in frank neurotic symptoms, or in subtle personality traits or, ultimately, as psychotic disorganization. He must demonstrate that obvious neurotic symptoms may be sharply circumscribed so as to leave the rest of the personality not only unimpaired but often highly endowed, both emotionally and intellectually, while the subtler manifestations of the neurotic process can escape recognition by hiding in the personality as a whole or in an entire way of life. The psychoanalyst hopes that ultimately the distinction between "neurotic" and "normal" will lose some of its misleading implications, as people come to realize that the one is a person with obvious symptoms and the other a similar individual who unwittingly has been able to conceal his symptoms in his personality.

In World War II, in every land and every culture, wherever a statistically adequate cross-section of all young adult males was called up for military service, psychological disabilities were found to be more wide-spread than any other, regardless of geographic, national, and cultural variables. In the United States these disabilities accounted for the rejection of one out of eight registrants for military service. Furthermore, despite efforts at preliminary screening, one third of the discharges from training camp were for similar disabilities. Among those discharged after combat, the psychological apparatus again proved to be the most frequent cause. Civilian experience demonstrates equally clearly that a subtle neurotic process is a universal component of human nature. Experienced internists point out that nearly seventy per cent of the patients who pass through their private offices suffer from psychological troubles. The same incidence is found in the outpatient departments and wards of general hospitals (1942b, 1947c).

From the top to the bottom of the economic and social ladder, in large urban centers, in isolated villages, on farms or in the woods, the same neurotic difficulties are found and in approximately the same proportion. To illustrate: one sturdy family had served for many decades as fishing guides on a remote lake in Canada. One summer they found a psychiatrist among the guests, and, before he left, practically every member of two generations of that family had consulted him about neurotic symptoms that were indistinguishable from those confronting him in his private office and in the outpatient clinic of a New York City hospital.

Attitudes to Psychological Ailments

When we speak of psychological difficulties so wide-spread that no one escapes them, obviously we cannot mean illnesses involving so profound a disorganization of the personality that the patient must be hospitalized for his own good and for that of his family and community. Such patients are numerous enough: in 1950, 630,000 beds in United States mental hospitals and at least 415,000 more needed. But of the sufferers from the psychological ailments we have been describing, the vast majority will never become sick enough to require hospital protection. It is safe to say that since every human being has some manifestations of the neurotic process, every psychotic patient in a mental hospital has also had a neurosis. Moreover, it is probable that in many of these cases early treatment of the neurosis *might* have averted the ultimate total breakdown. This does not mean, of course, that every neurotic, if untreated, is headed for a similar disaster.

Statistical samples indicate that in this country alone there are several million people who carry on their lives in the face of a daily struggle with troublesome psychological symptoms which hamper them without wholly incapacitating them: bouts of seemingly cause-less depression, sudden spurts of terror or anger, rigid obligatory rituals of thought or action (i.e., compulsive counting or compulsive handwashing), phobias that impose painful restrictions on their freedom (such as a terror of certain animals or of dirt, or an inability to go out in the street or more than a certain distance from home or higher than the lower floors of any building),

27

or uncomfortable physical symptoms—with or without disturbances of bodily functions—for which there is no organic cause. These are only a few of the more obvious of the wide variety of symptoms of the frank neuroses. They are found in almost a tenth of the adult population, and in early childhood they occur universally as transient episodes; yet they constitute the smaller part of the total problem.

Only exceptionally does the neurotic process occur as the result of some startling or unusual occurrence or some melodramatic life situation. The rule is rather that it results from the everyday stresses of family living. Indeed, there is evidence that it is launched together with the acquisition of man's highest gift—to wit, the use of symbolic speech. Until our educational and child-rearing techniques have solved this problem, the neurotic process will continue to haunt human development (1974a). Until we have learned a great deal more about these universal emotional stresses of human life, neuroses will continue to arise everywhere. A gradual recognition of this fact is making us humbler and more tolerant toward all manifestations of the neurotic process. From the study of individual patients, we can hope in time to learn how to prevent much of the neurotic suffering that attends human life today.

The ultimate prevention of the neurotic process can bring humanity to its first true maturity. We are emerging from an era of human history in which it has been assumed naively that it is easy to be psychologically well. Slowly we have learned that this is not so, and that to be a human being is so complex a task that the human race is not yet up to it. We have learned that wisdom about the world around us, scholarly erudition, high purpose, and religious faith have not singly or together been able to prevent neurotic distortions of human life. We must also humbly admit that we know so little about the processes of normal development that the adult who is truly normal is still a happy accident.

There is no valid evidence that man has become more neurotic. But clearly, in this age of increased life expectancy, growing population density, and unlimited destructive power, we can no longer tolerate those destructive influences of unconscious psychopathological processes the world could once accept with relative impunity. This is why the solution of the problem of the ubiquitous marked neurotic component of normal human nature is so pressing. Its solution affects the welfare of all, but can be found only through the study of the individual. Therefore, every time that analysis helps one human being to rid himself of his neurotic difficulties by tracing his neurosis to its roots, all of us have gained a fragment of knowledge that may help us to save the world. And every individual patient who subjects himself to analysis is making a contribution not to his own happiness alone, but to the general good as well.

Chapter IV

THE CONCEPT OF NORMALITY
AND THE NEUROTIC PROCESS

Psychoanalysis is uncompromising in its concept of mental health. The analyst is not content with a statistical definition of normality as being that which "most people" do or feel or think. Common colds are illnesses, even though everyone catches colds, and dental caries is not "normal" merely because most of us have cavities in our teeth. The physiologist does not think he has explained the subtle mechanism of the heartbeat by stating that everybody's heart beats. No more does the psychoanalyst feel that the mere fact that most people behave in a certain way makes it superfluous to seek the reason *why* they do so. The answer that "everybody does it" may be a statement of a fact, but never its explanation.

Nor is the analyst content to use conformity to the cultural mores of any time and place as his criterion of normality. It will be shown below that neither conformity nor rebellion is necessarily or intrinsically normal. Neither do the usual medicolegal distinctions between the sane and the insane throw light on the essential contrast between normality and illness. These legal definitions deal only with the practical distinction between those people who for the good of the community should be held responsible for their conduct, and those who for any one of several reasons must be safeguarded like children from the consequences of their own impulses. Whether or not a man "knows the difference between right and wrong" in the archaic and unreal legalistic sense, or whether or not he believes that he knows both *what* he is doing and *why* he is doing it, is of limited significance. Many insane people know the difference between right and wrong quite as clearly as a clergyman; and many who think that they can fully explain their own conduct are merely deceived by pseudorational explanations. Nor does the difference between normal and neurotic conduct depend upon the degree to which an act contributes either to the welfare of society or to its destruction, or on whether the behavior is extravagant and fantastic or orderly and sedate. Certainly, from the point of view of society, all of these are important attributes of human behavior; but they are neither constant nor explanatory as a basis for the distinction between the normal and the neurotic process. In the mere act of handwashing, there is nothing eccentric or antisocial or deviant from any culture; yet it is not normal to wash one's hands thousands of times a day. This is not because the act itself becomes different when it is repeated, but because there is a fundamental difference in the purposes the act serves. Similarly, to stand on your head in a tumbling act is normal, whereas to stand on your head in church is not—

31

unless perhaps it is done to pay an election bet or as a hazing stunt. The critical difference evidently lies not in the act, nor in its setting, but in the psychological mechanisms that determine the act. It will be shown that it is the nature of the constellation of inner processes producing them that determines whether personality and behavior are normal or neurotic.

The Role of Conscious, Preconscious, and Unconscious Processes

Through psychoanalysis we have learned that every moment of human life and, indeed, everything that we do or think or feel is determined, not by one psychological process operating alone, but by whole constellations of processes. In fact each instance of behavior, each act, expresses the sum of concurrent biological changes plus conscious, preconscious, and unconscious processes, some of which we are aware of and of others totally unaware. Starting from this basic fact, psychoanalysis has made it clear that human behavior is normal precisely to the degree to which it is determined not exclusively but predominantly by conscious processes, and neurotic insofar as it is determined predominantly by unconscious processes. This holds true equally for individual acts and for personality traits as a whole.[1]

[1]It may be that the normality and maturity of a culture or an entire civilization depends equally upon the extent to which conscious purposes determine its customs. This is a proposition for sociologists and cultural anthropologists to examine.

At this point the reader might ask why it makes so much difference whether conscious or unconscious processes drive the engine and steer the car. It is because the processes we are conscious of can be influenced by appeals to reason, by argument and exhortation, by success and failure, by human loyalties, by need or its satiation, by rewards and punishments. Consequently, those psychological processes predominantly consciously determined have the capacity to adapt flexibly to signals arising from changes in the external environment and to internal cues arising from changes from within the body. To the extent, therefore, to which conscious processes govern our lives, we are free—free to learn and to grow in wisdom and understanding, free to change and to go on changing (1968a). Such freedom, indeed, is the only psychological freedom psychoanalysis recognizes, and it is the essential core of normality. In contrast to this, those thoughts, feelings, behavior and personality traits which are determined *predominantly* by unconscious psychological processes are for that very reason rigid and inflexible. Precisely because the determining forces are unconscious, they cannot be swayed by argument or reason, by exhortation or persuasion, by appeals to feelings or to loyalty, by rewards or punishments. Furthermore, since unconscious forces pursue the symbolic representations of unknown goals which they can never attain, those cravings determined by unconscious forces are insatiable, and the behavior which expresses such needs must repeat itself endlessly, repeating errors as frequently as successes, regardless of the happiness or unhappiness it occasions. To the extent to which behavior is driven by unconscious forces it can learn nothing from experience and can never develop, change, or grow. In the truest sense of the word, it is enslaved (1956a, 1958a, 1959, 1964d, 1965c, 1966e, 1967d). That is why the relative roles of conscious and unconscious psychological processes in human affairs is perhaps the most important single fact to be determined about human personality, human behavior, and human institutions.

Neither conscious nor unconscious processes ever operate separately. A mixture is always at work, and the distinction between normality and neurosis is relative rather than absolute. The more preponderant the influence of conscious forces, the more normal is the resulting behavior, and vice versa. It is a further corollary of this definition that there is no single human quality and no human act, thought, or feeling that cannot be either normal, neurotic, or both. Benevolence can thus be both normal and valuable, but when it is compulsively overdriven by unconscious necessity it is destructive both to the giver and to those it attempts to serve. Similarly, a high tolerance for pain, frustration, or uncertainty can be a most valuable human trait, but when it serves an unconscious need to suffer, the capacity to endure becomes a measure of illness and not of health. Similar reservations must be made about the human drive to work, to play, to eat, to fight—indeed, about anything that

man does. This brings us back again to our fundamental principle, namely, that it is not what we do but
why we do it that counts. Or to put it more explicitly,
it is not in the quality or value of an act or trait to
oneself or to others or to society, but in the inner forces
that determine it, that we find the essential distinction
between psychological sickness and psychological
health (1954b, 1963c, 1974b).

This is far from being a purely theoretical
distinction. Quite the contrary, it has practical consequences from infancy to the end of life. Take as an
example the disturbances of behavior that occur in the
development of every child. Those which are determined predominantly by conscious and preconscious
processes can be corrected quickly and easily by simple
common-sense devices: e.g., by distracting the child,
by punishing him or rewarding him suitably, by argument, by affection, by sternness, by flexible modifications of the situation, and the like. When, on the
contrary, the identical behavior is determined predominantly by unconscious forces, it will resist all such
efforts and can be modified only if and as changes
occur in the unconscious forces producing the behavior
(Skinner notwithstanding).

Thus, our unconscious needs and our conflicts over
our unconscious needs become the source of all that is
obsessive, rigid, and compulsive in human behavior.
They enslave reason and subject it to their own purposes; and when reality frustrates them, or when they
are deadlocked within us, they give rise to all of the

35

familiar manifestations of anxiety, depression, confusion, and anger that haunt men's lives. This implies that the neurotic in human nature causes all that is ridden with anxiety, driven by unreasoning anger, paralyzed by depression, and lost in confusion. This occurs whenever our important inner conflicts take place on levels to which our conscious self-perceptions cannot penetrate without outside aid.

Our consciously organized processes contrast sharply. Because they are conscious, the individual is able to consider them with clarity. He can gauge his chances of achieving his goals by one path or another. He can be experimental and adaptable in his efforts. He will appraise the difficulties realistically, and, if they are great, they will deter him from attempting the impossible or spur him on in the legitimate hope of eventual success. In short, the man who is normal in this sense can accept the guidance of reason, reality, and common sense. The outside world may be unyielding; but he remains flexible, modifiable, and educable and, therefore, in a pragmatic sense, *free*. This indeed is the Fifth Freedom, the most important freedom of all— the freedom from the tyranny of the unconscious. It is the essence of the psychoanalytic concept of normality.

In this sense, even in the complete absence of outspoken neurotic symptoms, a man may be "neurotic" to the degree to which his life consists of compromises with unconscious conflicts and unconscious purposes. By compensating for them as best he can, he may achieve some degree of mastery over them without ever becoming free from their secret influence.

Over the years, such compromises gradually work less and less well until finally there is some kind of collapse, commonly called a "nervous breakdown." This may be nothing more than a period of depression or of pseudophysical illness; or it may manifest itself in sudden and perhaps unwise changes in marriages, occupations, or homes, or through some more serious mental disturbance. What Abraham Lincoln said of the people is equally true of what goes on inside Everyman in his dealings with his own unconscious. We may be able to fool part of ourselves all of the time, and all of ourselves part of the time, but we cannot fool all of ourselves all of the time. This is why we pay so high a price for the unresolved neurotic forces that lie hidden in all of us.

To the analyst, therefore, normality means freedom from the masked as well as the overt neurotic tendencies of the personality. Freedom such as this is manifested in the strength to withstand the pressure of external events, in the ability to tolerate uncertainty without generating excessive anger, on the one hand, or paralyzing anxiety or depression, on the other, through the absence of blindly compulsive and repetitive activity, and, above all, in the freedom to change and to go on changing.

Much remains to be discovered about how these unconscious processes arise in infancy, how and why they split off from the stream of conscious and preconscious events to initiate the neurotic process, and how this process may be checked or at least guided into less destructive channels.

(1) We know that, for various reasons, early in infancy painful psychological conflicts are subjected to a process called "repression," in the course of which all memory or awareness of them is pushed out of consciousness.

(2) We know, furthermore, that these buried conflicts do not thereupon become inert or inactive. Instead, processes which have their roots in these repressed conflicts become detached from them, to exercise a powerful although unrecognized influence upon our conscious processes. Consequently, behavior is always a product of conscious, preconscious, and unconscious processes acting concurrently; and the latter are represented in disguised and symbolic forms in all of our actions, thoughts, and feelings.

(3) As a result, any human need, however legitimate it may be intrinsically, can be either compulsively overdriven or anxiously denied and inhibited whenever forces derived from unconscious processes acquire a dominant role. This is how a child's natural and healthy need for food can be distorted into a total refusal to eat or an insatiable need to eat to the point of vomiting. Any unconscious necessity, as long as it remains unconscious, can be gratified only symbolically, which means that in reality it is never gratified at all. These unconsciously determined processes are the scars of the buried conflicts of infancy and childhood. Since they may remain with us throughout life, they are the source of those insatiable and repetitive needs, fears, activities, and "habits" that make up so much of human personality as we know it.

(4) The neurotic process is always a symbolic process, and the split into parallel yet interacting streams of conscious, preconscious, and unconscious processes starts approximately when the child begins to develop the rudiments of speech. Early speech is at first a language of action and not of words; but there is good reason to believe that the evolution of the capacity to use language is linked closely to the process by which we first repress our unconscious struggles and then represent them by conscious symbolic processes. Consequently, everything we do, feel, and think throughout life is both symbolic and realistic at the same time; and the extent to which any piece of behavior serves as a symbol for something else measures the degree to which it has been shaped by unconscious forces. It may be accurate to say, therefore, that the neurotic process is the price we pay for our most precious human heritage, namely our ability to represent experience and communicate our thoughts by means of symbols, attempting, albeit unsuccessfully, to discharge at least some of the psychic tensions we bury in ourselves during our struggles with our instincts and our life experiences. Thus, the highest potentialities of the human psyche and its susceptibility to neurotic distortion are closely interrelated, and all hope of any fundamental progress in human nature depends upon our learning how to preserve the creative potential inherent in the symbolic process, while limiting and controlling its vulnerability to neurotic distortion (1958a).

The transient neurotic episodes that occur in every childhood are the first manifestations of this neurotic distortion of symbolic functions. Familiar examples are the nightmares, the commonplace facial twitchings and tics, the stereotyped behavior habits, the exaggerated loves and hates, the blind rebellion and equally blind submissiveness, the timidity, self-consciousness and shyness, the food habits and eating compulsions. These universal troubles of childhood are the larval manifestations of the processes out of which adult neuroses evolve, and, because at the present stage of the evolution of human nature these episodes are universal and are never wholly erased, some residue in adult years is also universal.

Hence, what passes for normality in our world today is not in any fundamental sense normal. It is rather the unstable equilibrium among conscious, preconscious, and unconscious processes by means of which men have hidden the unconscious mechanisms that infest their daily activities. The resulting activities may not be peculiar or strange in themselves; they may be socially acceptable and even valuable; and they may meet all the demands of conscience. They can, nonetheless, express the distorting influence of unconscious forces. The way we live, eat, work, make love, and bring up our children, our attitudes toward politics, economics, and international affairs, how we play, our choice of companions, how we dress and sleep, attitudes toward pain and suffering (both our own and that of others), our tolerance for uncertainty, our proneness to anger or to depression, our tendencies to dependence or independence, how we react to success and failure, our morals, the balance in us between generosity and selfishness—all these and many other personality traits are consequences in the adult personality of the residues of the unresolved neurotic problems of childhood. These residues make us what we are as craftsmen, artists, professional men, citizens, husbands, wives, parents, and friends. They determine the peace of mind, serenity, and gaiety with which we are able to live, or the veiled tensions, anxieties, and angers that discolor our lives. They can be the source, equally, of greatness of spirit or of meanness and crime; and they can cost us much of the happiness that would otherwise be ours for the taking. They lie at the heart of the oldest of human problems—human discontent. They are the veiled and universal neurotic component of so-called "normal" human nature (1951b).

Some Additional Comments

The foregoing discussion of normality and the neurotic process is reasonably accurate, but not quite the whole story. There are three potentials in the make-up of every human being—a neurotic, a psychotic, and a creative potential. These three potentials are not only universal (except among the mentally defective), but relatively constant. Out of them, three enormously variable processes evolve slowly—a neurotic, a psychotic, and a creative process. Not only do these three processes interact continuously; they are also molded constantly by the concurrent influence of varied indi-

41

vidual experiences, cultural pressures, genetic and physiological differences. Hence, the processes change progressively as they evolve. Some of the forces that determine the course of these three streams are intrinsic to the personality and arise out of our earliest life experiences; some are dependent upon the impact of physiological variables; others result from the varied social conditions under which people live. At critical junctures in life, states of illness may occur, precipitating either the clinical neurosis or the clinical psychosis; or states of free creative productivity may be reached. The full story of the complex, interwoven evolution of these three ingredients in human nature is the story of human life, of human creativity, and of human tragedy. It is into this complex stream that psychoanalysis attempts to introduce its influence.

Chapter V
THE GENERAL NATURE OF NONTECHNICAL PSYCHOTHERAPY

Psychotherapy existed long before there was a name for it. Indeed, psychotherapy is as old as medicine and nearly as old as religion. Its story would be a history of human civilization. Yet only the last century has brought scientific knowledge of its scope and limitations; and it is only in the last century that anything new has been added to its techniques.

The term, though young, has already acquired too vague and general a meaning. It is applied to the mystical healing rites of a priest-physician of ancient Greece, the drum-beating and voodoo practices of a modern primitive, David strumming his lyre against Saul's melancholy, classes in rhythmic dancing in a modern psychiatric hospital, forced labor in an old prison asylum, the monotone of a class in basket weaving, lectures on ideals of healthy living, dramatizations of human conflicts, an assortment of modifications of hypnotism, or the most subtle and sophisticated psychoanalytic technique.

In this broad sense, psychotherapy includes every effort to shape human thought, feeling, and behavior, whether by education, precept, or example, by command or exhortation, by reason and logic, by humor or emotional inspiration, by distraction and diversion, by stern discipline, or by indulgence and deliberate escapism, by punishments and rewards, by direct material relief or by gross or subtle alterations in the external environment. It can include the influence on the individual of such cultural forces as religion, music, the arts, and literature. These devices are by no means new, nor were they invented by psychiatry. They have always been resorted to by parents, teachers, religious leaders, and social workers. The Greeks in their healing temples used music and occupational therapy as adroitly as does the modern hospital; and while these are most effective if applied with patience, tact, intuitive sympathy, and practical wisdom, they require little technical psychiatric knowledge. Nor are they the specific tools by which the neurotic process as such can be altered, much less cured; and no matter how imaginatively they are used, they can never by themselves resolve the unconscious conflicts every adult inherits in some degree from his own infancy and childhood.

It is our thesis that psychotherapy as a science begins where these simple yet venerable methods leave off. It is usually good sense to give water to a thirsty man, but this is not science until we know the role of water both in the normal body and in illness. So, too, with all such simple psychotherapeutic sips of water as sympathy or advice, or rewards and punishments: we can use them with scientific precision only when we know their relation to normal and disturbed functions of the mind on both conscious and unconscious levels. Thus, the term psychotherapy is used in two senses: (1) as a name for all homely common-sense aids to wise and peaceful living, i.e., nontechnical psychotherapy; and (2) as a technical term for certain specific methods of altering the neurotic process, methods that take up where simpler remedies fail.

The psychotherapies can be classified in various ways. It frequently is useful to group them under three headings, like three partially overlapping bands in a spectrum. At one end is simple, nontechnical, non-analytic psychotherapy, which deals primarily with conscious situational problems and conflicts. Without considering unconscious conflicts, it offers instruction, guidance, rewards and punishments, vocational training, material relief, distraction, encouragement, and exhortation, and usually helps the patient to master or suppress troublesome conscious problems and impulses. In the next category or band is analytically informed psychotherapy, which may be both palliative and in some measure expressive. Here the therapist is alert to the interplay of unconscious forces in his patient's life and takes them into consideration in dealing with symptoms, but he makes no effort to impart this understanding to the patient. Finally comes analysis itself, the crux of which is the effort to share with the patient full insight into unconscious mechanisms. This is done by interpreting to him his transference phenomena, resistances, free associations, waking fantasies, dreams, and the patterns of his daily living, as well as his frank neurotic symptoms. These analytic devices will be dealt with in subsequent chapters. The simpler components of psychotherapy will be considered here.

Obviously, psychotherapy cannot always achieve or even aim at the eradication of causes. As with any other medical therapy, it must sometimes content itself with palliative measures in which the homely common-sense maneuvers may play a major role. As the late Austen Riggs once said, "Psychotherapy is the effort to heal or influence another human being through the instrumentality of the other's own mind."

Nontechnical Psychotherapy as a Practical Test of the Severity of a Disturbance

Nontechnical psychotherapy performs several essential functions which fall naturally into three categories: (a) *practical support*, consisting primarily of advice, guidance, and assistance through social service in the management of life situations and environmental difficulties, occupational guidance, etc; (b) *emotional support*, consisting essentially of sympathy, exhortation, admonition, encouragement, humor, art, recreation, companionship, and the like; (c) *reorienting education*, consisting primarily of efforts to alter the patient's habitual conscious attitudes of guilt, fear, hate, and depression by educating him to recognize and tolerate his own conscious needs and cravings, his instinctual hungers, and his familial jealousies and hates, etc.

Deliberately or inadvertently, this third category often penetrates to unconscious levels. When it does so, some knowledge of the workings of unconscious psychological forces is required. It also harbors certain dangers, which will be discussed below. The first two categories, however, are the homely nonspecific weapons of every wise parent and teacher, and these must always be tried first. Indeed, where they succeed alone, one may be sure that the maladjustment was external rather than internal, since it is precisely the failure of the simple therapeutic devices that demonstrates the presence of the rigidity that stamps behavior as neurotic, in the sense that it is shaped predominantly by unconscious forces rather than by conscious forces or external stresses. This, again, is why psychotherapy as a technical science begins where the simpler methods fail.

A banal example may make this clear. A child of three or four wakens at night, slips out of his bed, and comes pattering into the room in search of his parents. On the first occasion he is picked up, hugged, and carried back to bed, and after his wants are attended to he is tucked in, kissed, and left there. A few minutes later, however, he reappears. The same procedure is followed, perhaps a little more brusquely, but nonetheless kindly. Even if it did not work the first time, it might work now. But again the youngster appears. The parents successively try leaving the light on, the door open, a toy in his bed, cuddling, promises, bribes, scoldings, threats, and punishments; but in spite of their versatile efforts the child reappears over and over through the course of many evenings. The parents become distracted. They run through the whole gamut of feelings—from affectionate patience to irritability, anger, and finally a panicky feeling that something must be wrong and a guilty conviction that they are failing in their responsibility as parents. They do not realize that their seeming failure is a necessary therapeutic test, proving the roots of the child's disturbed behavior to be on a level inaccessible to surface manipulations. Their handling of the situation demonstrates that they confront one of the typical, transient, neurotic episodes of childhood.

Common-sense maneuvers thus constitute a practical test of the severity of any psychological upset. Where they succeed, their success shows that the roots of the disturbance are superficial. On the other hand, where after persistent use they fail, the failure demonstrates that the disturbance is more deep-seated. This fact is self-evident, yet is too often overlooked. Patients, their families, and their physicians often blame themselves for the time that has been consumed in giving these simple preliminary measures an adequate trial. Such self-reproaches are justified only when we try to terrorize symptoms out of sight by excessive penalties, or bribe them into silence by overindulgence, or when, in spite of repeated failures, we persist too long with futile efforts. Mistakes such as these are most likely to occur either where no technical psychiatric help is available, or among those harboring a blind prejudice against turning to psychiatry under any circumstances (cf. Chapter XV).

What is true of the small child is equally true of the adult. Rewards and punishments, discipline and education, argument and reason, the sensible manipulation of the environment, occupational therapy, comfort, solace and exhortation—all these are helpful preliminary steps in the approach to any psychotherapeutic problem. They clear away external complications. They effect cures when the situation rather than the individual is sick. They are at once an antechamber to deeper treatment and a practical therapeutic test of its necessity. Where they achieve lasting therapeutic results, it is certainly folly to go deeper; but where they fail, it is even greater folly to persist, because until the internal obstacles are eliminated the neurotic patient cannot make effective use of such aids no matter how badly he may need and crave them. Indeed, technical treatment of a true neurosis must usually precede or at least accompany practical nontechnical assistance, otherwise even the wisest and most benevolent guidance will usually be sabotaged by the neurotic process.

Palliative Psychotherapy

Palliative psychotherapy consists primarily of an effort to teach patients how to live with some measure of comfort within the confines of their uncured neuroses. By itself this can sometimes relieve much suffering. For instance, what is called "agoraphobia" may at first manifest itself merely in an uneasy feeling when the patient is out in very large, open spaces. At this stage the neurosis will make relatively little difference in his life. Gradually, however, the anxiety will become more all-pervading, until finally the patient may be unable to go out of doors at all, or unable even to leave his own room lest he be confronted by the challenge of a room that may be even slightly larger than his own. His neurosis gradually imprisons him, and with each successive encroachment on his freedom, his life and that of his family become more circumscribed. Ultimately, all whose lives touch his in any way begin to pay with him the price of his illness. If, through ingenious manipulations and his personal influence, the psychotherapist achieves no more than to keep the patient from succumbing to these successive neurotic restrictions, if he merely keeps the prison walls from closing in, he will contribute greatly to the comfort and happiness of the patient and his family.

At the same time, the palliative levels of psychotherapy often provide an invaluable foundation for ultimate curative treatment. By the time a patient comes for help, a severe neurosis may have caused such complete disorganization in his life that he can neither work nor play nor love, and thus is cut off from all sources of gratification and self-esteem. The patient's life has become "sicker" than the patient or the process of illness itself. Intelligent preliminary psychotherapy and guidance may help such a patient to engage again in healthy, diversified activities, without which it might be impossible for him to undergo prolonged and intensive treatment.

Let me illustrate this with the problem of a man who came complaining of a severe height phobia. He was a doctor. Up to a point, his practice had expanded well as a result of a warm personality and because of his exceptional zeal and intellectual ability. Gradually, however, he had found himself increasingly crippled by the fact that he did not dare to go above the third or fourth floor in any building. If a colleague or a patient or a hospital ward or a laboratory or even a friend's apartment happened to be on a floor higher than this, he found himself in the grip of an attack of acute anxiety, sweating, his knees knocking together, short of breath, in fear of death, possessed by fantasies of throwing himself from the nearest window, unable to think or talk. The immediate effect upon his professional and social life was devastating.

But that was not all. The patient had suffered from these symptoms for several years before seeking help. As the futile struggle continued, he had acquired many tricks for fooling himself and others. He had learned a thousand dodges to avoid going up in high buildings and to bring others down to him. On an auto trip, if anyone happened to suggest a route that would take him over a high bridge, what had started out as a pleasure trip became a moral battlefield. Should he fight his terror and literally sweat it out; or succumb to it and insist on some alternate route, and then hate himself for his "cowardice?" He developed a tendency to exaggerate minor physical upsets or even to fake illness in order to dodge the anxiety-provoking situations. And with every evasion, his self-hate and his despair increased, as well as his envy and rage against those who were not hampered as he was. This bitterness inevitably had infected his relations with his wife and children and his professional associates, since those who were closest to him provided the most frequent occasions of his fears and were the witnesses of his retreats. Gradually the world became a finger pointed at him in derision. Although it was built on a simple neurotic disability, this complex superstructure of fantasies and feelings carried with it the threat of a major psychosis and had worked at least as great an injury to the patient's life as had the original phobia. This is a characteristic story of a process of incapacitating psychological illness evolving out of a simple phobia. It is the conclusive answer to the myth propagated by Thomas Szasz (1961) that mental illness itself is a myth.

Faced with this quite typical problem, palliative psychotherapy attempted first to remove the elaborate secondary structure, while at the same time attempting to show the patient less destructive ways of living within the confines of his neurosis, i.e., with a minimum of interference with his own life and that of his family. It taught him to handle his symptoms so as not to visit their consequences on his family and friends. It aimed to restore harmony and mutual tolerance and understanding both in his home and with his professional associates. Valuable as all of this was, however, it left unaltered the underlying neurotic conflict, which remained for analysis to remove if the patient was ever to become "well" in the sense of regaining his freedom to change and grow and learn.

Such palliative help is of great human value as long as there are neurotic patients who cannot be cured completely because they live too far from anyone equipped to give deeper therapy, or because they are unable to devote sufficient time to treatment, or because of elements intrinsic to the neurosis itself, or because others in the family are opposed to intensive treatment, or because they have postponed seeking treatment until it was too late for fundamental help. Skillful palliative therapy, although it should be highly valued, should be used only where for any of these reasons more fundamental treatment cannot be undertaken.

Dangers of Palliative Psychotherapy

In connection with these general introductory measures, the psychotherapist must often undertake considerable emotional re-education. As we have said, this consists of a cautious effort to increase a patient's tolerance for his own instinctual needs, for the bitter jealousies born in the nursery, and for the hostilities, fears, and guilts arising out of such conflicts. In this aspect of treatment, group discussions are sometimes helpful and effective.

There are limits, however, to what can be achieved by any such direct educative procedures. When pushed too far, patients will often reject those very truths about themselves which are most obvious to others.

Indeed, the more obvious the unwelcome truth, the more inevitable it is that the patient will be unable to accept it until the reasons for it and for his fear and guilt about it have been worked out with him. It is here that psychotherapy as a fumbling if benevolent art must give over to psychotherapy as a disciplined, scientific technique.

Indeed, the most serious error to which every would-be psychotherapist is liable occurs in this connection. We are constantly tempted to short-cut the tedious processes by which a patient's blind spots can be eliminated. If we keep a critical watch on what we say and do, we often find ourselves trying impatiently to cram insight down a patient's throat, like fattening a Strasbourg goose, forcing on him the guidance and instruction for which he is not ready. Many years ago the late William A. White said that the most difficult lesson a psychiatrist has to learn, and one which he has to relearn every day of his life, is to allow a patient to maintain that two and two is five, until psychiatrist and patient discover together why he has had to believe it. It is the discovery of the reasons for the patient's unconscious need tenaciously to cling to error that alone makes lasting correction of the error possible. It often happens that as the result of months or even years of work, with great surprise and excitement a patient discovers facts about himself that have always been obvious to his friends and relatives, who are then likely to say, "Why, we knew that all along. We could have told you that! You didn't have to go to a psychiatrist to find that out." In saying this they indicate their failure to understand the essential principle of psychotherapy—namely, that "telling" the patient is always useless until the therapeutic process removes from the patient's mind the unconscious preconceptions and resistances that have made it impossible for him to recognize the obvious. Before these barriers are removed, no one can effectively tell a patient anything; once the inner barriers are gone, no one has to tell him.

This fundamental principle runs counter to a great deal of what is called common sense; and since even experienced psychiatrists often violate this law of therapy, it is small wonder that physicians, nurses, laymen, clergymen, educators, and parents so frequently get into difficulties through their failure to appreciate its importance. They offer a patient excellent arguments, reassurances, consolation, or sound corrective advice, all of which he may seem to agree with eagerly. Then nothing happens, and the well-meaning advisers wonder why the patient fails to make wise use of their helpful counsel. Or, to their even greater dismay, the patient may react with panic, resentment, or depression instead of with the relief, reassurance, and encouragement his advisers have naively anticipated. This sort of disappointment is a daily experience for the psychotherapist who does not realize that the most critical step in therapy is the elimination of internal obstacles to clear vision.

It is nevertheless worthwhile to reiterate that even

such failures as these need not be without value, provided only that the advice and confrontation has been offered gently, tentatively, and in small doses. The failures may become actually dangerous only when the adviser obstinately and angrily persists with his confrontations even after the patient has failed to profit by them. If, however, he realizes that the patient's recalcitrance arises out of unconscious resistances, and if he modifies his approach so as to point the patient's attention to these resisting forces, he will then have helped his patient to take a long step toward the solution and cure of his neurotic difficulties.

There is one other lesson every psychiatrist has to learn over and over again throughout his professional life because he so often forgets it: however much it may relieve his own feelings, it does a patient no good to call his illness names. When a patient comes with a frank symptom, such as a handwashing compulsion, we know that it is a waste of breath to tell him solemnly that he suffers from a compulsion neurosis. In one way or another the patient tells us that himself. Our technical nomenclature can help him neither to control his symptom nor to get rid of it. Nevertheless, when dealing with subtler compulsive patterns this is often forgotten; and some psychiatrists hopefully describe to patients their "neurotic trends." There is no parent who has not told his child the same thing in laymen's terms, when he calls his child lazy or balky or ungrateful or disobedient. Pseudoscientific name-calling is no more effective than parental name-calling as a way of altering the repetitive nucleus of neurotic manifestations.

It is impossible to overemphasize the futility of naive confrontations and their dangers, when they are offered too insistently, because this is the most frequent mistake of the immature psychiatrist and of the well-intentioned general practitioner who has read psychiatric theory without having been subjected to rigorous drill in procedure. Even superficial confrontations without careful preparation may precipitate resentment and mobilize defenses. Confrontations that reach to deeper levels, challenging the patient to recognize some of the buried sources of his difficulties, *must* be rejected by the patient if they are not to precipitate him into unmanageable terror, guilt, or depression. One learns slowly not to force a patient to look at painful facts about himself until some understanding of their origins and purposes has been achieved. Sometimes, one may have to patiently withhold interpretations during many months of exploration.

It may at times even be dangerous to attempt to argue a patient out of cherished ideas and beliefs about such seemingly impersonal affairs as science or politics. Occasionally, such an argument can be as dangerous as confrontation. If it succeeds too suddenly in breaking down the defensive barrier of symptomatic ideas, all that will result is an eruption of emotions before these can be digested. There may be similar danger even in reassurance and consolation. A patient said, "I was feeling all right until my sister happened to telephone me to tell me that her household was well. Then all of a sudden I found myself in such a panic and depression that I stood at the window and thought of throwing myself out." Thus, one slowly learns that the only wholly safe thing to do with a patient is to listen to him until one understands enough about him to be in a position to relate one's comments to the patient's unconscious psychological processes.

"Mental Catharsis"

Most neurotic patients live in a state of constant inner tension of one kind or another. This gave rise to the notion that to express the pent-up feelings would work an automatic cure. Such a process of discharge is sometimes spoken of as mental "catharsis," and from time to time much is made of it in psychiatric literature. It is important to realize that catharsis alone is never enough. The concept is poorly understood and generally misused. Any "discharge" of emotional tension can give temporary relief, be it a temper tantrum or an uncontrolled outburst of crying and laughing. Indeed, every neurotic symptom gives some momentary relief. A patient with a hand-washing compulsion relieves a certain amount of tension each time he washes his hands. In a broad sense, this is "catharsis," too. Unfortunately, however, until the source of tension is removed it reaccumulates rapidly.

It is cathartic in a somewhat more lasting sense, to enable a patient to express pent-up feelings he has previously been unable to face. A man who has never been able to admit that he hated some member of his own family may feel marked relief when the psychiatrist's noncritical and permissive attitude enables him to acknowledge this feeling without acting it out destructively. Even here, however, unless a fresh upsurge of guilt or anxiety can be avoided, such a cathartic maneuver may precipitate the patient into subsequent depression and terror. No mere expression of feelings, whether from the surface or from the depths, can accomplish lasting benefits unless it is preceded or accompanied or followed by a gradual eradication of the unconscious sources of the feelings. Without this, the tension will inevitably recur.

The Role of Insight in Psychotherapy

In any organic disease, lasting therapy depends upon the elimination of the causal agents. This is equally true for those psychiatric illnesses arising out of a cluster of unconscious conflicts and their derivatives. In order to dispose of these hidden troublemakers, it is necessary first to bring them out into the full light of consciousness. Some of them thereupon prove to be no longer disturbing because they were based upon childhood desires and misconceptions. Others can then be dealt with by conscious controls without the production of disturbing symptoms. This is the generally accepted concept of the role of insight in the therapeutic process. Unfortunately, this most fundamental of all elements in psychoanalytic therapy has never been adequately tested and verified experimentally (see Chapter XXVI). Indeed, it is fair to say that this cornerstone of the modern conception of a dynamic psychotherapeutic process confronts us with many complex and unsolved problems. The word "insight" itself is applied to quite different levels of self-understanding. There is a superficially descriptive insight that is merely the ability to describe honestly, and if necessary unsparingly, the way we have behaved. Even for those who can recall daily events with reasonable accuracy, this is not simple. In keeping with the needs of our differing personalities, we usually color our memories, sometimes flatteringly sometimes unfavorably to ourselves. Furthermore, our ability to appraise our daily experiences depends upon our ability to recall them. This is a variable faculty taken for granted when we have it, but one that seems wholly unattainable when we lack it. There are some people who go through their days as though they were traversing a long corridor of doors, each of which they shut firmly behind them as they go, literally obliterating from their minds every detail of the day's journey and ending the day blank, except for a state of diffuse, unattached and unexplained emotion, which inevitably gives painful coloring to the dreams that follow at night. At the other pole are those who can give a play-by-play account of every moment of the day, with an automatic and amazing facility for total recall of everything anyone said and did and felt. Most of us come between these two extremes. There are significant reasons for these marked differences, reasons that have to do partly with variations in the structure of the nervous system but chiefly with variations in human nature. The capacity for spontaneous recall markedly influences our accessibility to therapy, because the exploration of links with the past must start from current events. Inasmuch as the present is a screen on which the past throws its shadows, we must study the present to find clues to the past, and the habitual obliteration of daily material blocks the exploratory process at its inception.

Experience consists not of events alone, but also of feelings; hence, factual memory and factual recall are by themselves only one component of insight. Here again there are marked variations in people. Some recall only feelings and no events; others only events and never their feelings. Some recall only what others did, and some only what they themselves have done. Again, most of us fall between the extremes; but our position on the spectrum makes a difference in the ease with which we can acquire inclusive insight.

Finally, we find that for some people memory has only a short and recent span, whereas for others it tends automatically to go far back into early years. Memory is always full of gaps, however, and the first step in "insight-therapy" is the effort to fill in these, whether they are in the recollection of recent or of remote experiences. Insight begins to have a therapeutic effect only when it leads to an appreciation of the relationship between buried experiences and the unconscious conflicts out of which both the neurotic components of the personality and the neurotic symptoms themselves arise (1965c).

Let us take as an example a young sailor who had gone through overwhelming stresses in battle. After a particularly trying experience on a landing craft, he broke down with severe gastrointestinal difficulties. When he came for treatment he had only one complaint, namely, a persistent diarrhea; he recalled much of the details of combat, but he saw no connection between the two. The first goal of therapy was to give him an understanding of this connection. His own associations to this material soon revealed another area of his life into which he lacked insight. This concerned the relation between battle stress and certain painful situations of his early life. He had been raised in a home that had, in fact, been a living nightmare. He had been beaten and kicked and painfully mauled by older brothers and two young uncles, and had reacted to this treatment with incessant rage and terror. This was when his diarrhea had started. He remembered a fair amount of this, but again he felt no connection between this and what he had gone through in battle. He did not realize that the gastrointestinal disturbance precipitated in battle was a facsimile of a prolonged intestinal disturbance from which he had suffered in childhood, and that the battle stress was itself a re-experiencing of the misery of his earliest years. This was a second step in the acquisition of insight. Typically, insight must be acquired in just such a series of steps, which consist of the recapturing of the memory of events, and of emotional reactions to disturbing events until finally an understanding of the relation between old and recent pain, and between pain and symptom, is attained. This frequently means going back through one level of investigation after another. (Controversial aspects of this are discussed in Chapter XXVI.)

It will become apparent at once that in this discussion we have left far behind the narrow limitations of nontechnical psychotherapy. The first step in the acquisition of insight (i.e., the correlation of a present symptom with an immediate strain) may be quite simple and may require no specialized technical skill. Deeply rooted neurotic symptoms or traits, however, are rarely relieved by this maneuver alone. Usually, they must be traced to their roots in earlier experiences that have sensitized the patient to his current problems. This requires facility in the specific techniques of analytical psychotherapy. And it is to these that we will turn our attention in the succeeding chapters.

Chapter VI
THE EXPERIENCE OF BEING PSYCHOANALYZED

In the anticipatory fantasies of a prospective patient, psychoanalysis is neither a system of theories nor a technique of treatment. It is an experience through which he is about to pass. It is therefore natural that he should want to have some idea of what this experience is going to be like. A detailed preview is neither possible nor desirable; only those who are overanxious about the undertaking will demand it. Much of this anxiety has its origins in unconscious problems and cannot be put to rest by descriptions of the process of analysis, however reasonable or reassuring. Hence, this chapter cannot hope to resolve the blind terror with which some patients approach analysis, but only to allay the most reasonable misgivings of the rest.

Some anxiety, however, is based on misconceptions persisting in the minds of even supposedly educated people, such as the notion that most patients are wealthy women with nothing else to do who come to analysis out of furtive, erotic curiosity; that the analyst asks the patient a great many embarrassing and exciting questions; that the patient, in the popular sense of the word, "falls in love with" the psychoanalyst; and that an analysis is conducted in an atmosphere of self-indulgent emotionalism. Some patients hope to carry away at the end a pearl of analytical wisdom in the form of a written or oral digest of all their problems, together with an outline of guiding principles and directions as to what they should or should not do in the future. Fragments of these fantasies persist in the minds of most laymen and even of some physicians.

The realities of psychoanalysis are quite different. Patients usually approach analysis with hesitation and misgivings, under the pressure of their own wretchedness or because of the urging of family, friends, or physician. Throughout the analysis they encounter an atmosphere of friendly courtesy and quiet formality and reserve. They find that the psychoanalyst's private life, his tastes, his opinions, and his personality are exhibited as little as possible, and that outside of the analytic session social contacts with the psychoanalyst are avoided. Indeed, if the psychoanalyst they first consult has had a prior relationship as friend or adviser, they discover to their surprise that he will usually send them to some other analyst who is a total stranger.

Once launched in the work of the analytic session, they find that instead of an affectionate and comforting friendship, they do not even hold ordinary conversations with the analyst. Usually they will lie on a couch with the analyst seated behind them so that he is able to observe them without being under scrutiny himself. Therefore they cannot watch his expression or respond to his apparent approval or disapproval; and when they try to laugh or joke with him about their troubles in an attempt to smooth them over, they find him bafflingly silent and unresponsive. They may talk for long periods with scarcely an interruption, while at other times they will be checked by insistent comments, comments that sometimes will make them more comfortable but, quite as often, prove to be disturbing.

Furthermore, the analysis makes formidable demands. It may require at least five sessions each week. Each session starts and stops punctually and lasts as precisely as is possible for the period of fifty minutes, which usually is agreed upon ahead of time. Patients are not encouraged to miss sessions for other obligations, whether pleasant or unpleasant, except when this is clearly unavoidable. They learn that they will usually be charged for scheduled sessions which they miss *unnecessarily*, and discover that it is difficult even to change the hour of an appointment. In short, the analysis turns out to be an exacting taskmaster.

As the analysis progresses, sooner or later the patient experiences periods of emotional turmoil and distress, intervals of peaceful satisfaction, moments of excited eagerness and hope, or arid weeks in which he cannot see where he is going or what progress he is making, and phases of anger, affection, friendliness, coolness, interest, impatience, boredom, resentment, skepticism, and a host of other unpleasant feelings.

The hypothetical patient who comes to analysis solely out of morbid curiosity or because he anticipates erotic titillation soon finds his shallow motivation frustrated and exposed. His interest wanes, and he does not long continue to waste his own time or the analyst's before dropping out of the picture. On the other hand, the sincere patient somehow manages to carry on despite the pain, the time, and the expense, on the arid plateaux as well as over the mountaintops, through one or more years of intensive work.

At this point many questions arise about these grim features of the analytic process: why it takes so long, whether there are no shortcuts, why it goes on day after day for all that time, how one can find things to talk about for so long a period, and what one gains from it all in the end. We hope to answer all of these questions in the succeeding chapters.

Chapter VII

THE DURATION OF ANALYSIS AND THE FREQUENCY OF THE SESSIONS

The Duration of Psychoanalytic Treatment

The ills that are subjected to psychoanalytic treatment are never acute or passing ailments. For the most part they are chronic illnesses with occasional periods of acute exacerbation. The quiescent chronic phases of neurotic illness may often be mistaken for normality, just as the sufferer from tuberculosis may seem to be normal in the intervals between attacks, or for years before his infection first manifests itself openly. There are illuminating analogies between the problems of treatment in the two illnesses. In each, the acute episodes may be of short duration, but the physician who is willing to discharge a patient as cured immediately after such an episode is either incompetent or unscrupulous. It is only when a sufferer from tuberculosis has become temporarily symptom free that the long march toward enduring health begins. The same principle is valid in the treatment of neuroses. It is unreasonable to think that lifelong illnesses, be they low-grade chronic infections or masked neurotic traits, can be cured in a short time. In both, one measures the

68

duration of adequate treatment in terms of years and not of months. The psychoanalyst who fails to explain this before beginning treatment or who, at the end of a few months of apparently successful analytic work, interrupts the treatment without making it clear that the job is only partially complete, does his patient no service.

Many short methods have been sought, but none has yet been found. It may be that it is in the nature of these illnesses that none will be found, although any such pessimism is as yet unjustified. The techniques of emergency treatment developed during World War II have instigated many new investigations, some of which may eventually bear fruit.

These investigations are experimenting with various types of hypnotic phenomena in combination with analysis, with and without the use of various drugs. All these methods aim at the induction of states of controlled dreamlike dissociation in an effort to facilitate the reliving of painful and forgotten experiences and the clarification of the multiple meanings of obscure symptoms.[1]

When he hears enthusiastic claims for new and rapid methods of treatment, the layman should bear in mind the fact that no other kind of research is as full of pitfalls as is research in therapy. In no other field are

[1]For those interested in a more detailed discussion of the theory underlying these investigations and their results, and in the literature on this subject, see Kubie, 1945; Kubie and Margolin, 1944, 1945; Brenman and Gill, 1947.

we equally vulnerable to the fallacies of wishful thinking. To offer a sick man a swift road to health is to offer him something for which he yearns. The conscientious psychoanalyst who warns prospective patients of the probable duration of treatment frightens many away. The temptation is great, therefore, to raise false hopes of rapid help. Unfortunately, results have not yet justified these hopes.

The Frequency of the Sessions

The practice of psychoanalysis has evolved out of the experience of many mistakes, and each technical detail plays a part in avoiding their repetition. There is a reason for the sacrifices the analysis requires. Of these sacrifices none is more irksome than the daily session. As the therapeutic work of the analysis proceeds, the incessant fluctuations of mood and tensions are observed and correlated with the impact of daily events. As this goes on, "forgotten" patterns of unhappiness are gradually brought to light: old fears, sorrows, guilts, angers, losses, conflicts, and frustrations. These come up for discussion in each day's work until their relation to the external events in the current daily life of the patient and to his psychological reactions becomes clear, and until he comes to understand how his own buried past distorts his daily attitudes and his ability to deal effectively and realistically with his current problems. The present is thus shown to be a screen on which the past constantly throws its shadows. To demonstrate these subtle correlations requires a continuous searching backward and forward between the past and the present.

Consequently, the psychoanalyst keeps an attentive eye on the minute details of the patient's current life. Any interruption in the information he receives about the stream of daily life temporarily deprives the psychoanalyst of that contact with current events without which the dynamic significance of the past may be lost. Even weekend interruptions sometimes check the momentum of the work. A schedule of two or three analytical sessions a week almost inevitably tends to slow up the pace of the analytic process and in some cases will stall the analysis completely. Nevertheless, in certain centers, psychoanalysts are trying to determine if and when it may be possible to do equally effective analytic work with a less continuous schedule, and with what types of illness, and with what changes in technique. That this can be achieved in certain cases has long been known, but the limits of the effectiveness of a discontinuous schedule are not yet clear.

There are many reasons why physicians and patients are tempted to diminish the frequency of the analytic sessions. For the patient, it means a strain upon his time and pocketbook. Furthermore, it seems to him that a day of freedom between analytic sessions gives him a breathing spell in which to carry on his usual life without interruption. Certainly these are practical advantages, but the loss of continuity in the work may prove to be too high a price to pay. Furthermore, the prized day of "rest" may become a day in which the

patient withdraws from the analysis, both intellectually and emotionally, and to a degree this may
jeopardize his progress.

Because it is popularly believed that long drawn-out
treatments and daily sessions are financially advantageous to the analyst, it is worthwhile to point out
that, on the contrary, precisely these features of analysis place a ceiling on the analyst's income. Indeed,
from the analyst's point of view, every consideration of
self-interest would tempt the busy practitioner to
reduce the frequency of the analytic sessions. Were he
to give each patient fewer appointments per week,
each patient would be able to pay more per session;
fewer sessions per patient would enable the psychoanalyst to take care of more patients at one time, with
the result that the loss of one patient would make less
difference in his income. For an analyst, as for any
doctor, the more patients he has at any one time, the
more secure is his income. He can earn more, and his
earnings will be more secure, if he takes care of more
patients for short treatments and with less frequent
sessions. The dismaying prospect of long months of
daily work frightens off many potential patients; and
the psychoanalyst who refuses to compromise in these
matters has to content himself with a relatively modest
and sharply fluctuating income. It is nevertheless a
fundamental principle of analytic practice to determine the frequency of the sessions, not according to the
patient's pocketbook, but by the technical requirements of his neurosis. Thus, although it is both legiti-

mate and essential to make experiments in varying the frequency of the sessions, if any analyst ventures to proclaim that "most patients do not need to come so often," he must be very careful that he is not using this statement as a rationalization of his own financial interest. We should study with an open mind the therapeutic results achieved in recent experiments with less frequent sessions, but at the same time they should be scrutinized with cautious skepticism.

Chapter VIII
THE TECHNIQUE OF
FREE ASSOCIATION

In psychoanalysis the daily search for unconscious material is conducted by means of a technique called "free association." In the early development of psychoanalysis, a series of experiments with other methods led to an increasing dependence upon free association as the tool without which it proved impossible to penetrate to unconscious levels of psychological activity.

Physiological Basis

The method of free association is in essence an application of the obvious fact that it is impossible for psychological processes to move from one thought to another unless there is a connection between them, just as it is impossible for a train to move from one station to another without a connecting track. The old saying that "one thought leads to another" is a popular statement of the same fact. We now know, however, that many associative links are unconscious, and it is the function of the psychoanalyst to discover the nature and meaning of unconscious as well as conscious linkages. He does this by studying the patient's free association.

The psychoanalyst notes not merely the conscious logic of a patient's communications, but also the sequence in time of his ideas and feelings. In his work on the conditioned reflex, Pavlov showed that in a hungry animal no two experiences could impinge upon the nervous system without setting up a connecting link, and that the nature of this link was dependent in part upon the time interval between them. Similarly in psychoanalysis, it has been possible to prove that ideas, feelings, and actions that occur together are bound to one another in a meaningful pattern. The nature of that bond and of the inarticulate ideas that underlie it is often hard to ascertain, and much of the work of psychoanalysis is devoted to the investigation and translation of these bonds into conscious thoughts and feelings (1934, 1941a, 1942a).

Thus, it has been the contribution of a great Russian school of neurophysiology to prove that time relationships have a vital significance in psychophysiology; and it has been the contribution of the psychoanalytical school to make use of this fundamental principle in the study of unconscious psychological processes of thought and feeling.

Its Application

In applying the principle, the psychoanalyst asks the patient to make use of the simplest and most primitive of all ways of thinking: to allow his thoughts to flow without guidance or direction, bumping along from one idea to the next as a blindfolded man would bump from tree to tree in a forest. The patient is instructed never to withhold anything, never to substitute one thought for another because the other seems more relevant, never to omit anything because it seems impolite or unfriendly, a violation of confidence, embarrassing, or trivial and unimportant. In short, he is instructed to tell everything that passes through his mind, and, as nearly as this is humanly possible, to tell it in the order and in the form in which it comes to him. Thus, he is asked to think aloud in the presence of the psychoanalyst with that simple and naive form of undirected musing which everyone uses in the solitude of his own chambers and which is at the same time the most spontaneous and creative of all forms of thought.

It is not always realized that free association is the natural process by which the mind of the artist and scientist creates. Free associations enable the psychological processes to roam through the mental highways and byways, unhampered by conscious restrictions, gathering up ideas and impressions and putting them together in varying combinations until new relationships and new patterns come into view. Both in science and in the arts, free association is an essential tool in the process of creative search. Subsequent logical scrutiny subjects the new patterns to a necessary secondary process of retrospective checking and testing. In psychoanalysis, the free associations are provided by the patient, the logical scrutiny by the analyst.

It is important to realize that this dependence upon free associations is the basis of all that is new and

scientific in psychoanalytic technique. Ordinary con-
versational speech, logical and chronological thinking,
the asking and answering of questions, arguments and
expositions are the product of a continuous auto-natic
scanning and screening of the psychological process.
This scanning and sampling selects certain ideas for
attention because of their logical and chronological
relationships, rejecting others as irrelevant. On this
depends our ability to organize thoughts and to communicate them. The product of this selective process,
however, is what the statisticians would call a weighted sample of our psychological processes and consequently is not truly representative of all that goes on.
Free associations, on the other hand, may approximate
a random sample of our psychological processes. It is
this special virtue of the technique of free association as
a method of truer sampling that makes it more valuable than any previous method of studying human
personality and human psychology.

There are three psychological "levels" of linkages,
conscious, preconscious, and unconscious. If we allow
ourselves consciously to pick and choose from among
the thoughts that come freely to mind, it becomes
impossible to study the influence of unconscious forces
on the stream of psychological events. If, on the other
hand, all conscious choices are eliminated, then the
unconscious influences are exposed. Free associations,
therefore, are the key to the unconscious, indeed, the
only key we now possess.

When the patient allows his thoughts to roam freely,

he gathers together a surprising array of apparently unrelated items. The well-trodden highways of his mind are soon abandoned, and he finds himself in a seemingly trackless forest, following paths from which he can emerge only slowly. Sometimes it is possible to see almost at once the direction of the patient's thought processes; but more often the analyst's task is slowly to piece together a picture puzzle. Each day's work brings its additional bits of data; and only as the fragments of the puzzle accumulate over weeks and months can the pattern of the whole be made clear. Therefore for both the patient and the psychoanalyst there are periods of searching during which no rewarding answers and no immediate emotional gratification or relief from symptoms can be expected. *However, as long as free associations continue to come from the patient without hindrance, the analysis progresses.*

This would seem to be a simple requirement. Yet in the course of every analysis, free associations repeatedly become entangled in an intricate network of conscious and unconscious emotions, the resolution of which is one of the important therapeutic experiences of the analytic process.

The Value of the Struggle to Produce Free Associations

"Why does just lying down and talking do anyone any good?"

When he attempts to produce a flow of free associations, the patient, to his dismay, finds it to be an unexpectedly baffling task. This most spontaneous of

78

all forms of thinking, which in solitude is also the easiest, proves in the analytical situation to be the most difficult. From moment to moment the patient struggles with impulses to hold back or not to talk at all, or to rearrange his words into pleasanter and more acceptable forms; that is, into forms more flattering to his self-esteem and to the impression he wants to make on the analyst. The mere presence of the silent analyst exercises a profound influence on this process. The intensity of this inner struggle varies from time to time. No patient achieves unguided speech continuously. Usually, indeed, the psychoanalyst has to work for weeks or even months before he succeeds in ridding a patient of inhibitions that make free associations impossible. Since without free associations we cannot penetrate to unconscious levels, one of the primary functions of the psychoanalyst is to help the patient surmount the inner obstacles to the production of free associations. Indeed, throughout an analysis, the freedom with which such associations keep flowing is one of the important indicators of progress. In especially difficult cases, certain drugs have been tried in an effort to help patients to overcome this difficulty. Their success has not yet been fully established. It is important to bear in mind the fact that true free associations are not easily come by and make up only a small portion of any analytic session.

The analytic work required to clear away the emotional obstacles to the production of free material turns out to be fruitful in many ways. In the course of an analysis, each time it becomes necessary to resolve feelings that are obstructing free associations, an alteration occurs in the patient. Thus, even when the struggle to maintain the free production of psychological data turns some phases of an analysis into a pitched battle with the psychoanalyst, it leads to a deepening understanding of the patient's problems.

Patients have many special difficulties in producing free associations. There are those who cling to logic out of terror, as a frightened bather in the ocean clutches the ropes when he jumps up and down. There are those who exploit logic obsessionally, using it as their only weapon of attack and defense, under the spur of an unconscious hate. There are those who flee from free associations out of shame at what they might say, fear lest free paths of thought should trap them into an admission of something they are ashamed to confess (e.g., a man who had stolen from his father, a woman who had suffered from compulsive promiscuity, etc.). There are obstacles to free associations which arise from the symbolic values that words themselves, or the mere act of uttering them, may have for certain patients.

All such difficulties, and many more, have to be resolved in the course of the analytic work itself, and tax the skill and ingenuity of the analyst to the utmost.

Among these various obstacles to the processes of free association, two have special significance: (1) the complex anxieties patients feel at giving themselves up to the processes of free association at all, and especially in the presence of another person (the inner nature of these anxieties will be discussed later); and (2) emotional storms which sweep over the patient in his relationship to the analyst. These, however, constitute major obstacles to freedom in all human relationships. This is one of the several reasons why self-analysis, even to the limited degree to which it is possible at all, cannot achieve by itself the same therapeutic goals as the analytic process in the presence of a human psychoanalyst, before whom the patient must have the humility to reveal himself, and on whom, in conscious and unconscious fantasies, the patient works out his problems. The analyst as a target for the patient's difficulties is therefore an essential ingredient in the therapeutic process.

The Impossibility of Recalling One's Own Free Associations

Certain theoretical and practical consequences result from this dependence upon free associations. The patient who is allowing his thoughts to flow in this unguided fashion soon becomes lost in the labyrinth of his own associations. It is as impossible for him to recall all of his scattered, interrupted, and fragmentary thoughts as it is to recall a long chain of nonsense syllables. If after each session any patient has a clear recollection of the sequence of his ideas, it is easy to show that they have been produced not freely, but under the influence of some guiding preconceptions and purposes. The worker in academic psychology used to be trained in the classical techniques of the introspectionist and was supposed thereby to be able to observe and to report his inner psychological processes unmodified. Actually, by the very process of systematic observation and report, he automatically restricted the freedom of his associations. Therefore, in order to study the uncharted paths of associations, an observer must be present to note the patterns traced by the patient's productions, or else one must use some method of mechanical recording.

For this same reason, not even the trained psychoanalyst can be his own analyst. One cannot simultaneously be the miner and the assayer. One cannot produce ideas freely and at the same time note them and evaluate them, because the act of observing and recording will in itself alter their sequence. For research purposes, therefore, methods of mechanical recording are an indispensable adjunct to the human observer; but no matter how perfect the recording apparatus may be, for therapeutic purposes the human observer is essential. There are further reasons for this, which will be discussed in Chapter IX.

From time to time, orderly sequences of thought occur during the flow of free associations, the stream of ideas assuming a logical, narrative, chronological, or argumentative form, without interrupting deflections. The experienced analyst will be as suspicious of a stream of thought that is always fragmented as of one that is always carefully organized. But the patient who never produces free associations never gets analyzed.

The Couch

Usually, the patient is requested to lie on a couch during most if not all of the analysis. The purpose of this is primarily to facilitate the production of the free associations we have been discussing. It is necessary to conduct an analysis in the presence of a psychoanalyst, but it usually helps a patient to relax if he does not have constantly to observe the psychoanalyst and to adapt to his presence. When a patient is face to face with the psychoanalyst, it is inevitable that he will respond continually to the analyst's facial expressions and gestures. Whether the analyst shows his feelings in his expression or whether he maintains a stony immobility, the watchful patient will find meanings in his stance. This introduces distorting external impressions into a stream of thought that is most useful when it proceeds spontaneously from the patient's inner psychic life.

Furthermore, it is to the patient's advantage that the psychoanalyst should be relaxed, because only in this way can the analyst listen to the patient's productions with the greatest possible freedom. If the patient were merely to turn his back to the analyst while seated in a chair, the psychoanalyst could not observe him at all. If, on the other hand, the patient reclines on a couch, with the psychoanalyst sitting just at the head of the couch, it becomes possible for both the patient and the analyst to be relaxed, at the same time affording the analyst an opportunity to observe the patient's gestures and his facial expression. Thus the analytic couch, about which there has been considerable discussion and perplexity, is actually a minor detail of psychoanalytic technique, nothing more mysterious than a helpful and sensible expedient.

It has one further value. By keeping out of the patient's direct line of vision, the analyst remains less "real" to the patient than he would become in the course of a long analysis, if this were conducted vis-à-vis. The couch therefore helps to preserve what has been called the "analytic incognito" and thus increases the value of the analytic work on transference manifestations. These are discussed in Chapter IX.

In spite of these considerations, however, the use of the couch is not indispensable. For various reasons some patients become completely blocked if they lie down. Some become panicky or depressed. In such cases the difficulty has to be analyzed before the couch can be used helpfully. Consequently, some patients vary between sitting up, walking around, and the couch. It is probably true, however, that the ability to produce free associations fluently while on the couch is a fairly reliable index of analytic progress, and I would never feel entirely secure about an analysis in which the patient had *never* been able to use the couch.

The Direct Question vs. Free Association

The psychoanalyst makes only limited use of direct questions. There are times, of course, when these are essential either for eliciting precise information or as a stimulus to further free associations. But for the most part it is better to allow the historical data of the patient's life, and his opinions and feelings, to express themselves spontaneously and without the guidance of systematic inquiry. This means a freer and at the same time a more disconnected and less orderly history than would be produced in response to leading questions. The reconstruction of such a history takes longer, but the historical data comes to light against a rich background of associations, which in turn give emotional significance to the bare facts. There are occasions, of course, when the psychoanalyst must use questions to gather facts, as with children, with families, and occasionally to corroborate or correct the data elicited from patients themselves. In general, however, the facts assembled through questioning can be used only as the patient elaborates upon them freely. Histories that are put together in response to persistent questions are, in general, shallow compared to histories that are compiled more slowly by the use of the method of free association.

"Homework" during the Analysis

During the course of an analysis a patient often asks whether or not he should think up things to talk about ahead of time, whether he should write them down, whether there is work that he should do outside, and whether he should read psychoanalytic literature. There are no generally binding rules for these questions, but the guiding principles are implicit in the foregoing discussion of the process of free association. Certainly, both in and out of the analytic session the patient is free to think or write anything he pleases. It is essential not only that when he comes to his analytic hour he should not confine his thoughts to the paths he has traversed already, but that even when he uses his previous thoughts or notes as a starting point, he should thereafter allow his associations to roam as freely as they please. Such "homework" is useful when it serves merely as a springboard from which the patient dives into his own free associations. Beyond this, one may say that the amount of thought a patient devotes to his analysis when he is away from it may be an index of the sincerity of his analytic purpose. On the other hand, an obsessive preoccupation with the analysis or an extreme inability to think about it at all is equally indicative of the presence of unresolved emotional problems that must be dealt with in the analysis itself.

The values and dangers of analytic reading vary with different patients and in different phases of each analysis, and in each case have to be determined as the work proceeds. This is often an issue of special importance in the training of young psychiatrists who are naturally eager to read as much and as early as possible in the course of their training analyses. Experience has demonstrated that it is usually well to limit such reading at first, and to postpone it until late in the analysis. Otherwise, a patient is likely to intellectualize the analytic process and may unwittingly make his associations fit his reading. He will have greater confidence in the spontaneity of his own productions and in their freedom from suggestion if he has not read a great deal of theory before he has uncovered his own material.

Popular Misconceptions Concerning Introspection and Free Association

Psychoanalysis is often accused of making patients morbidly introspective. If true, this would be an important objection; it must therefore be considered in relation to, first, the approach to psychoanalysis, and second, the process of psychoanalysis itself.

As will be seen in Chapter XV, on the approach to analysis, every patient goes through a stage in his journey toward treatment during which he must be brought to a realization of the extent of his needs. During this phase he will inevitably become preoccupied with his problems and his symptoms, since it is only by allowing himself to think and feel about himself that he will finally accept the fact that he needs help. During this preanalytic struggle, the patient may well appear to be "morbidly introspective." Moreover, through the course of an analysis there will be recurrent phases in which the patient turns into himself emotionally and struggles anew with his consciousness of illness and his realization of his own maladjustments. During each such struggle, the "introspection" reappears. This is both necessary and constructive, since, unless the patient is willing to face inner realities, no psychotherapy, whether psychoanalytic or otherwise, is possible.

Between this and what may rightly be called "morbid introspection" lies a wide gulf. What common sense objects to is that form of introspection *which is itself a symptom of illness and not a phase of treatment.* It is a form of obsessive and solitary rumination that moves in closed circles without ever reaching any goal. It does not lead to the frank acknowledgment of illness, the necessity for which we have emphasized. Nor is it related to the process of free association. Instead, it is an obsessional symptom, a distortion of the intellect in the service of unconscious emotional needs. Free associations, on the contrary, are used to dissect and break down such obsessive introspection so as to make possible a more effective form of self-observation.

Patients who suffer from obsessive rumination will at times distort the analytic instrument through this morbid symptom. When this happens, the psychoanalyst uses it to give the patient further insight into the symptom with which he is struggling. It is fair to state, therefore, that despite the fact that psychoanalysis turns the attention of the patient on himself, it does so in a form which is fundamentally different from that profitless type of introspection which is itself a manifestation of neurotic illness. The validity of this statement is attested to by the fact that a successfully analyzed patient becomes far less subjective than ever before, indeed less subjective than the average man.

Connected with this issue is the widespread notion that all those who have neuroses are "introverts." By this term, the layman means people who are continuously charged with highly personal emotions and who are concerned primarily and exclusively with their own thoughts and feelings. Actually, there are many patients of whom quite the reverse is true, and of whom their friends and relatives say, "He's the last person in the world I would have expected to have a nervous breakdown. He always seemed so cheerful. He never seemed to worry about himself. He was always busy and active." A reluctance to let oneself face one's own thoughts and emotions may be just as serious a symptom of maladjustment as an obsessive inability to pay attention to anyone but oneself. Therefore, although the popular condemnation of obsessive introspection is valid, this condemnation should not include the properly guided psychoanalytic study of psychological problems by means of the technique of free association.

Summary

It is fair to say, then, that psychoanalysis makes use of two basic procedures. The first is to survey the play of unconscious psychological forces in the patient's free associations. The other is to show the influence of these unconscious forces upon the pattern of the patient's daily life and upon his relationships to other human beings. Consequently, the psychoanalyst himself plays a dual role. In one, he maps out for the patient hitherto unrecognized psychological linkages. He describes in a quiet, friendly, impersonal manner the significant connections he sees between the various components of the patient's free associations. Because these sequences of thoughts and feelings must ultimately refer to the patient's own life, the interpretation of them leads step by step to a deeper understanding of the patient's personality and history.

The patient soon discovers that this work does not proceed in an emotional vacuum. No matter how quietly impersonal the psychoanalyst remains, and no matter how little the patient knows about him in reality, the analyst soon becomes a storm center for the patient's highly charged emotions. This, indeed, is the second major role of the analyst; and in order to make it possible for the patient to produce his associations freely, these stormy, personalized emotions must be analyzed with the patient. That is, they must be watched for, anticipated, and described to the patient, sometimes before he is aware of them himself, and they must then be resolved by making clear their sources. This is known technically as "the analysis of the transference." If it is neglected, the production of free associations soon ceases and the analysis reaches an impasse. This process will be the subject of the next chapter.

Chapter IX

THE ANALYSIS OF THE TRANSFERENCE IN INDIVIDUAL AND GROUP THERAPY

The Phenomenon of Transference

In psychoanalysis the word transference derives from the fact that in adult years our relations to others are compounded of both conscious and unconscious elements, the unconscious elements consisting largely of attitudes, needs, feelings, and purposes carried over (i.e., "transferred") unconsciously from the attitudes, needs, feelings, and purposes toward others developed in infancy and early childhood.

A great deal of misunderstanding exists about "the transference" and the "analysis of the transference." It sometimes is pictured as something that is put over on the unwary patient, as a Machiavellian maneuver by which the analyst artificially induces in a patient a peculiar attachment to himself; as a method male analysts reserve for young and beautiful women and never use with the poor or the ugly or, for that matter, with men; as a highly pleasurable state of infatuation with the analyst; or as something that develops late in an analysis and only as the result of some mysterious and possibly malevolent, obscure, or lecherous attitude of the analyst.

In every detail, these notions about transference are false. In the first place, transferred feelings run the whole gamut of human emotions, including hate, fear, distrust, rivalry, and envy, quite as much as love, faith, and confidence. Secondly, "transference" is not a "method used in psychoanalysis." Psychoanalysis recognized and named it; but it is a universal phenomenon, occurring in significant measure in every human relationship. This unconscious transference of feelings occurs spontaneously and from the onset of the analysis, out of preformed attitudes existing in every patient before he ever comes for treatment. Although it evolves through many changing phases in the course of any analysis, one never needs to "wait for transference to develop." It begins even when a patient starts to consider being analyzed—indeed before he has even met his analyst—with his dim fantasies of what the analyst is going to be like. Transference never has to be cultivated by any analytic artifice. Peculiar to psychoanalysis is only one fact, namely, that in analytic therapy the transferred feelings are demonstrated to the patient and are studied with him and traced to their origins. The purpose of this is to make clear to the patient what parts of his conscious feelings are appropriate and what parts inappropriate, and how these feelings have arisen out of earlier relationships. This is of great value to the patient because it shows him how such transplanted feelings have the power to distort other human relationships. There is consequently never a psychoanalytic treatment, whether of an old man or a young woman, of adult or child, rich or poor, ugly or beautiful, in which transference does not occur and in which the transference is not analyzed.

Perhaps a few examples will make this clear.

A man came for help who was poor, homely, sick, and in desperate need. Analysis was started at once, but it was many months before the risk of suicide and of complete mental disintegration had been averted. Because the patient's illness had destroyed his business and rendered him penniless, he was treated for free. For this he was sincerely grateful; yet in spite of his gratitude, day after day the patient exploded at the analyst with furious bitterness, resentment, hostility, and fear. The violence of his feelings about the analyst is hard to describe; yet, for a long time its causes remained obscure. The analyst knew only that the patient had had equally violent and equally unprovoked emotional storms in many other relationships. Then one day the patient related a dream that suddenly brought back to his mind something that had occurred in the analyst's waiting room on the occasion of the patient's first preliminary visit. As the analyst had entered the waiting room with his hand outstretched to greet the patient and before a word had been spoken by either man, the patient suddenly had the thought, "He has an impediment in his speech." As he rose to shake the analyst's hand, he repressed this fantasy, not to recall it until several months later when, during the stormy course of his analysis, it came back to him in connection with his associations to his dream. Further associations brought to light the fact that the most important person in this patient's early years was an uncle who had alternated between effusive affection for the patient and stormy rages against him. This uncle, long dead, had in fact suffered from the impediment in his speech that the patient had momentarily attributed to the analyst. From this and other data it became clear that even before he entered the analyst's office, the patient had been prepared unwittingly to identify the analyst with his uncle; and it was this unconscious anticipation that had led him first to imagine that the analyst suffered from the uncle's speech defect, then to repress this notion, and then to feel for the analyst the violent fear and hate which, as a small child, he had felt secretly for his uncle. This led to the discovery that similar feelings had been transplanted into the patient's relationships with his wife's father and brother, with friends and teachers in school and college, with his business associates, and even with his own sons. The clarification of the source of these transferred feelings threw light on one of the roots of this man's illness and eliminated one of the most disruptive forces in his life, making possible a spontaneous improvement in all his human relationships. This is an example of what psychoanalysis means by "the analysis of the transference." It is hardly the exploitation of a "transfer of affection to the analyst." Hostile feelings were a transplanted and distorting force that had to be analyzed.

Again, there was an emaciated little woman of forty-eight, looking as though she were deep in her seventies, who would flare into savage rages at those to whom she was most deeply attached and for whom she had worked loyally through many years. Inevitably, in the course of time, the same angers occurred in relation to the analyst. One day, as this frail wisp of a woman shouted at the analyst in a towering rage, she suddenly became aware that she felt as though he were the living embodiment of everything that she had feared and hated in her own mother. This mother had in fact been a tyrannical and unfair woman; and the discovery that the patient's feelings about the analyst were derived from her feelings about her mother proved to her that the same process distorted many other relationships, initiating a gain in insight which gradually freed her from this persistent and destructive residue of her childhood.

Or consider a beautiful, gifted, yet tragic woman who for years was haunted by crippling anxieties and phobias. Like an automaton she swung from love to hate and back to love again in her relations with her husband, her children, her family, and her friends. In the course of treatment, she showed the same swing in her feelings for the analyst. Through the study of the sources of these feelings, she came to understand that she was superimposing on the analyst the image of an older brother who had brought her up. The intonations, inflections, gestures, and mannerisms of the analyst all reminded the patient of this brother, although no other person who had known the brother would have recognized the fancied resemblance. The gradual elucidation of the fact that her violent and inconsistent feelings about the analyst had nothing to do with him, led the patient to realize that the same transplanted emotions had distorted her relations to her husband, her sons, and her friends and that this had caused much of the havoc in her life.

Finally, there was a beautiful young woman whose analyst was an attractive man, not more than ten years her senior. Here, if ever, was a situation for the conventional assumption that "the patient falls in love with the analyst." What actually happened was quite different. From the first day, because of a bitter lifelong rivalry with her four brothers, her attitude to this analyst was one of well-masked hostility. With exceptional cunning she would set traps to fool him, making up stories, inventing dreams, and often protesting a love for him which masked her deep and abiding hatred of all men. Fortunately, he was taken in neither by her pretended affection nor by her bursts of violent rage, until finally his quiet detachment made it possible for her to see that her efforts to seduce him were part of her unconscious need to destroy all men, a need that had wrought devastation all around her. This discovery was the turning point toward health.

Thus, this process which analysts call "transference" can make a man treat a business associate as though he were his brother, an employer as though he were a father, a teacher as though she were a mother. It can make us behave in ways that may have been appropriate in childhood but are inappropriate in adult years. It is one of several forces that can lead people to hate those against whom they have no grievance, to love those for whom they have no valid basis for affection, to fear those who are no threat to them. By distorting relationships, transference hampers and cripples the universal groping for maturity and for an integrated existence which all men seek. Therefore, it is important for sociologists and cultural anthropologists and for ethical and religious leaders to understand the destructive role of this universal process in human affairs. To learn how easily we can fool ourselves about both our loving and our hating is a humbling lesson, having profound significance for man in his struggle to become civilized.

Regardless of the age and sex of the psychoanalyst, the patient reacts to him with patterns characteristic of his attitude to men and women in general. All human relationships are compounded of various admixtures of yearning plus the frustrations of this yearning, which lead to anger, fear, and sorrow. These feelings may exist even when they are masked or disguised. The psychoanalyst helps the patient to greater clarity by giving him insight into the ways in which these feelings work in him, the disguises they may assume, and the distortions they introduce into his relationships with his fellows. For a considerable period in every analysis

97

it is chiefly as these feelings manifest themselves toward the veiled figure of the psychoanalyst that it is possible for the patient to recognize the unconscious and fantastic sources of these disturbing emotions. It is in this way that the analysis of the "transference" helps to clear the air not only within the analytic situation, but in the patient's other relationships as well.

That the transferred feelings could be exploited by an unscrupulous or untrained analyst is obvious. It is for this very reason that analytic training is so exacting; and it is also for this reason, as will be explained below, that the skillful and scrupulous analyst avoids all social relations with his patients.

The So-called "Negative Transference"

What has already been said should make it clear that the term "negative transference" refers only to a phase in the analysis during which the patient feels a conscious antipathy for the analyst. This may be quite as valuable therapeutically as a phase of positive feelings.

Even in launching an analysis it is not always necessary for the patient to like the analyst. Some years ago a woman was referred to an able and experienced colleague who happened to be an unusually mild and gentle man. Nevertheless, for reasons which had not been anticipated, the patient reacted to him with an immediate violent antipathy. To her, this gentle analyst represented the embodiment of evil. She rushed from her first interview to telephone the referring colleague, full of fury and outraged reproaches, and begged him to send her to someone else. For various reasons, she was prevailed upon to return to the same analyst the next day. For four successive days her antipathy continued unabated. Then it began to lessen, only to recur from time to time at lengthening intervals and with diminishing violence. In the meantime, under the whiplash of this overwhelming reaction, an immense number of repressed and highly charged fantasies about men in general were thoroughly ventilated. The patient's reward for not running away was that her analysis progressed with exceptional speed. Under these somewhat unusual circumstances, the fact that the patient battled through her frantic terror and revulsion at the very start of the analysis probably saved her many months of polite but evasive sparring.

One does not deliberately risk so difficult a challenge at the start of an analysis because the analyst cannot yet know enough about his patient to be in a position to clarify the reasons for any violent hostilities. In most instances, rage at the start would make it wise to shift the patient to someone with whom the patient could launch the analysis more calmly. The foregoing episode is nonetheless worth citing to emphasize a point of general significance: that a patient's positive or negative feelings about his analyst arise predominantly out of the unconscious fantasies the patient brings preformed into the analytical situation and then drapes around the analyst. Whether the patient likes or dislikes an analyst is intrinsically of little significance to the outcome of the treatment. What is important is that the feeling must be thoroughly analyzed. Once analyzed, positive and negative feelings are of equal value for the solution of a neurosis. What is called "negative transference" is not negative in the sense of vitiating the treatment. Only if negative feelings make it impossible for the patient to work with the analyst and to produce free associations in his presence will they necessitate a change of analyst. It should be kept in mind that positive feelings for the analyst, unless correctly analyzed, can create quite as formidable an obstacle to the production of free associations as do negative feelings.

The Dependence of the Analysis of the Transference upon the "Analytic Incognito"

From the point of view of the patient, the analysis of the transference is one of the most valuable of the experiences his treatment brings him. The reason for this is simple. The psychoanalyst as an individual must be unknown to the patient. He therefore keeps himself as much in the background as possible, out of clear focus and definition, quietly friendly, but always impersonal and reserved. He makes no show of his life, his work, his tastes, his pets, his family, his feelings, or his opinions. Insofar as is humanly possible, he remains a peg on which the patient can hang his conscious and unconscious fantasies. By being unknown to the patient at the start, and by maintaining his formal reserve, i.e., his "analytic incognito," throughout the analysis, the psychoanalyst makes of himself a neutral sample of all humanity in the patient's emotional life. This is what gives value to the study of the origins of the patient's feelings. Toward the shadowy image of the psychoanalyst, the patient experiences anxiety, anger, hate, affection, jealousy, and the like. In the early phases of the analysis, most patients are unaware of these feelings until the analyst points out some indirect or disguised expression of them. By demonstrating the existence of such groundless affects in the analytic relationship, it becomes possible for the psychoanalyst to prove to the patient that similarly unfounded storms can warp his relations with other human beings. By unearthing the original sources of these feelings in early childhood, the analysis makes it possible to eliminate them, or at least to lessen their intensity and their influence.

If, on the other hand, the patient knows the analyst personally or knows a great deal about him through mutual friends or relatives or comes to know a lot about the analyst during the course of the analysis, it becomes impossible to use the patient's attitude to the analyst to illuminate the sources of his buried feelings toward others. The more the patient knows about his analyst, the more firmly will the patient's feelings be anchored in reality; and feelings which are a composite product of unconscious fantasies and realistic knowledge about the analyst are difficult to use to increase the patient's self-knowledge. Since realities are obvious, they mask the subtler role of fantasy.

That is why it is essential for the patient that the psychoanalyst be a stranger about whose personality he knows as little as possible, and why it is unwise for a psychoanalyst to capitalize on his social contacts and his friendships to build up his analytic practice, and, finally, why it is destructive to an analysis for an analyst to establish friendly social relations with a patient. It is only with an unknown figure that the analysis of the transference can be used with full therapeutic effect.

It is nonetheless inevitable that in the course of an analysis subtle hints will betray to the patient something of the analyst's personality as a real person. This cannot be wholly prevented even by the strictest precautions. What can be avoided, however, are frank avowals and confirmations of the patient's guesses and speculations. And this is worthwhile because it limits the contamination of the transference by realities and thereby preserves much of its value as an analytic instrument.

The Analytic Incognito as a Protection for the Patient

Another important purpose served by the conventional formality and impersonality of the relation between an analyst and his patient is to protect the patient from the human frailties of analysts. In spite of the careful training to which an analyst is subjected, and in spite of every effort to reduce to a minimum any sources of confusion from his own unconscious, an analyst is not and cannot be a saint. He cannot achieve a state of disembodied contemplation, free from all earthbound cravings and lusts, invulnerable to frustration or deprivation, and devoid of anger. He is at best a fallible human being with his own weaknesses and pains, and no matter how carefully he has been analyzed in the course of his training, not all of his frailties will have been eliminated. How, then, can the patient be protected from these residual weaknesses? This is achieved by maintaining a strict formality between patient and analyst in the therapeutic situation and by the rigid exclusion of all business or social relations between them. Why this is so should be clear. In any social relationship, we serve our own conscious and unconscious emotional needs. If any social relationship with a patient were to be meaningful, the analyst would have to bring his own needs into it. If he did not, the relationship would be a sham. Yet the moment he made any such conscious or unconscious demands, the relationship would serve two masters; and, from that moment, in any further efforts to analyze his patient he could not have the same objectivity he had before. It would become impossible for him to be certain whether he was serving the patient's needs or his own. A single-minded concentration on the patient's needs can be achieved only when the patient is to the analyst solely a patient. Once he becomes a friend, the patient's needs and the analyst's needs become inextricably mixed. The analyst has every right to serve his own needs elsewhere, but never at the expense of his patients, and therefore not through social relationships with his patients (1968d).

It is clear that the conscientious psychoanalyst is not free to expand his practice by social contacts with the friends and relatives of his patients, as is entirely proper for other physicians. The analyst must subject his personal advantage to the needs of his patients, and practice his particular medical specialty with a code more austere in this respect than that necessary for other medical and surgical disciplines.

The Unsolved Problem of Group Analysis

The increasing efforts to conduct the analytic process in groups instead of individually raise many difficult problems concerning free associations and the transference and its resolution. There are further unsolved problems concerning the composition of groups, questions that have to be considered separately in relation to analysis as an exploratory process and analysis as a therapeutic process (1958c, 1973c).

Chapter X
THE ROLE OF DREAM ANALYSIS

The Quality of Dreams

Readers may be surprised that there has so far been no mention of the analysis of dreams, which usually receives much emphasis in discussions of psychoanalysis. In reality, the exploration of dream material, while of great value, is only one ingredient in the complex technique of analysis: an ingredient used freely in some analyses, sparingly in others, and to varying degrees in the different phases of all. Dreams have always seemed fascinating and mysterious. The nightmares of childhood may retain their vividness throughout life. The conjunction of the possible and impossible in dreams keeps alive the old yearning to be able through them to prophesy the future. None of this, however, has anything to do with the use of the dream in analytic therapy. Here, the analysis of the dreamed experience is conducted as soberly as is the analysis of a waking experience. Reality is woven into the fabric of a dream, just as fantasy weaves its way through actual events; and the differences between the psychological significance of dreams and of real events are relative rather than absolute. The analysis of the two yields much the same sort of information, although each has its own special advantages.

Certain questions about dreams are asked regularly. People want to know why we forget our dreams, why dreams can be so confused and fantastic, why a dream that lasted only a fraction of a second may take so long to tell, whether dreams "mean" anything, and the like. It is not possible to be dogmatic in answering all these questions, but certain facts are clear.

It is certainly not the clarity or emotional intensity of a dream that determines whether or not the dream is remembered. Vivid dreams may be forgotten quite as often as vague ones. Everyone has had the experience of dreaming something in sharp detail, of waking with the dream clearly in mind and a determination to remember it, only to find that within moments or by the next morning it is completely gone, perhaps to return to memory suddenly a few days later. Evidently, even when a dream is clear and vivid, active forces of some kind must determine what is forgotten and what is recalled, and when. The therapeutic value of dream analysis is largely a result of alterations produced in these forces by the process of analysis. Much of the research work on dreams deals with the nature of these opposing or "censoring" forces; how they distort the content of dreams through processes of displacement, condensation, reversal, and the symbolic representation of the sources of the dream, and how they determine whether a dream is forgotten or recalled.

Our memory of a dream always includes a lot of "filling in." Hardly ever do we dream as much of any dream as we think we do. There are occasional epic dreams which are remembered in every detail, but even these often prove to be a synthetic product of clear fragments and conscious or unconscious secondary elaborations. Most dreams consist largely of a series of vivid and highly condensed tableaux, not unlike old-fashioned charades or living pictures, or a series of "stills" from a motion picture. A sequence of such images can flash across the screen of our thought processes in a fraction of a second, but it may take half an hour to tell the story they represent. This is due partly to the tedious process of putting into words the quality of a single word or gesture, partly to the time it takes to fill in the gaps between the clear flashes, and partly to the fact that a dream is a condensed way of saying many things at once. Together, these features of the dream process account for much of the apparent confusion of the dream. It is fortunate, however, that the confused and uncertain parts of any dream and, indeed, the uncertainty itself can be quite as meaningful for an analysis as are the clear elements.

Many special features of the thought process in dreams are a direct result of the fact that in the dream we think primarily by means of visual images. In this respect, dream thinking resembles the thought process of the human child, and probably that of all lower animals. Certainly, most of us recall the look of things more readily than we can recall their sound, taste, smell, or feel. This is partly because form and color remain relatively constant, whereas other modalities of sensation are transitory experiences which can less readily be re-experienced unaltered. Furthermore, vision is the only sensation which, during sleep, can be completely eliminated at the level of the sense organ, that is, at the source. This is done through darkness and by shutting the eyes. Sound, taste, smell, the various forms of touch, and internal bodily sensations can never be excluded to the same extent during sleep. At best they are diminished by rendering them more or less constant, and by a process of central muting in the brain, called "inhibition" (1962a, 1966e, 1972a; Kubie and Margolin, 1944). As a result, sounds are rarely heard clearly in dreams, but are usually represented by a thought of the sound; and taste, smell, and bodily sensations are seldom experienced as such in dreams. None of these is totally excluded, but their roles are quite secondary to visual imagery, which is the principal language of the dream process. This is why the dream is predominantly a visual hallucination. For most people the visual images of dreams consist largely of black, white, and grey. Colors appear relatively rarely and are usually limited to one color which picks out some particular object for special emphasis. The physiological reasons for this are not known.

The Meaningfulness of Dreams

An understanding of the value of the interpretation of dreams requires a statement of certain elementary facts, most of which are obvious, but whose significance is often overlooked.

(a) The same physiological apparatus, the same brain, and the same human being is the instrument of the psychological processes in the waking state and in dreaming.

(b) The psychological processes of the dream serve the same purpose as do the psychological processes of the waking state. This purpose is primarily to express psychological tensions that accumulate in us during the day. Dreams may serve this purpose in many ways. Even combat dreams that waken us with terrifying hallucinations protect the dreamer from even worse states of tension; more often, by expressing tension the dream enables us to remain asleep.

(c) The immediate instigator of the tensions that accumulate at night is the residue of the day's unfinished business. Each day brings some experiences that yield a quiet glow of satisfaction and others that end unhappily, leaving behind them a bad aftertaste. Some of these daily events make us feel confident, relaxed, and reassured; others leave us shaken, uneasy, depressed, and frightened. Some give us a feeling of virtue; other episodes awaken feelings of guilt. Some leave behind them feelings of peace and good will; others stir deep tides of rage. If we could make an algebraic summation at the end of each day, we would find that some days add up to a contented frame of mind, and others to a deep and restless discontent. The former usually lead to a relatively dreamless sleep, the latter to restlessness or wakefulness, or to sleep broken by dreams.

Such dreams regularly begin as more or less dis-guised attempts to resolve the emotional residue of the preceding day. They are efforts to find happier endings for the day's pain. This is a basic psychological law—what Freud called "the pleasure principle." Holly-wood, too, puts a happy ending to an unhappy tale. The child who wakens from a nightmare makes up a happy ending to the dream so that he can go back to sleep. Long after a dispute in which we have been worsted, we continue to think up the crushing argu-ments that did not occur to us in time. The man who has taken a beating in a fight thinks afterward of all the blows he should have landed. The nation that has lost a war dreams of revenge.

This is precisely what happens at the end of the day. First come the spontaneous reveries that take posses-sion of us as we drift off to sleep. Then comes the dream process, which begins as a continuation of these reveries. As we drift off to sleep, however, these gradually lose their anchorage in external reality. In spite of the fact that our thinking becomes increasingly fantastic as sleep deepens, it continues to serve the same psychological purpose. Automatically, therefore, as we slip away into sleep, our thought processes revolve around those problems brought to the forefront of our minds and hearts by the less happy events of the preceding day. This is why the springboard from which every dream starts is the residue of the day's misadventures. Daydreams are efforts to solve frag-ments of these problems. Sleeping dreams are condensations of many fragmentary daydreams, which through sleep have lost their moorings in reality, but which continue the same old search for a happy ending.

(d) This does not mean that the dream process deals with trivial disappointments. On the contrary, those frustrations sufficiently highly charged to upset us derive their emotional importance from the fact that they represent deeper struggles. The unhappy occurrences of each day are merely the most recent of a long line of earlier experiences which have sensitized us. Although every dream starts from the unhappy residue of trivial current experiences, each represents a condensation of our past. Every person and place and event in a dream is a fused image of people and places and events from many periods in the dreamer's life, plus the inner problems with which these are connected. Indeed, these condensations can be so all-inclusive that the drama of a lifetime may be recaptured in one series of vivid and fantastic dream images. Hence, every dream has not one but many "meanings." This is a further cause of the apparent confusion of dreams. Because of this condensation, the successful analysis of a dream uncovers a rich vein of gold, leading back from the present to remote and more deeply buried sources of trouble. The tracing of a dream to its immediate source in the trivial hurts of the preceding day is merely a first step toward an understanding of the experiences that have sensitized the dreamer to pain in the past. This is what led Freud to call dreams the "royal road to a knowledge of the unconscious activities of the mind."

Summary

One may summarize in general terms the present state of psychoanalytic theory of dreams. What we dream seems sometimes to be quite orderly and clear and at other times wholly confused. In either case, the obvious content of the dream, technically known as the "manifest content," always represents much more than itself. By various technical procedures this can usually be deciphered, and the "latent" or underlying significance of the dream can then be brought to light. When this is done, the dream is seen to represent many levels of buried feelings, wishes, and problems. Each dream, then, is an attempt to solve unconscious conflicts touched off by experiences of the preceding day, but originating in those earlier struggles of infancy and childhood which have become inaccessible to conscious introspection. In the compromises, displacements, and symbolic imagery constituting the dream, the early emotional and instinctual struggles are represented in condensed visual images. These fundamental conflicts are the power source of the dream. They are like the field of force between magnetic poles, the residues of the unhappy experiences of the preceding day arranging themselves along the lines of force like iron filings in a magnetic field. The interpreter uses them to discover the shape and character of the field of force, i.e., of the fundamental problems and conflicts latent in the dream.

In recent years a group of extraordinarily versatile and well-trained investigators (Fisher, 1965; Dement, 1972) have studied the phenomenology of dreams and the dynamics of dreams from both the electrophysiological and the analytic point of view. Those who have been most active in these investigations have been both analytically and physiologically trained and experienced. These recent developments represent one of the first successful attempts to bridge the gap between the two fields of investigation. Whether or not one agrees with their interpretations, one cannot diminish the importance of this breakthrough (1962a, 1966e).

Chapter XI
THE CHOICE OF A PSYCHOANALYST

The Influence of Individual Differences in Psychoanalysts

It is often asked how much difference it makes who psychoanalyzes a patient, or whether the same results will be achieved no matter who conducts the analysis. This question is of concern to every prospective patient, who naturally wants to know how he can be reasonably sure of finding the analyst who will be "right" for him.

The first step is to consult the nearest recognized psychoanalytic society or institute in order to ascertain whether the man under consideration is a member of an accredited psychoanalytic society and has been trained at a recognized institute. In this way one may at least be sure not to fall into the hands of someone who is untrained. That there are differences in skill among various members of any such group is inevitable, just as among the members of a society of surgeons, and opinions will differ concerning the relative skills of various members. Membership in a psychoanalytic society does guarantee a minimal level of intelligence, integrity, and specialized training.

114

Beyond that, the prospective patient must depend upon the advice of physicians and friends who may know something of the work and reputations of different analysts. Minor differences in skill have less influence than is generally supposed on the success or failure of an analysis.

Assuming, then, that only adequately trained analysts are under consideration, the question remains what differences in the course of the analysis and in its therapeutic outcome will result from differences in the personalities of various analysts. The effects of personality traits have to be considered separately in relation to three phases of an analysis: (1) the initial steps of the analysis, (2) the analytic process in full swing, and (3) its ultimate results. In the introductory steps and in the early phases of the work, the analyst's sex, voice, manner, appearance, and other individual peculiarities evoke specific responses. Consequently, the beginning of the ascent of the analytic mountain will take a path with one analyst that will not be identical with the path along which some other analyst would guide the patient. Issues will arise and obstacles will be surmounted in different sequences. Naturally, it is easier to launch an analysis when a patient's first response to the analyst is comfortable and full of confidence. I have, however, seen analyses work out successfully even when the patient's initial reaction was one of blind hostility, panic, and distrust. (An example of this is given in Chapter IX.)

As the treatment proceeds, if the analysis is conducted by one *who is careful to remain as unobtrusive and inconspicuous as possible*, the effects of superficial differences gradually disappear. Behind the mask of the analytic incognito, the personal quirks of the individual analyst become inconspicuous through habituation, and lose most of the emotional significance they may have had at the start. The personality of the analyst thus becomes progressively less important than the fantasies with which the patient invests him. In the end, the view from the top of the mountain will be the same, however much the upward path might have differed had a different analyst been the guide. This will be true, however, only if the analyst conscientiously maintains his analytic incognito (cf. Chapter IX).

Indeed, if the analyst remains inconspicuous, in most instances the influence even of his sex may be disregarded; and whether the analyst is a man or a woman, old or young, will make less difference in the ultimate outcome than one might imagine, even when it has made a considerable difference in launching the analysis and to the order in which the patient's material is uncovered. Again, this is because the patient's fantasies can treat the same analyst sometimes as a man and sometimes as a woman, sometimes as old and sometimes as young, irrespective of the actual facts. The naive idea that all male patients should go to male analysts and all women patients to women, need be given little serious consideration.

To this general rule, however, there are certain

exceptions. For instance, in the treatment of certain psychosexual problems the sex of the psychoanalyst may be quite important. In such cases, it is not always possible to predict which will be better. In the course of the analysis, a male analyst will sometimes find it advisable to send his patient to a woman analyst, or vice versa, in order to facilitate the clarification of some special aspect of the patient's problems. This will involve a temporary loss of momentum in the work and a short period of recapitulation; but after such a change the two pieces of analytic work will fit together quickly.

We have already emphasized the necessity of going to a psychoanalyst who, apart from his professional reputation, is unknown to the patient personally. It may be hard to convince patients of the importance of this rule. Patients are usually frightened at the mere prospect of being analyzed, and thus it seems easier to them to start with someone they know and in whom they have confidence. They cannot, however, foresee the difficulties that knowing the analyst will create for them as the treatment develops. It should be understood that these future difficulties are for the patient not for the analyst. Chapter VIII (on free association) and Chapter IX (on transference) will have made clear the reasons for this. A conscientious analyst will refuse to analyze not only his own friends and relatives, but even their intimate friends, since these would inevitably have learned a good deal about his private life and personality from the casual

117

conversations of their mutual friends or relatives. The careful analyst will consent only to guide them into the hands of competent colleagues.

The major responsibility for adhering to this rule falls on the analyst; but the patient who comes to an analyst asking to be analyzed and who is refused feels deeply hurt at the rejection and finds it hard to understand or even to believe the analyst's explanation. It will lessen this hurt if the patient understands that in turning him over to a colleague the analyst is merely following a practice that applies to all patients because its value has been proved repeatedly.

There are times, however, when it is impossible to adhere strictly to this rule. A very disturbed patient may refuse to go to anyone else. The family physician or the responsible relative may take a similarly intransigent position. Under these circumstances, especially when there is danger that delay might allow the illness to get out of hand, the analyst may be forced to take into treatment even a relative or friend, if only temporarily. Usually, he will at once begin to prepare that patient for an ultimate transfer to some colleague unknown to the patient. He will try to do this within a few weeks, but there are occasions when for technical reasons it may take months to accomplish.

Concurrent Treatment of Patients who are Friends or Relatives of Each Other

Similar considerations must be weighed whenever the question arises whether to treat concurrently or in close succession two intimate friends or two members of one family. Here, no unvarying rule can be laid down, but whenever possible this is to be avoided. Analytic work is difficult enough without going out of our way to complicate it unnecessarily by adding the competitive jealousies certain to arise between any two patients who know each other well. No two analyses progress with equal speed, and each patient is likely to watch the progress of the other with an anxious eye, at times unhappy, at times triumphant, depending on who seems to be out in front at the moment. Even the patient who seems to gloat over his friend's tribulations will at the same time have his own confidence shaken by the other's upsets. To some extent all of this can be used as grist for the analytic mill; but it tends to focus attention on the intra-analytic struggle and to obscure those problems which are indigenous to the patient's life. Furthermore, in such situations patients are likely to lose their confidence that what they say is for the ear of the analyst alone. A nagging doubt arises about whether the analyst has carried tales from one to the other. Nor will it be easy for the analyst himself always to be sure which of two patients has given him which version of episodes in which both patients have been involved. As a result, in his discussion of events with either patient, the analyst may involuntarily betray one to the other. The analyst may thus find that he has given the appearance of taking sides, which will endanger his therapeutic usefulness to one or the other patient, or both. It should be emphasized that these complications add to the difficulties of analysis for the patients, not for the analyst. Such complications should therefore be avoided by observing the simple rule of not analyzing two close friends or relatives simultaneously.

Even to analyze relatives or close friends in quick succession is not without some risks of this nature. There may be an unfair pressure on the first to finish up in a hurry so as to make room for the second. Should he then need to return, he may find the path blocked. Furthermore, *as time goes on the analytic incognito cannot remain wholly intact,* because, as he continues analysis, any patient inevitably picks up a certain amount of personal information about the analyst. Late in the analysis this will make relatively little difference; but the friend or relative who follows can learn more about the analyst from his analyzed friend than is good for an analysis just beginning. Such considerations as these should be taken into account whenever this issue arises. One exception should be added: the recent experiments with group analysis have sometimes included parents and children, siblings and friends in the group. These experiments present many difficulties, but nevertheless merit careful exploration.

Chapter XII

THE RELATION OF THE ANALYSIS TO THE PATIENT'S LIFE DURING THE COURSE OF TREATMENT

The Pledge

Before the start of an analysis it is customary for the analyst to advise the patient that for the duration of the treatment he should attempt not to make any basic changes in his life until the actual and immediate necessity for the change and its unconscious meanings have both been thoroughly explored. This restriction applies to such matters as living arrangements, jobs, occupations, schools, and marital status.

There are two reasons for imposing this limitation on a patient's freedom during an analysis: one is to protect the patient's own best interests, the other is to make sure that fundamental psychological problems will not escape analysis. No such rule would be needed were it not for the fact that so many people find it less disturbing to act than to think; and once a patient has acted, it becomes difficult and often impossible to lead him to re-examine the subtle conflicts out of which his action arose. Furthermore, without an agreement not to act in the dark, such patients may endanger their healths, their lives, their careers, and their most important human relationships through impulsive behavior which may be a transient product of the analytic process itself. This single analytic restriction on a patient's liberty is justified because it both facilitates the analysis and protects the patient during the analysis.

There are certain patients, of course, for whom no such rule is needed because their personalities are so organized that they are frightened more easily by doing than by thinking. These patients often try to use the analysis as an excuse for doing nothing and for postponing action. One extreme example of this misuse of the sound principle not to make major changes in life during the analysis is a patient who used it as an excuse to postpone accepting a job opportunity, to postpone engagement and marriage, and even to leave his Ph.D. thesis incomplete until it was too late to reap the harvest that should otherwise have been his from all three. Unless delay might bring such a patient into critical danger, the analyst can usually wait for the analysis of the patient's anxieties to release him for spontaneous and effective action; but sometimes the patient pays a high price for this.

Setting the Stage for Analysis

In planning the analysis of a child or adolescent it frequently is possible to make substantial changes in the setting of the patient's life for the duration of the analysis, changes designed specifically to facilitate the progress of the treatment. This can only rarely be done with adults, partly because they usually come for analysis burdened with responsibilities that cannot be delegated to others even temporarily, and partly because low-cost neurosis treatment centers where patients could live cheaply during the early stages of analysis do not yet exist. In fact, merely because it is not easy to make the necessary changes, far too little thought has been given to the problem of how to *set the stage for an analysis* so as to launch it under the best possible circumstances (1956b).

Patients come to analysis with their lives badly snarled; they are unhappy and defensive over the pain their neurotic conduct has cost others, and often in need of protection, especially at the start, from the resentments their illness has aroused. All too often the analyst discovers that he is dealing, not only with the patient's neurosis, but with the neuroses of those with whom the patient's life is interwoven. To sort this out, and to make the patient see where his neurosis ends and those of others begin, is never easy. Often it would be simpler to do this if the patient could be transplanted temporarily to a neutral and relatively impersonal atmosphere. From this vantage point it is possible for the patient to look back upon his life with some degree of objectivity and perspective. It is human to be less defensive about the past than about current confusions and mistakes.

Before there were any analysts in America, patients

had to go to Europe for analysis. The Atlantic Ocean separated them from much of the confusion of their daily lives, and they could then analyze this confusion from a helpful distance in time and space. This did have one obvious disadvantage, namely, that the analysis could not continue when the patient returned to his home. During the Second World War, the armed services also recognized the need for treatment facilities that would help the patient to a perspective on the situation in which his illness had arisen. For this purpose, special neurosis treatment centers of various kinds were organized, not as psychiatric hospitals, but as camps in which patients could receive psychiatric treatment while maintaining an appropriately reduced level of military activity. In civilian practice the need for such centers is barely recognized. There have been some moves in this direction, sufficient perhaps to demonstrate its importance, such as the Cassel Hospital in England, and especially the Austen Riggs Center for the Study and Treatment of the Neuroses in Stockbridge, Massachusetts. Many more are needed, especially in connection with general hospitals, and on a self-sustaining and economical basis.

There are other subtler and more powerful reasons why it would frequently be helpful to have a patient start his analysis in such an ivory tower, out of reach of the stresses and turmoils of his daily life, and with a moratorium on all daily problems, where no issues would press for immediate decision and where he would live for a time without external demands, deprivations, frustrations, or frictions. Since there would be no immediate external stresses, any unhappiness he experienced and any symptoms that occurred would obviously have to be traced to residues from the recent or remote past. The role of buried and unconscious conflicts would thus become evident to the patient much more quickly and vividly than is possible when he can use current problems as a smoke-screen behind which to hide the persisting and distorting influence of the past. Later, when such a patient returned to his home to complete his analysis, he would bring to his old problems the insights he had gained in the ivory tower—insight into the continuing influence of his own past, insight into the structure of his own personality, and insight into the reverberations in his present life of old unresolved and hitherto unconscious conflicts.

I think of a patient with whom chance made it possible to conduct his analysis in just such a series of steps. The analysis began far from his family and friends and with no work responsibilities. After some time, in graded doses, he returned to work. Then he reached out for some friendly social contacts with new acquaintances. Still later he began to see something of his family and old friends, until finally he resumed his full domestic responsibilities, including the challenge of a difficult marriage. Only rarely, however, is it possible to arrange so precise a sequence of events. Usually, as a matter of fact, it is only during a retrospective survey of an analysis that the analyst understands enough about a patient to know how to plan such a schedule wisely.

In the workaday world which the analyst and the patient share, all of this is scrambled together: the past, the present, and the future, the old buried sources of difficulty and the immediate external trials and tribulations. It is conceivable that as new types of neurosis treatment centers are developed it will be possible to approximate such a strategy for the introductory steps in the analyses of rich and poor alike. At present, however, this is only a hope for the future.

Analyst or Guide

Experience has proved that it is not possible for the analyst to advise and guide a patient in his practical affairs without seriously undermining his value as analyst. There are many reasons for this. First of all, direct advice automatically limits the spontaneity and freedom of the patient's associations. Furthermore, in the process of advising the patient the analyst reveals himself to some degree, since his advice will disclose his standards, his tastes, his own ideas about how life should be lived, and his moral judgments. Inevitably, the patient's subsequent productions will be colored by these disclosures. The effect may be slight at first, but the cumulative influence of continual guidance can only distort and mask the expression of the patient's problems. Similarly, if the analyst should attempt actively to influence the patient's conscience, he will lose still further his analytic incognito and his impartial detachment. This will again deprive the patient of a part of the psychological freedom which is essential if analysis is to penetrate to unconscious levels. To the extent to which this occurs, the patient's associations will conform to an imposed stereotype and lose their value as clues to his own unconscious attitudes and feelings. In addition, toward the analyst who plays the role of a parental guide, the patient will ultimately react with both the automatic submissiveness and the automatic rebelliousness characteristic of the child. In "obedient" phases of the analysis the rebellion will be masked. A sham compliance will simulate an improvement, which will break down again as soon as the more independent and rebellious phases of the patient's responses assert themselves. Without this ultimate rebellion against the analyst who has presumed to interfere, the patient's final independence will be jeopardized. The more actively authoritarian the analyst has been, the more impossible will it be for him to analyze with the patient the fantastic transference roots of either his submissiveness or his rebelliousness.

For all of these reasons, the psychoanalyst cannot give a patient advice and guidance without impairing his analytic value. In general, therefore, his role is to allow wise decisions to grow spontaneously in the patient as a gradual outcome of the analytic work and with a minimum of advice.

Obviously, where a patient is too sick to be entrusted with the freedom to make decisions for himself or where there is a strong tendency toward impulsive and dangerous acts, someone may have to serve as counsellor and guide, or even as custodian. In such cases, it is best for the analysis if this function is performed by someone other than the analyst. Sometimes this guardian can be a member of the family, sometimes another psychiatrist, sometimes the family physician, sometimes a nurse or social worker working under the analyst's direction. In general, however, the analyst divorces himself as completely as possible from direct control of the patient's life.

The Basis of Active Interference During Analysis

There are exceptions to all such rules. For various reasons the analysis itself may sometimes require direct or indirect interference with a patient's life, his habits, and his relations with people. This occurs chiefly in the service of two fundamental but little understood requisites for successful treatment: i.e., the needs to accept deprivation and to face anxiety.

(a) *The Principle of Deprivation*

In the treatment of neurotic problems easy victories rarely last, and during his treatment every patient must be prepared to face periods in which his only gratification will be a slow and barely perceptible growth in understanding. This demands of the patient the ability to wait, and the patient who cannot tolerate even this degree of deprivation, who demands quick results and immediate gratifications, cannot be psychoanalyzed unless and until this attitude can be altered. So important is this principle of deprivation that the psychoanalyst must sometimes intervene to cut off temporarily or limit even normal sources of satisfaction in the patient's life so as to force the patient into a state of active need.

The same school of Russian physiologists that gave to psychoanalysis the experimental proof of the validity of the method of free association (cf. Chapter VIII) furnished valuable support for this other fundamental principle as well. They demonstrated that it is only in a state of craving that important new connections can form in the central nervous system. The psychoanalytic version of this fact is Freud's observation that an analysis makes best progress in the presence of deprivation. Hence, when there seem to be no fundamental deprivations in a patient's life, the analyst may have to introduce them. The form this will take varies with every patient and in different phases of every analysis. For one person it may mean living away from home; for another giving up reading or the movies; another who hides his problems in a compulsive work drive may have to take a vacation from work; a fourth may have to give up a favorite sport or stop even moderate drinking; a fifth may have to avoid normal social life with friends and family. What is cut off will depend on which activity has been used persistently as a major escape from inner problems.

It is difficult to apply this principle skillfully without being either too lenient or too severe. As much as any other analytic maneuver, this puts to a test the analyst's understanding of his own unconscious and his freedom from anxiety and from unconscious hostility. Whenever an analyst intervenes actively in a patient's life, he finds that the practical consequences involve not the patient alone, but also all of those with whom the patient's life is interwoven. For this reason, it may be necessary to explain the matter to them in some detail. Otherwise the analyst may find himself warring with a mystified and resentful circle of family and friends. (Cf. Chapters XIII and XIV.) The better resolution is to have the patient himself make the explanations, when this is possible.

(b) *Uncovering Hidden Anxieties and Masked Symptoms*

The second reason for active intervention in the daily life of a responsible adult patient is the need to uncover anxieties or other mood disturbances which, without such intervention, might remain masked. This never applies to painful neurotic symptoms. Every patient wants to rid himself of these. But many important manifestations of the neurotic process are not painful to the patient himself, and in the defense of these subtler difficulties, the patient runs from cover to cover, seeking to hide all revealing symptoms and moods. It is significant that when dealing with organic disease we so frequently try to prove how sick we are, whereas when dealing with neuroses we try to prove how much healthier we are than our doctors, friends, or families maintain. A patient may come to an initial consultation only to find himself compelled quite unexpectedly to make light of his difficulties. Not infrequently he may actually be unable even to remember the symptoms that brought him. The same automatic defense against the acknowledgment of neurotic illness continues to operate recurrently throughout the whole course of treatment. The patient may attempt to minimize his symptoms to his analyst while trying at the same time to overdramatize them to his friends. The psychoanalyst must often dig out the elusive evidence of illness from an evasive patient. This he does by cutting off all of the masking devices the patient has been in the habit of using. Unless the analyst succeeds in this, the patient may be able to fool himself and his friends, as well as the analyst, with an illusion of health that will last only as long as the treatment.

Certain implications of this are especially important. It is traditional and legitimate for most physicians to adopt a pacifying, reassuring, and comforting role with their patients. The psychoanalyst, on the other hand, must often do just the opposite. He will be tactful and judicious in his warnings, but in the end he must be merciless in forcing a patient to face his neurosis. Indeed, just as he must sometimes intervene actively to produce situations of deprivation, so he often has to tumble the patient into those very situations that arouse his fears, depression, and anger. In some illnesses, the need for this is so clear that even the casual onlooker will understand. It is evident, for instance, that at some point in the course of the treatment a patient with a phobia of high places must be encouraged to go up to face this fear; or that a patient with a handwashing compulsion must at some point restrain his ritual, no matter how much anxiety this may cost him. In such maneuvers the analysis meets with no objections from the patient's family and friends. On the contrary, they have had to endure so many inconveniences from the patient's symptoms and eccentricities that, if they hear about the analyst's recommendation, they welcome it approvingly. Their attitude is, "It's about time someone made him stop that nonsense."

There is always a long preliminary period, however, before any such recommendation can be made. The psychoanalyst must learn the meaning of the particular symptom or disturbing way of life, and this knowledge must be shared with the patient before such intervention is possible. Therefore, each symptom must be allowed to play its part in the analysis as it has previously existed in the life of the patient. The soldier who never goes into battle never gets killed; and the symptoms that never appear actively in the analysis never are analyzed.

During this long period of waiting, the interested onlookers may well become impatient and critical. They begin to complain, "Why doesn't he do something? Why doesn't he stop that? What good is all this talking, anyhow?" The only answer is that premature interference will fail and will also prejudice the value

of any later efforts to intervene. The wise psychoanalyst waits patiently; it is a fatal error to allow himself to
be hurried by the impatience of the patient's family or
friends.

Unfortunately, the task of the psychoanalyst is rarely
confined to maneuvers, the wisdom of which is evident
to the onlooker. Frequently the patient's problems lurk
behind seemingly unrelated details of his life. Where
these involve no one but the patient, the analysis deals
with them without reference to the outside world. No
one but the patient and his psychoanalyst is aware that
anything has happened when some detail of a patient's
patterns of sleeping or eating or dressing has been
altered in the effort to unmask obscure anxieties. It is a
different matter, however, when important human
relationships or the patient's occupation must be inter-
fered with. It is not easy for old friends to find
themselves out of bounds, much less for those relatives
or the physician who may have spent years struggling
over the patient's health. Yet the analysis sometimes is
forced to act as a wedge temporarily separating the
patient from these very relationships. To those who are
excluded, this seems like inexplicable ingratitude, just
one more evidence of the unreasonable nature of the
whole procedure. But the good intentions of these
well-wishers have little to do with the use the patient
may make of their loyalty. It is as impossible to create
self-sustaining health for a patient who is constantly
being propped up as it would be to strengthen a limb
that is kept in a cast. For this reason, if for no other, it

may be necessary during an analysis to lead a patient through a period of relative isolation from those on whom he has depended in the past.

Ultimately, the successful analysis will bring the patient back again to renewed closeness to all whose intimacy has stood the test of analytic scrutiny and where the basis of the relationship has proved to be fundamentally normal. The path to this goal may be long and tortuous, though, and requires an unusual degree of patience and confidence.

(c) *Dealing with the Neurotic Exploitation of "Normal" Life*

Sometimes the analyst may even take a parent or a child temporarily out of his own home, or a man away from his occupation. This latter may become necessary precisely because men sometimes hide their emotional difficulties in their most normal activities and relationships, making their lives endurable and masking their anxieties through an unconscious exploitation of relatives and friends, of work and play. When this occurs, the psychoanalyst is forced to strip away these masking devices one by one until the difficulties the patient is hiding are revealed. If these devices were always in themselves abnormal or unnatural, there would be relatively little difficulty about doing this. Unfortunately, however, what one man hides in compulsive drinking, another man may hide in an excessive work drive, or a woman in hyperconscientious preoccupation with her family and children, or in bridge or philanthropy or society. Obviously no one will doubt the wisdom of interfering with the habits of the drinker; but it seems strange to the onlooker when the analyst interferes even temporarily with other activities or relationships which are intrinsically healthy but which are being misused in the service and defense of the neurosis. Nevertheless, where practical considerations make it impossible to limit such activities, the analysis may be seriously hampered.

The ideal analytic situation is one in which the patient can be brought to understand the need for this type of self-denial and will impose it on himself of his own accord and without active pressure from the psychoanalyst. Difficult problems may arise when a patient persistently refuses to accept all such deprivations and is reluctant to face anxiety or pain in any form. This, indeed, is one of the factors that can make it peculiarly difficult to successfully analyze a patient who is absorbed in a love affair or who has great wealth. No human being accepts deprivation readily, and where the consolations of love or wealth or successful work are easily available, it takes a patient of exceptional stamina to turn his back on them. It is characteristic of analyses of the affluent that they are frequently interrupted by self-indulgences—a trip to Florida, a hasty marriage, a hunting trip, etc. One unfortunate man who sought help for psychic impotence and attacks of overpowering anxiety, ultimately refused analysis because his wife was disappointed on learning that during the course of the analysis he might be unable to accompany her on their periodic hunting and fishing expeditions.

An analysis, therefore, may from time to time become involved in a struggle against a patient's methods of garnering the momentary pleasures with which he has been accustomed to mask his fear, anger, depression, and the like. In his effort to unmask hidden difficulties, the psychoanalyst must at times block even healthy outlets of love, work, and play, while at the same time, paradoxically, allowing a patient to skirt danger or even to flounder into it if there is no other way to prove to him the neurotic basis of his conduct.

(d) *The Essential Conflict between the Needs of the Analysis and the Immediate Desires of the World Outside*

The little world circling around the outskirts of every analysis finds it hard to understand any of this. Its purposes are often directly opposed to the needs of the analysis. It is always trying to reduce the tensions the analysis must sometimes inflate. It is outraged during those phases of the analysis which may isolate the patient from daily realities, i.e., from work, family, friends, society, or play; and it may be equally perplexed at those other moments when it becomes essential for the patient to have the closest possible contacts with these situations.

Similarly, this small world always hopes that the psychoanalyst will intervene quickly to cut the patient's Gordian knots. In contrast to this "practical" point of view, when a patient is in a state of obsessional indecision, whether it be over buying a hat or contracting a marriage, the analysis tries to defer all impulsive pseudosolutions of the problem. At such a juncture, to postpone acting may take courage and the ability to stand deprivation and uncertainty until the psychic tension that is mobilized brings into the open the unconscious forces out of which the paralyzing indecision has arisen. Therefore, the psychoanalyst must turn a deaf ear to the importunities of the outside world when it says, *"Oh, why doesn't he tell him what to do—he must know by now—it would be better to do anything, just to get the suspense over."*

Here again we see that when dealing with an adult patient whose illness does not make him wholly irresponsible, the psychoanalyst cannot play the role of guide and protector without masking those inner problems it is his primary function to uncover and resolve. Important plans and decisions may grow out of the analytic work, but, except as a temporary measure, they cannot be imposed by the analyst if he has his patient's ultimate independence at heart. It is only in dealing with children or with psychotic patients who are not fully responsible that the psychoanalyst must either take on this double role himself (which may seriously hamper his analytic function) or else turn it over to others.

Chapter XIII

THE RELATION OF THE OUTSIDE WORLD TO PATIENTS UNDER ANALYSIS

The Patient's Self-Protective Secrecy

A patient often enters analysis determined to tell no one of his plans. Sometimes this is because he realizes that if he took anyone into his confidence the news would gradually reach the ears of others who would gossip about it or who might even try to interfere. A patient is wise to avoid being drawn into futile arguments when his undivided attention is needed for the analysis itself. At such times some measure of discreet silence, at least until the analysis is well under way, is sensible. Secrecy, however, can also arise from an unnecessary sense of shame. Because he fails to realize how universal neurotic difficulties such as his are, the patient feels mortified at any public acknowledgment of his need. He often pretends to himself that no one knows of his condition, and may try to hide the fact that he is in treatment, even when every close friend and relative is aware of his illness and is hoping that he will have the courage to face it and to seek help for it. Not infrequently a patient will go to great lengths to hide an illness which everyone has long since recognized, even rejecting the treatment he may desperately need. In a successful analysis, such false pride and unnecessary shame will gradually be eliminated.

The patient who resolves to keep his analysis secret frequently does so because his own doubts about analysis make him fearful of the skepticism of others. Here again, as the analysis proceeds and as anxieties lessen, friends and relatives gradually are taken into the patient's confidence. In this way, a little world of interested spectators slowly gathers around almost every psychoanalytic venture. The behavior of these onlookers, individually and collectively, can make a great difference to the comfort of the patient during his analysis and to his freedom from distracting external influences.

Any hothouse protection for psychoanalytic patients is neither possible nor desirable, but the patient has a right to a decently respectful attitude of noninterference. Patients go through phases of great emotional sensitivity. It was no act of kindness for a friend to call across a formal dinner table, "I can't believe you're having an analysis. You're young. You're attractive. Are you in love with someone else? Are you out of love with your husband?" How could the patient answer such an attack? How could she speak of the years of misery she had always kept hidden? Nor was that other "friend" considerate who said, "Darling, I hope you're enjoying a perfectly lovely transference," to a patient who was in a turmoil of rage and terror with regard to her psychoanalyst. Such jibes are deeply hurtful; yet they occur frequently, making it difficult for patients to work out their problems in peace.

Less gross, but nonetheless disconcerting, may be the solicitous inquiries of respectful and interested friends. "How are things going? What are you getting out of it? Is it proving worthwhile?" are legitimate questions for a patient to ask himself at various points along the road and again at the end of the way. But an outsider has no way of gauging into what distressing phase of the analysis his question may fall. Nor can he be aware of the impossibility of answering such a question, except by reassuring generalities or evasions. The wise patient is rarely willing to divulge to his well-meaning friends the intimate personal difficulties that can profitably be shared only with the psychoanalyst, because to pour out his heart to his friends will only impede the progress of his treatment.

Sometimes, however, the patient himself draws this little world of interested and curious spectators into the vortex of the analysis. Patients go through phases in which consciously or unconsciously they want to sabotage their analyses. At such times a patient may build up two groups of allies: on one side, those who support the analysis and, on the other, those who are hostile to it. According to his mood, he associates now with one circle and now with the other, and within the span of a single day he may unwittingly give to members of each group wholly opposite accounts of what is going on in the analysis, thus leading them to respond with conflicting counsel.

This may begin with the first analytic session. A patient who had come to analysis eagerly and yet with deep reluctance resolved to tell no one about it. She left her first session to make an unpremeditated call on a relative in whose presence she made a slip of the tongue which betrayed the fact that she had begun an analysis. This relative was the person who was most influential in the patient's life and most certain to oppose the analysis bitterly.

Such episodes are likely to happen in each recurring period of difficulty in the course of any analysis. It is an exceptional and fortunate patient whose friends and relatives refuse to allow themselves to be drawn into the struggle and who say to the patient, "Keep your confidences for your analysis, and work out your problems there."

The Patient's Need for Periods of Isolation

The reasons the patient needs periods of isolation from his family and friends may be summarized as follows: (1) Frequently these relationships have been invested with all the patient's neurotic problems. (2) They are often used as a target for his symptomatic behavior. (3) These symptoms and difficulties will frequently become exaggerated whenever the patient is among his old friends. (4) On the other hand, the patient may also use friends and relatives in order to cover and escape from the difficulties the analyst is trying to make him face. (5) Friends and relatives may have an oversolicitous concern for the patient's welfare, and, since they know him well, they may be sensitive to his every mood swing as he works through difficult phases of his treatment. This in turn may be hard both on the patient and on them. It often is an act of kindness to the family and to intimate friends to give them a respite from their responsibilities and from continual contact with the patient, inasmuch as such a respite may both shorten the treatment and spare everyone distress. (6) Often it would permanently damage the relationship if either the patient or the analyst were to tell friends or relatives of the fear, envy, hostility, and suspicion the patient may have harbored in secret and which the analysis is aiming to eliminate. Because the analyst can rarely be totally frank and open with the patient's friends or relatives, they are likely to sense his reservations and evasions and to resent them. They will think him either indirect or a boor. (7) On the other hand, when friends have been badly used by the patient because of his neurosis, the justifiable resentments they have sedulously held in check for years are likely to come out just when the patient is beginning to shed his neurotic attitudes toward them. The long pent-up resentments are frequently ventilated at this point against either the patient or the analysis or both. It may be necessary to shield the patient from these pent-up feelings until he is well on the way to recovery.

From time to time, all these considerations, as well as those mentioned in Chapter XII, make it wise for the analysis to serve as a buffer, temporarily dividing the patient from his usual associates. When this happens, unless it will excite in the patient a dangerous amount of distrust and jealousy, the analyst must be ready to satisfy the misgivings of responsible members of the family and to allay their anxieties as much as he can. Where, because of the patient's attitude, it is not safe for him to approach the family or friends directly, he must make this point clear to them through the family physician or through some trusted intermediary. It is best if the patient can see the wisdom and fairness of allowing the analyst to make his own explanations to those who would otherwise be hurt or mystified; but early in a treatment it is rarely possible to do this.

For his part, the conscientious and considerate analyst ought never forget that both by the very nature of his work and because he must often hold the family at arm's length, he puts a great strain on all of those who love the patient and who are anxious about him. The analyst does not relish this role; yet, occasionally, in the interest of his patient, he is forced for a time to ride roughshod over the feelings of a family. Since his therapeutic responsibility to the patient must come first, when this becomes necessary, all he can do is ask the family to have patience until he has reached a point in the analysis when it will be possible for him to talk to them freely without endangering the treatment. Sometimes such a talk can safely take place only in the presence of the patient himself. In all of these matters, however, there are no absolute rules. The reason for mentioning them here is to emphasize to patients, to the families of prospective patients, and to their physicians that there are times when the analyst is forced to put their feelings to one side lest he jeopardize his therapeutic leverage with the patient.

Chapter XIV
THE RELATION OF THE REFERRING PHYSICIAN TO THE ANALYSIS

The Referral

The selection of patients for analytic treatment is based partly on technical aspects of the patient's illness and personality and partly on practical considerations, many of which cannot be evaluated accurately ahead of time. Consequently, it usually is wise to begin an analysis tentatively, deferring for some weeks the final decision regarding its wisdom. Patients are therefore advised to consider the first weeks or months as a trial period, during the course of which the patient and the analyst will decide together on the advisability of continuing the analysis. This is why psychoanalytic clinics assign their most experienced leaders to the task of selecting patients.

It is essential that the general physician be equally cautious when urging a patient to consider analysis. When an internist refers a patient to some other medical specialist, he does not attempt to dictate what treatment that specialist will employ. He does not usually refer a patient to a surgeon for operation, but

145

rather for an opinion about the advisability of operating, the kind of operation, if any, its timing, etc. The same procedure should govern the referral of patients to psychoanalysis. It is well not to refer a patient to a psychoanalyst "for analysis," but rather for consultation with respect to the desirability of an analysis. Once a definite opinion has been secured on the advisability of this step, the effort to persuade the patient to go ahead can be undertaken without further hesitation. Otherwise the analyst may find himself facing a patient who has been persuaded by his physician that analysis is his one hope for health, when that patient may have an illness no sensible analyst would attempt to analyze.

The Family Physician During the Course of the Analysis

(a) Discretion

During the course of the analysis, the referring physician can rarely be taken fully into the analyst's confidence. In many instances patients themselves are explicit in their requests that nothing of what they tell the analyst should be communicated to their physicians. This can create an awkward situation for the psychoanalyst; but, unless the patient is psychotic or otherwise irresponsible, the analyst's responsibility to the patient must take precedence over his desire to be courteous to his medical colleague. In the course of the analysis, however, it may become clear that the patient's request arose from a neurotic distortion of his attitude toward the family physician. When this is the case, and when this aspect of the neurosis has been resolved, the patient will withdraw his request, leaving the psychoanalyst free, within reason, to take the referring physician into his confidence.

Certainly a patient's reluctance to have his story passed on to anyone other than the analyst is never entirely neurotic. To expect a patient to unburden himself without reserve in the presence of anyone is asking a great deal. To expect him to do this before two people may be asking the impossible. Yet that is what it would amount to if a psychoanalyst said to his patient, not, "What you say here is for my ears alone," but "What you say here is for my ears and those of your family physician." The patient's confident sense of privacy cannot be violated in this way without jeopardizing his ability to be completely frank.

At the same time, the analyst must always keep in mind the fact that it is wholly natural and legitimate for the family physician to have a personal interest in and sense of responsibility for his patient, as well as a scientific interest in the progress of the analysis and a reasonable amount of sheer curiosity to boot. Nevertheless, even when the patient makes no specific request to the analyst not to discuss the material of the analysis with his physician, the physician's interest or curiosity can be gratified only sparingly and in general terms during the course of the analysis. In the long run, such discretion is advantageous to the physician himself. During the course of an analysis, patients sometimes act out a great deal of rage on their friends, families, and medical advisers, as well as on their analysts. Therefore, it may actually protect the post-analytic relationship of the referring doctor to his patient if the physician does not become too intimately involved in the analysis. This policy can also protect the relationship of the physician to the patient's family. In the course of any difficult treatment, the family often attempts to learn more about the patient than is well for them to know at the time. They may bring heavy pressure to bear on the physician to make unwise disclosures. Lack of detailed information will be his best protection in this situation. If the physician says to the family, "I have confidence in the analyst, and I do not ask him to violate his patient's confidence," he both protects himself and sets them a good example.

When, for any reason, the analyst feels that he must take the family physician into his confidence, the latter should feel obligated never to divulge such confidence to anyone. Even when only a trivial fact is revealed, it may be fatal to an analysis if it leaks out via the physician to family or friends and thence back to the patient. The particular item may be something the patient himself may be ready to tell anyone; but the fact that it escaped the analytic chamber means to the patient that more important things can also leak. The temptation to minor indiscretions must therefore be resisted constantly. It is impossible to exaggerate the importance of this warning. The path of the grapevine of gossip may be tortuous, but it ultimately leads back to the patient with a fated precision. As an actual example: from the psychoanalyst to the thoroughly trusted physician of the family; from this physician, out of the goodness of his heart, to comfort the anxious mother; from the mother, because of her natural need for reassurance, to her "best friend"; from the best friend to her own daughter "as a warning"; from the daughter to her husband; from him to the patient's husband; thence to the patient; and from the patient back to the psychoanalyst. With the best of will, families and friends can be guilty of this kind of indiscretion, not out of malice, but either out of sympathy or the pressures of their own needs. Only if the analyst observes a code that makes of him a safe-deposit box to which the patient alone holds the key can the patient feel that he is the sole respository of his confidences. This is not mysterious psychoanalytic cultism. It is a policy that has been forced upon analysts by their experiences in dealing with doctors, friends, and relatives of patients; and it applies just as much to fellow analysts as to anyone else. Of all physicians, the psychoanalyst has the least right to talk about his patients, even to his colleagues, without protecting meticulously the identities of these patients. A good analyst is always close-mouthed.

(b) *The Problem of Divided Loyalties*

In many other ways the analyst and the general physician must have a clear understanding if they are not to impede the patient's progress. Not only do patients become attached to their physicians; physicians also become attached to their patients. Even after deciding to refer a patient for analysis, some physicians find it difficult to turn the patient over to the new adviser. The greater the effort the physician has made and the more he has played the role of trusted counsellor and friend, the more difficult it may be for him to relinquish his role to the analyst.

That this might cost anyone a pang of jealousy is only human and natural. Fortunately the transition is usually handled with generosity, although occasionally it creates serious trouble. It may lead the physician to hang on to a patient for years longer than he should, trying to cure the patient himself. Or, after finally bringing himself to give up the patient, the physician may find it so intolerable that his patient now confides in someone else that he may interfere in many ways. He may try repeatedly to learn what is going on, or he may try to anticipate everything the patient will say, making light of it, prejudging what is important, directing the patient what to tell the analyst, and, most disrupting of all, he may make the patient feel that not to confide first in him is an act of disloyalty. This may end with the patient using the family doctor as a spillway through which to pour out much of the material that should be brought to the analysis.

Not long ago two young women were referred to an analyst by two well-known physicians. To an amazing extent their neuroses were identical. They came from similar backgrounds. The pattern of their early lives had been remarkably alike. They had made rather similar marriages to men with not dissimilar problems; and they had developed almost identical neurotic symptoms and personality distortions.

There, however, the parallel ceased. One young woman had been brought to analysis at the age of twenty-three, within four months of the onset of clear-cut symptoms. Her doctor, who pretended to no knowledge of psychiatry, said to the analyst in the presence of the patient, "I am very fond of this young lady, and she of me. I have known her and taken care of her for many years. I have been her father-confessor. It isn't going to be easy for her to talk to someone else; and it will be impossible if at the same time she goes on talking to me. If she does that, all you will get will be warmed-over material. Everything will be predigested with me; and you'll never get anywhere. Therefore, at this point I am going to retire from the picture. I have told my assistant to take care of all routine medical problems, and to call me only in case of something special. I'll miss my young friend; but this is the best contribution I can make to her recovery." This wise and generous physician had the satisfaction of seeing his patient complete her analysis successfully in a remarkably short time.

The other physician prided himself on his knowledge of psychiatry and on his own personal brand of psychotherapy. He sent the patient to analysis when she was in her mid-thirties, after he had spent over twelve years in ineffectual efforts to treat her himself.

He actually told the analyst that he was sending the patient to him to get rid of her. Nevertheless, he could not give her up. He continued to see her almost daily, often on her way to her analytic session. He encouraged or permitted her to indulge in long talks with him, so that by the time she came to her analytic hour, her need to confide in anyone had spent itself, and she could say little or nothing to the analyst. She even held back a great deal of vital information because she had the feeling that she had already discussed it fully with her physician, and because this daily contact with her physician held her in a constant struggle between conflicting loyalties. Naturally, this patient made no progress.

For a long time the analyst did not even know that this was going on. When it finally was acknowledged, he recognized the neurotic basis of the physician's behavior and how it fitted into and fed the pattern of the patient's neurosis, and he set himself to break up the relationship. It took two years of completely frustrated pseudoanalysis before he was able to wean the patient away from her neurotic dependence on her doctor; and he could do this only by backing out of the picture himself and by insisting that she make a fresh start with another analyst and a new medical adviser. Only then did her analysis really start. This is an extreme example, but it happens in lesser degrees in many instances.

Of course, the analyst should be reasonably generous and tolerant to his nonanalytic colleagues, even when they make trouble for him and his patients. If he himself has ever had to sit beside the analysis of some well-loved friend or relative, he will know how hard it can be to keep one's hands off. This experience should help him to understand and sympathize with the position of his medical colleagues and of the families of his patients. When dealing with his own patients, the analyst is able to maintain a high degree of tolerance for their difficulties and to accept erratic or even dangerous behavior with considerable peace of mind. This is possible for him because he is not deeply involved emotionally and because he does not live with his patients and their symptoms twenty-four hours a day and finally, because he knows and understands what is going on. The patient's ups and downs make sense to him. When this same analyst sits in relative ignorance beside the analysis of some member of his own family, he will for the first time experience the difficulty of this position.

(c) *Physical Care During Analysis*

Throughout an analysis a patient must be guarded against the occurrence of physical illness. Rarely, if ever, will the psychoanalyst attempt to perform this function himself lest it interfere with his value as a psychoanalyst. Instead, at any hint of physical disturbance, he will expect the patient to turn to his usual medical adviser. This necessitates a good working understanding between the two, something hard to achieve if the general physician happens to be hostile to psychoanalysis. Should this make an understanding impossible, it may become necessary for the psychoanalyst to insist that the patient turn to another medical adviser for the duration of the analytic treatment. Nowadays, however, such disagreements are rare, and whenever a question arises concerning the organic or psychogenic or mixed nature of any physical disturbance occurring during an analysis, the two physicians must be able to confer without the usual reserve if they are to reach a point of view that does justice to all possibilities. Unresolved difficulties will only perplex the patient and not help him.

If a patient seeks a new physical examination at every moment of panic or if he is one of those who retreat into real or feigned illness whenever the going becomes difficult, some constructive method of handling this tendency must be agreed upon. Otherwise, to his own ultimate damage, the patient will play off the internist against the analyst and vice versa. If it becomes clear that the constant tendency to resort to medical help does not arise out of physical disabilities threatening the patient's fundamental health, it may become necessary for a limited time to forbid the patient to seek medical advice of any kind without the analyst's consent. Before this is done, however, the sanction and support of the medical adviser should be secured.

The opposite tendency may also be encountered. Some patients refuse to face the reality of organic illness, minimizing or hiding serious and even painful

154

symptoms, giving evasive and conflicting descriptions of them, and resisting the pressure of their families or of the analyst to seek medical advice. A patient with active tuberculosis refused for a time to take his temperature, to limit his activities, or to consult his physician. When such an impasse persists, it may force an interruption of the analysis, unless it has been possible to eliminate through the analysis the patient's objection to accepting medical help.

The relation of physical illness to emotional processes is far more complex than this brief note might suggest, and is connected with many scientific problems not directly related to these practical issues. These problems must also be considered in relation to the vexing question of whether nonmedical analysts should be allowed to do therapeutic analyses, an issue discussed in Chapter XXIV.

Chapter XV
THE APPROACH TO
PSYCHOANALYSIS

In a sense it is natural even if unwise that most people turn to psychoanalysis for help only as a last resort. As pointed out in Chapter V, simple remedies for psychological difficulties should be tried until they prove ineffectual. At the same time, one should keep in mind the warning given in that chapter against persisting in such efforts too long. Many years may be lost in heroic but futile and heartbreaking efforts at self-help or compromise. The psychoanalyst could often save these years by pointing out that these simple methods have failed after a reasonable trial. In the early stage of a neurosis, however, the analyst is only rarely able to persuade a prospective patient and his family and physician to accept this judgment. This is because turning to analysis for help presupposes an acknowledgment of illness and of an inability to help oneself, which people usually consider to be a sign of weakness. Accepting the need for external help requires, in fact, wisdom, humility, honesty, and courage.

For lack of these, patients regularly come to analysis

much later than they should, and their histories almost uniformly tell of a lifetime of ineffectual efforts to solve internal problems by external changes. Childhood problems were dealt with by changes in disciplinary regimen; difficulties in school were met by transferring to another school; or treatment was postponed while waiting to see if the symptoms would disappear spontaneously with the shift from elementary school to high school, from day school to boarding school, from school to college. In college it was expected that things would improve after graduation. Then the solution was sought in a job, in changing jobs, or in marriage, and in having first one child and then several, or, finally, in divorces and new marriages.

Ultimately, however, every adult reaches a point at which there are no further significant changes left to make in the outer forms of his life. At this point an intensification of persisting neurotic symptoms occurs, complicated now by depression and anxiety; and it is this which forces the average person to consider analysis, perhaps for the first time. He might have saved himself many years of suffering and frustration if he had had the humility and foresight to acknowledge that his illness was within himself. It is rare that external changes result in significant psychological readjustments because our internal problems usually follow us into new settings. Only when for special reasons the external change produces internal changes can it initiate lasting improvements.

The Tendency to Postpone Psychotherapy

There are two causes for the universal tendency to postpone treatment. To one we have already alluded—namely, the feeling of shame and guilt that attaches to psychological illness (cf. Chapters III and IV). This is only partly cultural in origin, but to this extent it can be modified by the processes of education, which are slowly producing more enlightened attitudes. Today, in many schools and colleges, psychotherapy is made available to youngsters who are in trouble; and in centers for the treatment of neuroses, to an increasing degree the patients are in their college years.

The other cause of delayed treatment is more difficult to alter. It arises out of the fact that the neurotic process does not always cause serious pain to the patient himself. Sometimes it is chiefly his family and friends who suffer. The existence of symptoms that hurt the patient little if at all is one of the special peculiarities of the neurotic process. Among these symptoms are many of the marked but ubiquitous neurotic elements in our personalities. They may make us work too hard, eat too much, play too hard, compete too violently. Or they may turn us into spectators rather than participants in life, philosophers or critics rather than doers. They can produce misanthropes or philanthropists. If we are gifted we can even turn these neurotic weaknesses into self-gratifying or socially acceptable activities. Although families and associates pay a high price for them, they cause little immediate suffering to the patient himself, certainly nothing compared to the gratifications they bring. Therefore, we tend to pride ourselves on such quirks as these and to defend them against interference, however therapeutic.

The spur that drives a man to seek help is usually his own suffering. Illnesses that do not hurt the patient himself are usually neglected, often until it is too late. Nowhere does this apply more than in psychiatry. I cannot make others suffer the pain of my broken leg, as I inevitably make others suffer through my neurosis. This is especially clear when the family of a patient allows itself to be ruled by the patient's symptoms. A woman with a phobia of the country forced her family to spend their vacations in town. A man with a fear of heights made his family live on the ground floor. A woman with a neurotic hostility to people, which took the form of acute anxiety in social gatherings, isolated her husband and children from all normal social life. A compulsive gambler put his family through repeated stretches of poverty. In each of these cases, it would have precipitated even more violent neurotic symptoms and much domestic warfare if the families had refused to submit to the tyranny of these symptoms. The patients themselves either would have cracked up or have come to treatment years earlier. Tender and loving patience, if misapplied, can actually block the road to health. As Macfie Campbell once said, a family is a dictatorship ruled by its sickest member, and a patient's chance of health may depend ultimately upon the steadfastness of his family in refusing to accept servitude to his illness. It is a sound principle that every patient must pay the price of his own neurotic incapacity. If the family pays these debts for him, then he will suffer little pain and there will be little to spur him on toward treatment.

Not infrequently a patient seems to feel that the only trait preventing his being a nonentity is his neurosis. Sometimes this protest is quite frank: "I want to get well, but I don't want to change," or, "If I am analyzed, I will turn out just like everyone else," or, "I'll lose my ability to write or paint." It is as though, stripped of their neurotic eccentricities, people would lose all individuality and all creative capacity. Actually, once freed of neurotic insecurity, human beings become more productive and less timid and conformist than before. Freedom from neurosis lessens the compulsive striving for pseudo originality for its own sake. No one is as conformist as the child, except perhaps the secret child hidden in every adult. I have fully discussed these issues elsewhere (1958a).

The prospective patient realizes none of these simple facts. He wants to blame situations, illness, disappointments, or other people for his neurosis, i.e., everything and anything but his own personality. Therefore, his personality as such is the last thing he wants the analyst to meddle with. Yet, as we have pointed out (Chapter V), basic therapy requires a profound personality alteration, not unlike that which sometimes occurs in the course of a deep and sincere religious conversion. It is the protest that we do not want to change and our proud and stiff-necked determination not to let any analyst "meddle with" our personalities that cause the longest delays of all in seeking psychiatric treatment, even when it is desperately needed.

The Reluctant Patient

In varying degrees, then, every patient is reluctant; and it is hard to stand aside and watch someone heading for avoidable disaster, especially when it is his pride or ignorance that makes him unwilling to accept help. Consequently, the patient's family or physician is sometimes tempted to beg, cajole, or bribe the patient into analysis. However well intended this may be, it usually is futile. The analyst can do little for the patient who comes against his own will. He can hold up a mirror to the patient in an effort to induce him to look honestly at his life, his personality, and his neurotic incapacities. He can hold out legitimate expectations of relief through long, hard analytical work. He can try to induce the family to remove all the devices with which they have been protecting the patient from paying the price of his own illness. Sometimes the analyst may even induce the patient to try some form of preliminary psychotherapy.

The patient who comes merely to please someone else confronts the analyst with a difficult problem. If the psychoanalyst paints an honest picture of the time and effort the treatment will entail, the patient will almost certainly run away. True, he may return years later; but to the extent to which this has cost the patient additional years of illness, it is a therapeutic defeat. If, on the other hand, the therapist minimizes the difficulties and duration of treatment and plays for a warm and friendly contact, he may succeed in luring the patient into treatment sooner. Furthermore, the patient may even improve for a time; but his lack of any sense of illness and the absence of a serious therapeutic purpose will usually lead him to break off as soon as the painful phases of the treatment begin. Such a patient usually goes off bitterly convinced that he has tried psychoanalysis and that it has failed. Therefore, even when it may seem callous, it usually is wise to send the reluctant patient away to wait until his increasing disabilities force him to return, this time with a conscious need and purpose that will carry him through the treatment.

The one important exception to this is in adolescence. The youngster who is resentful, resistant, and uncomprehending, may remain in treatment notwithstanding. He does this at first, not out of any understanding of his illness, nor because of any clear therapeutic purpose, but because he needs so desperately the substitute parent that the analyst represents. He needs the analyst as an ally against his own parents and against his own conflict-laden moods, and the analyst in turn can utilize this desperate need to help the adolescent to mature.

Psychoanalysis as a Preventive Measure

The growth of the general cultural influence of psychoanalysis has coincided with the development of the mental hygiene movement and with an increasing emphasis on preventive medicine in general. Before the introduction of psychoanalysis, the therapy of the neuroses was largely palliative, employing methods which even in ancient Greece had succeeded in making the lives of patients more comfortable (cf. Chapter V). Psychoanalytic technique has made it possible to investigate and sometimes to alter the complex psychological roots of neuroses.

Therapeutic triumphs lead naturally to attempts to use psychoanalysis as a preventive measure. Psychoanalysis frequently makes it possible to recognize incipient phases of illness, before either the patient or his family has become aware of the gravity or the imminence of danger. Secondly, serious mental illnesses sometimes start quite insidiously in seemingly mild neurotic disturbances, and in some of these cases the advance of the illness can be checked by using analytic methods early, before the pathological process has had time to become irreversible.

Yet this very ability to foresee future trouble may place the psychoanalyst in a difficult position. The old-fashioned psychiatrist played a simple role because he dealt almost exclusively with fully developed mental diseases. No effort was made to diagnose the process of illness until it was sufficiently advanced to be obvious even to the layman. When the psychiatrist said to the family, "This is a sick man who must be hospitalized," no one could accuse him of being an alarmist, or of looking at everything from a psychiatric bias, or of being mercenary.

The psychoanalyst, on the other hand, frequently

has to give people early warnings they do not want to hear. He may have to tell a family that a relative who to them seems fairly normal is really quite ill, and that he should go to an analyst in order to try to prevent the further development of this sickness. If the analysis succeeds and illness does not follow, there will always be some who doubt that it would ever have developed anyhow. Only rarely is it possible to prove that without treatment the alarming prophecy would have materialized. On the other hand, if the treatment fails and illness supervenes, the analyst is quite likely to be accused of having caused the very illness he was trying to prevent. Thus, whatever happens, there will be more than one friend and relative who will think that the patient has been misled into undertaking unwise or at least unnecessary treatment.

Under these circumstances, the psychoanalyst must expect and even invite frank skepticism from the friends and relatives of a prospective patient. Indeed, when responsible friends and relatives express all their doubts frankly to the psychoanalyst ahead of time, he has a chance to deal with these doubts before they can cause trouble. He can then establish a relationship of confidence, which will protect the subsequent course of the analysis. Furthermore, the relative who from time to time is free to blow off steam to the analyst, or to some representative of the analyst, is less likely to sabotage the analysis directly with the patient.

Even where all misgivings are handled openly, however, the symptoms the patient reveals to the analyst may have to remain hidden from the rest of the world. It might, for instance, do irreparable damage to reveal a sexual perversion a patient has hidden and for which he now seeks help. Therefore, when the patient is neither a child nor so ill as to be irresponsible, it is the psychoanalyst's duty to protect the patient's confidence by indicating to his interested relatives and physician only that there are serious symptoms which he does not feel free to discuss with anyone. Such evasiveness, however conscientious, cannot fail to arouse some measure of distrust.

Where distrust cannot be overcome, as, for instance, when dealing with a neurotic family, or with a family that has had its confidence shaken by previous incompetent or dishonest advice, it may be possible for the analyst to allay it only by refusing to accept the patient for treatment himself, insisting instead on sending the patient to a carefully chosen colleague. This can at least eliminate the suspicion that the psychoanalyst's judgment is influenced by mercenary considerations.

The basic solution of this problem lies, however, not in such devices, but in the growth of confidence in psychoanalytic integrity and judgment; and this in turn will come only as psychoanalytic judgment itself improves, and as the general public learns to deal only with those who are qualified to practice by the long and thorough training described in Chapter XXIII.

There is another form in which the problem of preventive analysis may present itself to the psychoanalyst. His advice may be sought by a patient who comes with an intrinsically mild neurotic disturbance, a complaint that might yield quickly to almost any kind of sensible and superficial help. Behind the specific symptom, however, the analyst may detect the signs of a more severe disturbance. The decision must then be made whether it is better to try to cure the symptom directly, since this is the burden of the patient's major complaint, or to use it as a lead to underlying difficulties.

Sometimes, curing a symptom only obscures a disease process, which will reappear with the next strain. This is comparable to the danger of masking the painful symptoms of an acute surgical emergency by a too free use of morphine. Only the opportunist in psychiatry will choose such a course. When an analyst uses a patient's symptom to direct the patient's attention to underlying problems, the patient will soon feel worse instead of better, whereupon the patient and the family may become indignant and alarmed, not realizing that this painful facing of hidden illness is essential as a first step toward health. If the patient has been properly forewarned, and if his capacity to stand the rigors of treatment has been gauged accurately, the ultimate results will justify these growing pains. To accept with unshaken trust an increase in the pain from which one is seeking relief demands an almost blind faith, and it is not surprising that patients and families rebel. Here again the only ultimate safeguard for the layman is the adequacy of the psychoanalyst's training. A full understanding of this complicated issue is dependent upon a clear comprehension of the relation of the neurotic process to psychotic disorganization which has been discussed at length in other papers (1966b, 1966d, 1967c).

The Use of Psychoanalysis as a Preventive Measure in Childhood

World War II taught us that the only way to prevent the full development of the neurotic state is by intensive treatment of the neurotic process as soon as its presence can be recognized. The best time to prevent neuroses, then, is in the early years of life. Let us recapitulate here what was pointed out in Chapter IV: It is inherent in the very nature of the growth process of the human being to have inner psychic conflicts in infancy and childhood. Because of our ability to use symbolic thinking, we represent these conflicts symbolically in thought and action and in their emotional concomitants. Finally, we render much of this conflict unconscious, so that the symbols of the conflict become detached from their original psychological sources to initiate what we call "the neurotic process." With the recognition of these basic facts, the various elements in a program of prevention become clear.

First, we would test the effects of different forms of social and family structure on the tendency to deal with conflicts by repression. Second, we would try to educate young parents in the methods by which the tendency of children to repress can be minimized. Finally, we would treat every neurotic upset of childhood as an acute medical emergency demanding immediate and intensive analytic help. The purpose of this would be to bring into the full light of consciousness the unconscious conflicts out of which those early neurotic episodes arose so that they would not leave behind them those residual unconscious forces which distort the later adult personality. This is the theoretical basis for child analysis—which may ultimately prove to be one of the greatest contributions of psychoanalysis to human progress.

Certainly the ancient technique of disciplining a child out of his symptoms has proved to be as destructive as the naively optimistic hope that, left to himself, the child outgrows his difficulties. At best, these devices merely bury the symptoms while allowing the underlying unconscious roots to persist. Furthermore, it is one of the deeply disappointing facts of human life that children even from happy families often develop serious neurotic problems. Evidently there are limits both to the preventive virtues and to the healing powers of family happiness as we know it today. Why this is true and what to do about it constitute one of the great cultural challenges of our times.

When Should Analysis Be Attempted?

How early in the development of a neurosis should analysis be undertaken? Let us consider a few examples. Take, for instance, a frequent problem—that of a spinster in her early thirties. She has never been happy in her social relationships. Whether idle or active, she has for years manifested veiled emotional and neurotic disturbances but has always been able to run away from them. She has escaped from them into work. She has gone on vacations abroad and at home. She has tried shifting from one social group to another. She has turned successively to Christian Science, social work, theosophy, and art. Yet, as the years have gone on, for reasons she cannot explain, frustration and defeat have followed her until suddenly she is confronted by one of the specters that she has always dreaded most—i.e., the fear of becoming an old maid. By this time, however, her fear is complicated by reality because she has reached an age at which most of the men she knows are already married. Indeed, many are husbands of her friends, which infects her limited social life with a secret rage and envy. Other men have remained unmarried for their own neurotic reasons. Therefore, as she reaches out blindly for inappropriate men, she suffers repeated disappointments. Finally, some particularly disappointing episode becomes too much to bear and precipitates her into a "nervous breakdown," i.e., into a fully developed emotional or mental disturbance.

The further course of such a patient reveals another significant fact: the fight is not won even when the patient recovers from this acute upset. She emerges from her illness to face the same external realities and the same inner psychological mechanisms until and unless analysis frees her from them. Even the patient who has been cured of a neurosis at this late date may be like a prisoner emerging from a long prison sentence. No magic can restore the lost years, or make the road ahead an easy one.

When should such a patient have been analyzed? There would have been an opportunity in childhood, when she first manifested temper tantrums, night terrors, a retreat into books or other work, an avoidance of contemporaries, or an excessive dependency on adults. There would have been an opportunity in adolescence when the patient had a short but serious emotional upset on going away to camp for the first time (euphemistically called "homesickness"). There would have been an opportunity in her early twenties when the patient's social uneasiness, her lost attitude in the world, and her excessive emotional swings became unmistakable. Sometimes these opportunities are missed because of the false pride of families who refuse to recognize the existence of a neurosis. Sometimes they are missed because the patient herself is proud and defiant, or secretive and ashamed, and rejects every effort to lead her to help. Whatever the cause of the delay, its ultimate effects on the patient's life are tragic.

Comparable to such a case is the fate of the bachelor who comes to the analyst at a similar age. He has been disappointed in his emotional relationships and in his work. He has met defeat because neurotic obstacles within himself have stood between him and success. Here again, even after successful analytic treatment, the patient comes out of the prison of his illness to face a world in which opportunities for further training and for employment may be seriously curtailed. His bungling progress through school or college or professional school, or through the early years of a business or professional career, has marred his record so that the latter does not do justice to his potential abilities. This in itself limits his future opportunities. Even if he achieves freedom from his neurosis, he faces a difficult task. Sometimes he must train himself for competition with people twenty years his junior. Sometimes he must abandon one field of work for another. These difficult readjustments are the inevitable consequences of years of neglected neuroses. For these lost years, analysis has no magical assuagement. It cannot turn back the hands of the clock.

The question may be asked when to begin analysis. In the early years, when the transient neurotic outbursts of childhood gave warning of possible future difficulties? In adolescence? Or at the recurrence of difficulties in the twenties? The specific time can be chosen only in terms of the needs of each patient, but the general principle holds that "the earlier the better," because the fresh neurosis is less resistant to therapy and because early treatment can save many years of tragic waste and frustration.

These are some of the considerations which make one recommend that treatment be instituted just as early as the patient can be brought to realize his need for help. It is rarely wise to wait long to see if a patient will "outgrow it," or, on the other hand, to protect a patient to a point at which it becomes easier for him to live with his neurosis than to face the rigors of treatment. Whether as therapy or as prevention, psychoanalysis can function effectively only for someone who has become convinced of the necessity of the step he is taking, who is ready to face his neurotic tendencies, who has abandoned the effort to blame his maladjustments on physical illness, external circumstances, or other people, and who comes willingly and largely on his own initiative. In many cases, and especially in the effort to prevent the development of illness before it is fully manifest, the analyst's first task is to prepare the patient for treatment by bringing him to this fully cooperative viewpoint. This antechamber to analysis may sometimes take a long time.

Who Can Be Analyzed?

(a) *Intelligence*

One is often asked whether formal education and intelligence are essential for an analysis. This is not a matter about which one may be dogmatic. It is clear that, in general, a fine intelligence is an asset, but that formal education matters little. There have been efforts to use psychoanalytic methods to study primitive savages, simple people in our own society, and the mentally defective, and in the latter case to alter their sudden emotional tantrums. The immediate therapeutic value of these studies is less certain than is their scientific interest.

172

(b) *Age Limits*

Are there age limits outside of which analysis is impossible? Certain special technical problems arise in the psychoanalytic investigation of infants before they have reached the age of spoken language. Technically, it comes down to the question of how far gestures, play, direct emotional expression, and the like can be used as a substitute for the spoken word in tracing the patterns of free associations to reach an understanding of the preverbal process by which the infant or child learns to represent symbolically the conflicts he represses. Much important research centers about this problem, but some theoretically illuminating and therapeutically gratifying results have already been achieved.

With older children, no such technical difficulties exist. The exploration of unconscious influences and their conscious resolution in this age group is an important phase of current psychoanalytic development. In adolescence, the main obstacle to successful work is the patient's temptation to blame his difficulties on the vicissitudes of home, school, and college, and to reject all personal responsibility for the task of getting well. Sometimes this may be so difficult to overcome that the youth must be allowed to flounder until he becomes convinced of his need. This is dangerous, however, and whenever the adolescent neurosis contains any premonitions of delinquency or severe mental illness, one dares not wait for the patient's awareness of his own illness to develop. By that time it may be too late for help. This problem is complicated today by the tragic prevalence of drug abuse in adolescence, not part of the picture in 1950 when this chapter was first written.

Old age, too, brings its perplexities. For those beyond a certain age, one would hesitate to recommend so lengthy a form of treatment. What that "certain age" is, however, must be determined for each individual patient. What one person can no longer undertake profitably at forty-five, another can carry through at fifty-five or sixty. Many considerations will enter into that decision: the duration of the neurotic difficulties; the patient's earlier flexibility and health in meeting the challenges of life; the social, familial, and economic problems the patient has to face, etc. The decision will rest on grounds of practical common sense, as well as on technical issues, and must be thoroughly discussed between the psychoanalyst and the patient or his family before treatment is undertaken. One thing is certain: some people gain in flexibility as the years go on and become more accessible to swift changes under the influence of analysis in the sixties or even the seventies than they had been in earlier attempts in the thirties, forties, or fifties. This surprising fact has only become clear to us in relatively recent years.

Chapter XVI
JUDGING THE COURSE AND OUTCOME OF AN ANALYSIS

That many analyses fail to achieve complete success goes without saying. To anticipate the same degress of therapeutic success in as heterogeneous a lot of illnesses as those brought to the psychoanalyst is to expect something that no other medical therapy can claim, namely, the ability to treat all illnesses with equal effectiveness. It is often forgotten that, under the cover of some such euphemistic term as "a nervous break-down," the psychoanalyst faces many diverse problems —drug addictions, the perversions, every known form of psychoneurosis, psychopathic personalities, delinquency, incipient insanities of various kinds, etc. One does not expect surgery to achieve the same results in cancer, a brain tumor, appendicitis, and a boil. We estimate the value of surgery separately in terms of each disease entity it attempts to help. In the same way, the therapeutic value of psychoanalysis must be judged separately for each of the conditions it attempts to treat. Furthermore, even when dealing with similar symptom clusters, the processes by which they evolve and the psychopathological soil out of which they develop may vary so widely that identical results cannot be expected.

The Data Essential for Judging

To judge accurately either the progress or the outcome of a psychoanalytic treatment requires exceptional patience and caution. This is because it is difficult for an outsider to know the essential facts without which no judgment can be valid. Some of these facts are obvious: (1) Was the patient analyzed by a competent and properly trained psychoanalyst? (2) Was the analysis approximately completed, or prematurely interrupted by circumstances over which neither the patient nor the analyst had any control? (3) What were the symptoms and difficulties that brought the patient to the psychoanalyst for treatment, and what would be the normal outcome of such a condition if untreated? (4) What would be the expected course and outcome of the psychoanalytic treatment of such a case (a) under favorable circumstances, (b) under unfavorable circumstances? (5) What especially favorable or unfavorable influences affected the progress of this particular analysis? (6) What was the condition of the patient at the end of the treatment in comparison (a) with his condition when he began, (b) with the best that might be hoped for? (7) To what extent had the patient's life been destroyed by his untreated neurosis before he ever took the plunge and came to treatment? Here it must never be forgotten that even a seemingly minor neurotic difficulty can destroy and disrupt a life so disastrously, that the life becomes "sicker" than the illness (1956d, 1965a, 1968a, 1968d).

Many other considerations are often important, but, with this minimal information on hand, competent opinion would usually be possible. Unfortunately these data are rarely accessible even to interested friends and relatives. No other patients are equally reticent about their symptoms, and nowhere else would the least abuse of professional confidence have such disastrous effects upon the treatment itself. As a result, the psychoanalyst frequently must accept criticisms that are unfounded, without being free to say a word in defense or explanation. As we have pointed out, it is sometimes impossible for the analyst to take anyone into his confidence, even the referring physician. This is a situation the psychoanalyst deplores but cannot change. There are many occasions when he would feel happier if he had the right to share his knowledge with others.

A few actual experiences, which are in no way exceptional, can best illustrate these difficulties. Neurotic problems are often dissimulated. More frequently than is realized, patients succeed for years in fooling their friends and families into thinking of them as people of more than ordinary stability and poise. They may carry responsibilities well. To the rest of the world, they may appear happy and successful. Yet all the while, and notwithstanding this courageous simulation of health, they may suffer almost continuously from neurotic symptoms they never acknowledge. When such a person finally comes to psychoanalysis, these hidden symptoms may soon be aggravated, so that the patient looks and feels worse than before he began treatment. At this time, the patient will usually take his family and his physician into his confidence, which naturally gives rise to the impression that the analysis is making the patient worse. Actually, this uncovering of hidden neurotic symptoms is an essential forward step without which no healing can even begin. This is one of the many situations in which it is wise whenever possible to give psychoanalytic patients a large measure of privacy from their customary contacts, and in which the well-meant solicitude of loyal friends may add a considerable burden of unnecessary strain.

A young businessman provides an example of such a situation. He was a man of exceptional ability, who early in life had achieved unusual success. In addition, he had carried the responsibilities of two households and managed the affairs of a large family, which looked up to him as to a figure of unshakable strength. No one but his wife had any suspicion that he was troubled by an array of phobias and by a severe psychosexual problem. For the sake of the many people who were dependent on him, this patient had kept his symptoms secret, as well as the fact that he was being psychoanalyzed. Had anyone known of this, however, within a few weeks the cry would have been raised that under the influence of the analysis the patient was getting worse, because by that time his old symptoms were intensified and, in addition, many new ones had come to light. Fortunately, in this case there was nobody who could interfere, and the patient had an opportunity to work through this symptomatic flurry early in his analysis and reach lasting health.

Equally difficult for the outsider to judge fairly is the case of the patient who comes to analysis and attends each session faithfully, but never does a stroke of analytic work. Sometimes he comes and says only selected things, consistently refusing on the basis of one excuse or another to follow the rule of free association. After a period of conscientious effort, the psychoanalyst may have to discontinue such a treatment. If the patient is seriously sick, however, the psychoanalyst may hang on doggedly, trying by every device at his command to break through the patient's defenses and win his confidence, because the analyst knows that unless he succeeds the patient will remain sick indefinitely. If he fails, the outsider will think, "What a racket this is, all that time and money for nothing." The defeated psychoanalyst is not free to explain that, although the patient came for many months, he may have done only a few days of honest analytical work in the entire period.

In another type of case the treatment is a race against time—i.e., a race against the downhill course of an illness that has already acquired great momentum. For instance, certain sudden disorders, which if untreated will regularly lead to serious mental illness, can sometimes be arrested by immediate psychoanalytic therapy. At some point, but rarely early enough, the patient is brought to the psychoanalyst. If the analyst has the courage to undertake the treatment of such a patient, he knows that he is entering a race difficult to win. Occasionally he will succeed in cutting short the attack and in returning the patient to health before he has to go through the entire cycle of illness. More frequently, however, before the analysis is even fairly launched, the patient may become so disturbed as to require hospitalization, either temporary or permanent.

An example of this type is the case of a man in his middle forties who had been subject to recurrent periods of severe emotional illness for nearly twenty-five years. In the incipient stages of a fresh attack, he was placed under treatment in the hands of an able colleague. In a short time, however, despite this analytic interference, the patient had to be hospitalized for a few weeks, at which some of his closest friends and relatives became alarmed and claimed that the psychoanalyst had caused the illness. Completely overlooking the fact that identical episodes of illness had occurred many times before psychoanalysis had ever been contemplated, they tried unsuccessfully to influence the patient's wife to interrupt the treatment. After a few weeks of hospitalization, however, the patient improved sufficiently to enable him to return to his analysis, at first continuing to live in the hospital, and later in his own home. It was soon found that the analytical work done before the severe upset was immediately related to that done during the convalescence. The final outcome of the two together was a return to uninterrupted health. In this case it was only the wife's firm confidence in the psychoanalyst that prevented a premature interruption of the treatment.

Perhaps more difficult to evaluate than any of the foregoing is the problem of the forlorn hope. There are desperate illnesses in the field of psychiatry, just as there are in other medical fields. That is to say, there are illnesses so severe that the patient almost never makes a complete recovery, or, at best, remains a crippled personality for the rest of his days. Sometimes such conditions develop out of seemingly innocent and insignificant neurotic disturbances. A patient may be brought to psychoanalysis for troubles that the family and the family physician look upon as trivial, when the patient may actually be on the brink of serious mental illness. Here, the diagnostic keenness of the psychoanalyst is of vital importance; and it is here that the adequacy of his fundamental psychiatric training is put to the test. If the pathological process has not gained too much headway, the psychoanalyst, after frank discussion of the dangers with the referring physician and some responsible representative of the family, may attempt to check the progress of the disease. Under such circumstances it is rare that anyone but the official representative of the family realizes that the psychoanalyst is knowingly undertaking a forlorn hope and that his chances of success are slight. Yet, if no analyst is willing to take this risk, the patient may be deprived of his only chance of escaping permanent sickness. In such situations, those who are on the inside tend to keep their knowledge to themselves, and, in the event of failure, it appears to the rest of the world as though a slightly "nervous" person has been driven into permanent illness by psychoanalytic intervention.

For instance, a severe case of paranoia was already well developed before the patient was brought to a psychiatrist. To the casual observer, the patient still seemed merely "a little nervous." At the insistence of the family, the patient was subjected to a cautious psychoanalytic investigation, which was abruptly interrupted by the family after only a few weeks. Two years later, when the patient required permanent hospitalization, this was blamed by many outsiders on the few weeks of tentative psychoanalytic probing. Psychoanalysis cannot claim to be that potent, whether for good or for evil.

A less subtle source of trouble for the psychoanalyst is the patient who comes with impossible hopes of what analysis should do for him. Unless the analysis succeeds in uncovering and resolving these fantasies, such a patient usually goes away disgruntled, even though he may have been relieved of serious symptoms. An artist in his middle thirties came to a psychoanalyst for the treatment of a neurosis that had had its symptomatic onset before he was fifteen years of age. He was a man of outstanding ability who had on several occasions been offered important positions in the world of art. On each occasion, however, his acute anxiety states, his fantastic compulsions, his neurotic seclusiveness and hostility, and his disordered psychosexual life prevented his realizing his ambitions. When he came to the psychoanalyst he had been unable to work for almost a year because of a purely imaginary (i.e., "hysterical") paralysis of one of his arms. As a result, he and his family were on the verge of starvation. For many months he was treated without charge and, during the course of that work, was able to resume his craft. He secured a good position as a commerical artist, so that he could support himself and his children. The larger part of his neurotic symptoms were reduced to negligible severity, although they were not completely removed. In fact, at the end, the patient acknowledged that he clung almost deliberately to the remaining symptom, chiefly as an excuse for not pursuing his earlier ambitions. Nevertheless, and in spite of his obvious improvement, after an unavoidable interruption of his analysis this patient became hostile. Because the psychoanalyst had not set the hands of the clock back twenty years so as to make him again the prodigy he once had been, he inveighed against psychoanalysis and the psychoanalyst. In these attacks he stressed only the large amount of time he had contributed to his treatment. As evidence of his unimproved condition, he pointed to the fact that he was still unable to realize his earlier ambitions. He did not mention the severe and crippling symptoms that had disturbed his entire life, throwing him out of work and rendering him helpless and penniless, and of which, to all intents and purposes, he had been relieved. His hearers heard only what he chose to tell them, and misjudged the value of his analytic experience accordingly.

With the patient and his family hedging his illness with secrecy and sometimes even with deception, it is small wonder that the outside world watches the progress of an analysis and its outcome with skepticism and misgivings. One can meet this only by urging the onlookers to bear in mind that it is impossible to judge the outcome except in the light of full information, and that they can only rarely be in possession of this information.

It has already been seen that the family physician can be taken into the analyst's confidence only with care and reservation (Chapter XIV). This is even more necessary in dealing with family and friends. Often enough, friends and relatives may be a focal point in the patient's neurosis, and any contact with them may stir up symptomatic activity long after this has disappeared in all other situations. That is one reason why so many patients can maintain a pretense of health in the presence of the outside world long after their families are well aware of their illnesses. It is also why patients who may show marked improvement on the outside continue to exhibit their old difficulties at home. Neuroses arise in the bosom of the family and persist there with greatest tenacity. This is not calculated to arouse in the families of patients much confidence in the therapeutic value of the analysis. It is likely rather to give them a one-sided and pessimistic picture of the patient's progress. Furthermore, despite adequate warnings, it is hard for the family and friends to believe that in the treatment of a neurosis, by whatever method, a patient must often get worse before he gets better. Yet this occurs almost inevitably, because every human being shields himself as well as he can from that which is neurotic in his nature. Every patient must first go through the painful and distressing experience of facing unsuspected depths of illness before he begins to turn toward health. This initial and sometimes recurring intensification of symptoms may be serious enough to cause grave concern to family and friends and medical advisers; yet it is something for which everyone who faces an analysis must be prepared.

At times, patients who have had full-blown psychotic episodes should be treated psychoanalytically during their intervals of health in an effort to avoid further recurrences. In such situations the referring physician and responsible representatives of the family should be warned that psychotic episodes may occur at almost any time during the course of the analysis and sometimes with little warning, and that it may be only after several such episodes have been analyzed that the patient's health will become in any degree secure. Without such warnings, misunderstandings that can lead to premature interruption of the work are almost certain to arise.

The Right of Consultation

This is not an argument that, merely because the facts are so rarely accessible to the critic, one should never criticize or question or doubt an analyst. Analysts are far from infallible, and mistakes occur in analyses as they do in any other form of medical therapy. Fortunately, there is a constructive way of intervening. Granted that before undertaking the analysis it is essential to have every possible assurance about the integrity and ability of the chosen psychoanalyst, and granted also that it is wise thereafter to leave things in his hands, situations do nevertheless arise in which the inalienable right of any patient and family to a consultation should be exercised. The only question is how to do this in such a way that the further therapeutic usefulness of the psychoanalyst will not be impaired. A simple course can be recommended:

(a) If not done at the beginning, it is essential to ascertain from a psychoanalytic society whether the particular physician is an adequately trained psychoanalyst.

(b) The next step would be to go directly to the psychoanalyst himself with all of one's doubts and questions.

(c) If this does not allay the anxiety that has arisen, one may then ask for a consultation with another psychoanalyst and the family physician. In arranging such a consultation, it is best to work out with the original psychoanalyst and the consultants how and when and whether the patient himself should be examined. In fact, unless there is reasonable doubt regarding the integrity and competence of the psychoanalyst in question, it is often well to defer any direct examination of the patient until after a preliminary conference among the psychoanalyst, the consultants, and the representatives of the patient. Sometimes the detailed discussion of the story of the illness and of the course of the treatment may make unnecessary any examination of the patient himself. This at times has great advantages.

One cannot be sure that these steps will always settle the disquieting issues, but it is as fair and safe a procedure as can be followed. Such steps are necessary only in exceptional cases.

Some Reasons for Failure

One might summarize as follows some typical causes of analytic defeats.

Some are due to faulty technique and/or faulty diagnosis. These can be reduced to a minimum by turning only to properly trained men. Some fail for external reasons—either they have been prematurely interrupted by unavoidable external circumstances or as a result of the impatient interference of those who influence the patient. This can sometimes be avoided when it is possible to give accurate warnings to the referring physician and to the responsible members of the family concerning what to expect, and where the family is sufficiently stable to hold to a course once it is agreed upon.

Soundly conducted analyses can fail because of forces inherent in the illness being treated. Sometimes the psychoanalyst has made a legitimate but unsuccessful effort to save a patient who was already desperately ill; sometimes the analysis fails, but only temporarily, because, in a race to stave off a process that has already gained too much momentum, the analysis loses. Such temporary failures may in the end turn out to be sound successes if, in a later and less stormy phase of the illness, the analysis can be resumed and carried through to completion.

Some analyses fail because of forces peculiar to particular cases: a patient who suffers from an otherwise curable neurosis cannot be induced by the psychoanalyst to undergo those essential emotional deprivations without which no real analysis is possible; or the life situation of a patient is so unalterably unfortunate that life itself can offer nothing better to him than the retreat afforded by the neurosis. (The first group is sometimes represented by patients who have been spoiled by great wealth and the second group by certain sufferers from great poverty. Subtler factors than these, however, may also play a determining role.) Or the failure may occur when a patient has so many emotional assets that, with every minor advance, he feels convinced he is well. There may be a complete if temporary disappearance of all symptoms, and the patient reaches a plateau of apparent health, while the analysis stalls.

Analyses fail because the patient cannot be induced to abandon deliberate plans to block the treatment: he may come for months, but can never be launched in the free production of his material, or he enters analysis reluctantly, under pressure from some external compulsion rather than because of an acknowledged internal need. Such patients often are firmly and unalterably resolved to withhold essential data, either in a deliberate effort to thwart the psychoanalyst and thus to take revenge on those who forced the analysis on them, or else to protect someone else. Or the patient has a secret but conscious determination not to get well because he feels that recovery would be a tacit admission that the whole illness was psychological and therefore "his own fault," instead of being physical or due to external forces. To blame the body or the outside world is always a temptation to the patient who looks upon his neurosis as a sign of shameful weakness.

This list could be vastly extended to include many technical factors, until the reader, in confusion, would begin to wonder how it happens that psychoanalysis ever succeeds. One may offer assurances on this score, however, and couple them with the reminder that one hears much less about psychoanalytic successes than about failures. Partly this is because the healed patient goes his way gratefully but quietly so that few people may know the nature or extent of his previous difficulties, and even fewer may know that he had ever been under psychoanalytic treatment.

The Final Test of Health

After an analysis is over it is fair to appeal to a wider court in evaluating its effects. Provided the judges have

189

some knowledge of why the patient sought analysis in the first place, it is fair to measure its results in terms of the patient's apparent happiness and peace, his satisfaction in his activities, his freedom from disturbing states of depression, anxiety, guilt, anger, fear, or jealousy, and, finally and specifically, his freedom from those neurotic symptoms that brought him to analysis in the first place.

Certainly it is not an analytic goal to alter fundamentally the life situation of every patient. The psychoanalyst hopes rather to make it possible for the patient to find health within the framework of the life which he is already living. This means that by and large the psychoanalyst prefers to leave marriages, occupations, and friendships unaltered. On the other hand, as is explained in Chapters XII and XX, this aim must always be secondary to the patient's health. Where a life has been built under the influence of neurotic mechanisms, nothing short of radical alterations may suffice to make health possible. In such situations the analysis becomes a surgical instrument, the psychoanalyst needs a surgeon's courage, and the patient the ability to endure pain. It takes a good surgeon to know when not to operate, and a good psychoanalyst to know when to leave things alone. But the final criterion of success is the health of the patient and not what has to be altered in the patient's life situation.

Such health, as we have already tried to indicate in Chapters III and IV, expresses itself subtly in every aspect of life. The patient will have gained an enlarged understanding of himself and of all of those with whom his life comes into contact, a deeper understanding of his own children and of their needs, freedom to give of his time, energy, and interest to the world at large, to his own business of living, and to his human relationships. He will have learned certain things about himself, which many of his close friends could have told him but which before his analysis he could not have understood. He might have recognized the words, but never the tune; and he would have been unable to use this knowledge because he would still have been under the tyrannical domination of his own unconscious mechanisms. This indeed is the greatest of his analytic gains—a true inner freedom, a broadening of the areas of life in which psychological forces of whose nature he is now fully aware will dominate his thoughts and feelings and purposes and behavior. To the extent to which his analysis has succeeded, therefore, he will have become flexible, adaptable, and dynamically mature and free. In short, he will have acquired the freedom to change, which he had lost through illness and which is the subtlest and most inclusive criterion of health. Without this, he cannot grow in maturity, and without this he cannot learn from experience (1968a, 1973a).

Chapter XVII
THE FINANCIAL ARRANGEMENTS
FOR AN ANALYSIS

It is customary to pass lightly over the financial arrangements between a professional man and his client or patient, both behaving as though money did not exist, and as though it were below their dignity to discuss financial arrangements frankly. This polite pretense is especially prevalent in the dealings between a physician and his patients. Even if he wanted to, the psychoanalyst could not follow such a course without jeopardizing the analysis.

It is the psychoanalyst's task to clarify to his patient the ways in which unconscious attitudes can disturb any aspect of his life. The analyst can therefore hardly permit his patient to evade the conscious and unconscious emotional significance of money. Nor could the analyst bring these unconscious attitudes into the open if he and the patient danced a polite but evasive minuet around their financial arrangements. Indeed, not infrequently it is how the patient plans to finance his analysis and how he pays his monthly analytic bills that first make clear the full complexity of his unconscious attitudes to money. Moreover, how this problem is handled may prove to be an important indicator of the nature of the patient's purposes in seeking treatment. Hence, for psychological as well as practical reasons, a full and frank discussion of finances is necessary when planning for an analysis.

The relation of the psychoanalyst and his patient is in essence an unwritten mutual contract in which, as with any physician, *the patient remains free to terminate his treatment at any time.* It is the analyst's hope, however, that the patient will not do this impulsively or without careful, joint deliberation. For as long as the patient chooses to remain in his care, the psychoanalyst, on his part, obligates himself to treat the patient in return for a certain agreed fee per session, and to remain responsible for that treatment until he feels that he has done everything in his power to help the patient toward health. The patient agrees to be financially responsible for the time assigned to him, whether he keeps his appointments or not, from the moment he begins his analysis until it is either terminated or discontinued. At the end of each month the analyst presents a bill, usually directly to the patient, based on the number of sessions scheduled for that month. Nor, if he is wise, will he allow the patient politely to evade repeated discussions of these monthly accounts.

The Missed Session

Even when the patient announces in advance his intention to miss a session, he may still be held responsible for it. Otherwise, he would be given a double incentive to miss appointments and to become irregular in attendance. Every patient has a natural temptation to avoid analytic sessions whenever things become difficult. Unless there is some strong deterrent, minor business or social demands may be allowed to interrupt the continuity of the analytical work precisely when such interruptions will be most deleterious in their effects on the analysis. If the patient were not charged for appointments he missed for inconsequential reasons, the analyst would, in effect, be offering him a financial inducement to escape painful sessions, since he could go off and enjoy himself, and save money as well. The steady, day-by-day continuity of analytical work is of such importance that every inducement must be brought to bear on a patient to hold him to his schedule. *On the other hand, when a patient is well launched in treatment and works consistently and faithfully, the analyst need not adhere rigidly to the practice of charging for missed hours.* In this matter, therefore, he is free to vary his practice, both from case to case and at different stages in the analysis of any patient.

Setting the Fee

It is never justifiable for a psychoanalyst to fix his charges at such a rate that all of the funds available for a patient's analysis will be used up within a few months, when a lower fee would carry the patient through a longer period of treatment to its successful termination. It is imperative to budget carefully for an adequate length of time. Although it is impossible ever to predict how long an analysis will take, it is a wise procedure to plan for at least two years of work, pointing out that it may take less than that, but stressing equally the possibility that it may take longer. To aid the psychoanalyst in fixing a fair fee, the patient will describe to him the facts concerning (1) his financial status, (2) his income, (3) his capital, (4) his prospects, (5) his responsibilities, and, if necessary (6) any accessory sources of funds which might be made available to help him finance his treatment. The patient who will not trust his analyst with these financial facts might just as well not attempt to be analyzed, because he will surely not trust his analyst with more intimate data. The analyst on his part must insist on this information so that he can be fair to the patient as well as to his own needs, and also to put to an immediate test the patient's trust. Together, then, with this information, they will decide what the fee should be, and whether it should be paid entirely by the patient himself, and entirely out of income.

Sometimes it is wise to look upon health as a form of capital, thus justifying the invastion of capital to finance treatment so as to lessen the immediate sacrifices entailed in paying for analysis out of income alone. A thousand dollars out of income in one year might cripple a family's budget whereas if taken out of capital it would reduce the family income by only a few dollars a year. This spreads the cost of the analysis over the many years during which the patient and his family can expect to enjoy the benefits of it. Perhaps it is relevant to add that the psychoanalyst contributes working capital to every treatment, in that he gives his patients his only irreplaceable capital goods, *time*. The hours he devotes to his patients are his only working capital, what he expends on one patient cannot be used for another. Therefore, when necessary, a similar contribution from the patient is not unreasonable, provided such a capital outlay does not jeopardize the fundamental economic security of the patient or his family.

Sometimes it is difficult to decide who should pay for an analysis, or how the cost should be divided. In general it is best for a patient to pay for his own treatment. Frequently, however, wives or minors may have no money at all, or very little, whereas the husband, parent, or guardian may have ample resources. In such cases, the psychoanalyst and the prospective patient together consider whether any of these accessory sources may fairly be called upon to support the patient's treatment, or whether the use of any outside source will obstruct the progress of the analysis. This issue is decided individually in each case. For instance, one patient who was heir to a large fortune was treated for many months for a token fee. He could have gone freely to his father for money but it happened to be essential that this patient undertake his treatment on an independent and self-supporting basis, and that it should be his personal sacrifice alone which made possible the analysis. He was therefore charged only what he himself could afford. Analysts cannot always do this, however, because, when an analyst reduces his charges for the benefit of some patient who could turn to others for financial help, that analyst thereby limits his ability to make concessions to other impecunious patients who have no supplemental funds available. Therefore, although in the example cited this concession made a major contribution to the success of the treatment, it also limited the contribution the analyst could make to others. Clearly, mere embarrassment at the idea of asking for financial help is never an adequate reason for allowing a patient to pay less than the financial status of his family as a whole would justify.

From the social point of view, a patient should be ready to borrow in order to pay for his analysis, if his own funds are not sufficient and if others to whom he is close have ample funds, whenever this will not hinder the analysis. If a patient who could borrow fails to do so and the analyst therefore treats him for little or nothing, the patient is, in effect, being treated at the expense of other poorer patients for whom no accessory funds are available. There are few psychoanalysts who can themselves afford to play the role of banker; but even if they could, such a relationship would seriously hamper the analysis. The recent introduction of various subsidies for psychotherapies of all kinds makes some modifications in these general practices imperative. These have been discussed elsewhere (1964b).

Psychoanalytic fees vary widely. There is no one

"fair" charge. A surgeon may be entitled to charge many hundreds of dollars for one hour of operative skill; the psychoanalyst's apprenticeship takes even longer than that of the skilled surgeon. The surgeon, however, makes his charge only once, whereas the psychoanalyst's fee goes on for many months or even years. Therefore, as we have said, the analyst charges only what a patient can afford to pay for as long as the analysis is likely to last. He must take into consideration the source of the money with which he is being paid, so that this, in turn, will not in any way hamper the progress of the work; and he must provide the patient with an opportunity to make some personal sacrifice for the analysis. To this end, when a patient does not pay the entire fee himself, he can be charged with the responsibility for some part of it at least.

Like anyone else, the psychoanalyst must earn a reasonable, steady income from his day's work. It is rarely possible for anyone to analyze more than eight to ten patients at a time and do them full justice. From the varying fees these patients are charged, the analyst must realize a certain average return. Therefore he must balance each patient who is unable to pay him more than a fraction of this average with one who can pay him above the average. Almost every psychoanalyst carries a few patients who can pay little or nothing, except those who make their contribution to society by giving time to hospitals and to teaching, without compensation. It is the rule of some psychoanalytic societies to exact a pledge from every member to accept at least one free patient who is referred from the psychoanalytic institute. Where no such pledge is exacted, much the same contribution is made through the personal recommendation of poor patients from one psychoanalyst to another on a voluntary basis. That is, a psychoanalyst whose schedule is full, or who cannot afford at a particular time to take on another free patient, guides such a patient to another psychoanalyst whose schedule makes it possible to accept him.

It has long been argued by some analysts that for a variety of reasons an analysis for which a patient makes no personal financial sacrifice is foredoomed to failure. This has not been the experience of the author. It is true, of course, that a patient may exploit an analyst's generosity for neurotic reasons. This neurotic drive may defy analysis for many months because of the gratification the patient derives from this behavior. Usually, however, such analytic generosity bears fruit in the end, as the patient begins to face his guilt, and the reasons for it. This entire issue of the therapeutic leverage of the free analysis requires critical reinvestigation.

Average Fees and Average Costs

We have said that the psychoanalysts' fees have a wide range. In 1936 the average fee for all psychoanalytical work done in New York City was under ten dollars an hour. Today the average fees are considerably higher. In the winter of 1948-49 a questionnaire was sent to every member of the American Psychoanalytic Association. Usable answers were received from about 42 per cent of the membership. They revealed a number of interesting facts: e.g., for the United States as a whole the average fee per session was $14.50, the range from 0 to $50.00. The various psychoanalytic centers showed less variation in the averages than had been anticipated. The range was from $11.30 in one city, to just about $18.00 in another, with the other large centers all averaging between $12.00 and $17.00.

Because only 42 per cent of the membership furnished usable information, it is not possible to claim absolute accuracy for these statistics. We have no way of knowing whether those who answered represent a random sample of the whole group, or whether the "high chargers" or the "low chargers" held back disproportionately. Since the replies were all anonymous, however, it is probable, that these figures are reasonably accurate. If statistics were available on the cost of analyses conducted by advanced students under supervision (cf. Chapter XXIII), the percentage of analyses at less than $10.00 per session would be enormously increased for every training center.

If these charges are compared with the consultation fees charged by most medical specialists, they are modest enough, and, compared with a surgeon's charges, they are minute. But when one takes into consideration the fact that the patient must pay this fee not once, but every day for many weeks and months or even years, it is clear that the ultimate cost is high. The exact amount will vary, of course, both with the fee per session and with the duration of the analysis. If one year is taken as a basis of computation, eliminating Sundays, most Saturdays, and at least one month's holiday in the summer and a few shorter interruptions, there will be about 200 to 225 analytic sessions in the analytic year. At ten dollars per session this will cost $2,000 to $2,250 for a year's analytical work. Today, of course, all of these figures would be higher.

Peculiarities of the Psychoanalyst's Economic Position

In spite of the fact that even at low rates the total expense for the patient is heavy, the analyst does not earn a large income. The psychoanalyst who sticks to his job, who does not accept too many consultations (since these break into the continuity of his therapeutic schedule), who works consistently with the same patients, who does not give his patients fewer sessions per week merely to make it possible to charge higher fees per session, and who does not crowd his days with too many patients—such an analyst cannot earn an income comparable to that of the successful consultant in internal medicine, the surgeon, or almost any other specialist. Indeed, the psychoanalyst's economic position tends to be somewhat precarious. Because his income is derived from work with a few patients at a time, it is relatively easy for him to become established on a modest basis. On the other hand, this income will fluctuate sharply as patients start or stop. In times of economic unrest it is not a rare experience for patients

201

who have been economically secure to be deprived of important sources of income suddenly in the midst of treatment, or to have to undertake unexpected financial responsibilities for other members of their families. It is then a matter of conscience for the psychoanalyst to carry that patient at a reduced fee for as long as possible, and not to drop him at a critical point in his analysis simply because of his lack of funds. The psychoanalyst is willing to do this for a few patients, but if he attempts to help many patients in this way, he may find that several hours of every day are devoted to uncompensated work. The psychoanalyst's own economic security will then be undermined, and he can make himself secure only by taking on more patients than he can treat with maximal efficiency, or by interrupting the analyses of some of his poorer patients in order to replace them with others who are more fortunately placed. No conscientious analyst does this unless he is forced to; but there is a limit beyond which he cannot go without impairing his own security, his peace of mind, and the quality of his work. This dilemma is always painful, but until there are endowment funds for the support of analyses of indigent patients, psychoanalysts will have to compromise as best they can between their own needs and their responsibility to their analysands.

The economic position of the analyst is unusual in one other respect. His years of training continue until he is between thirty-five and forty. Several more years are required before he gains full clinical maturity.

Therefore a life-expectancy which, after the age of fifty-five, drops below that of most other professional groups does not give him many years in which to serve the community, or in which to earn an education for his children or a modest independent security for his own old age. This has an effect on what he must try to accumulate during the relatively few earning years, and therefore on what he must charge for his services, and on how much free work he can do. These facts create a serious problem in medical economics which cannot be solved by analysts alone, but only by the coordinated efforts of the whole community.

Chapter XVIII

THE CONTRAST BETWEEN PSYCHOANALYSIS AND HEALING BY FAITH OR BY SUGGESTION

Many years ago Claude Bernard, the great French physiologist, pointed out that philosophers, theologians, and scientists are all alike as human beings; and that, since they are human, their minds obey the same basic laws. Thus, all of us operate under the influence of biases, prejudices, and preconceptions, and in our work we make use of variable mixtures of logic, guesswork, and intuition. Out of this our theories arise, whether these are scientific, philosophical, or theological. What then distinguishes the followers of these disciplines from one another? Claude Bernard pointed out that the scientist stands apart from the rest in only one important respect. If he is a true scientist, then the mere fact that any theory is his own, or that it seems or "feels" true and convincing, has no value for him as evidence. For the scientist, no theory, however logical, can ever be more than the starting point for an investigation. As this great physiologist put it, the scientist sheds his theories with his coat as he enters his laboratory; and not even logic is a substitute for evidence.

The psychoanalyst should maintain the same scientific attitude. When he interprets to a patient some bit of behavior or a fragment of his life-story or a dream, that interpretation should be put forward not as an article of faith but as a working hypothesis, a theory that might conceivably explain the psychological experience. It is a hypothesis to be tested against the patient's further material. What the patient produces at the time of the interpretation or in the subsequent course of the analysis will either confirm the hypothesis, correct it, or throw it into discard.

The psychoanalyst expects and invites from his patients a frank and open skepticism. Nothing should excite graver misgivings in him than the blind credulity and pious faith some earnest patients struggle to maintain. Experience has taught the analyst that unless he can break down such attitudes they will make lasting therapeutic results impossible. He knows that the patient's effort to look upon him as omniscient and omnipotent is a symptom of the patient's neurosis, a direct carry-over from infancy, and he sets out not to exploit this uncritical worship but to analyze it away. This is quite different from the attitude and practice of the faith-healer.

All methods of healing by faith have in common certain fundamental assumptions and processes. First there is a basic premise that recovery depends upon supernatural forces which affect all illnesses equally. It is therefore superfluous to make a differential diagnosis, and no detailed investigation of the natural phenomena of disease is necessary. Indeed, since all that is needed is faith in the supernatural force in order to call it into action on the side of a mystical healing process, one need not bother even to take a careful history, or to make a careful physical, psychological, or laboratory study. The faith-healer never knows what, if anything, he is "healing." In contrast to this, the psychoanalyst bases his therapy upon the detailed investigation and evaluation of each case as an individual problem. Indeed, even during the course of the analysis there may be long months of study before a definitive diagnosis is possible and before definitive therapy gets under way.

Secondly, all methods of healing by faith or magic depend upon some form of exhortation, a mobilizing of religious and personal emotional enthusiasms. This is not the technical meaning of "suggestion," but this is what the word connotes to most laymen: an emotional ecstasy that carries the patient out of one mood and into another and, in so doing, obscures or gets rid of his symptoms, at least for the time being. To the layman, suggestion also connotes the influence of ideas to which the patient has been introduced by the "healer." Such ideas may influence the patient by challenging the logic of his own thinking; or they may exercise their influence largely through the emotional hold of the person who has presented them, and irrespective of their objective validity. This emotional influence may in turn be conscious or unconscious, deliberate or inadvertent; and it may lead the patient to accept ideas without any effort at personal critical evaluation. Thus the operation of suggestion in this sense is always dependent on the human relationship behind the ideas, a relationship which induces the patient to abrogate his right to individual judgment. Consequently, once the relationship is broken the patient will sooner or later regurgitate the imposed ideas. This is one reason why hypnotism, *in its original form of direct suggestion*, failed to produce lasting therapeutic results. The psychoanalyst, instead of making use of suggestion in this fashion, is constantly on the lookout to combat any manifestation of a tendency to submissive suggestibility on the part of the patient. Much incompetent and some skillful palliative psychotherapy depends largely upon suggestive procedures. Nothing, however, could be further from the theory and practice of competent psychoanalysis.

It may be argued, on the other hand, that psychoanalysis also works through a human relationship. This is true; but the bond is utilized differently. In analysis the relationship between the patient and the physician is not used to influence the patient directly, but rather to facilitate the production of buried material which would otherwise remain inaccessible. As is explained in the discussion of the analysis of the transference (see Chapter IX) every effort is made in analytic therapy not to bind the patient to the analyst or to his fantasies about the analyst, but rather to clarify these fantasies so as to enable the patient to progress steadily toward greater freedom.

Let me repeat that what psychoanalysis demands of

the patient is diametrically opposite to that which faith-healing demands. Psychoanalysis demands confidence in the integrity and intelligence of the analyst, an intellectual willingness to cooperate, and a whole-hearted purpose to abide by the rule of the analysis that the patient produce material freely and honestly. This in turn requires a courageous willingness to accept pain, anxiety, and deprivation, and to face unpleasant facts. Psychoanalysis, however, not only does not demand blind faith, it attempts constantly to analyze it away, even when this is faith in the analysis itself. Credulity impedes the progress of analytic therapy and insight, by hiding secret disagreements under a mask of sham compliance.

Psychoanalysis also demands willingness to accept in every detail the reality of the body, in a fashion which contrasts sharply with the faith-healer's effort to deny the reality of organic disease. Therefore, even where the faith-healer succeeds temporarily in suppressing pain, the analyst views this not as a therapeutic achievement but as the reinforcement of a process of illness, since suppressed pain is not eliminated from psychic life but is certain to reappear in other forms and at other times with increased intensity.

In all of these fundamental respects, therefore, psychoanalysis and healing by faith or by suggestion are at opposite poles.

Illusory Faith Cures

This is not the place to discuss the many claims which have been made for the power of healing by faith. It is well to remind ourselves, however, that in evaluating such stories it is at least as difficult as in psychoanalysis for the outsider to know what condition was "treated," what changes may occur spontaneously in such conditions, and what was the real relation of the treatment to the course of the illness. Every psychiatrist has had the experience of treating a patient who was convalescing slowly. Sometimes in such cases some well-meaning friend or relative will make the suggestion that the patient should turn to some form of faith cure. If the patient had attempted this during the deeper stages of his illness, it would have brought him no relief. As his convalescence progresses, however, the patient's growing optimism makes it possible for him to respond to any hopeful philosophy; and as this happens he may find himself seizing hold of Christian Science or some other faith-healing cult. This gives him a further boost, and when recovery supervenes the patient may feel convinced that he was cured by faith, whereas in reality his ability to embrace the optimistic faith was a clear indication that his convalescence was already well under way.

In general, one finds that so-called "cures" by faith-healing or by suggestion usually consist of temporary alleviation of symptoms; yet, as we have said elsewhere, the curing of a symptom may mean the obscuring of an illness. In the long run, this may do serious harm to a patient who would otherwise have had a chance to rid himself of the underlying neurotic process. Occasionally, however, affiliation with a religious sect may be part of a more fundamental alteration in a distorted personality, a change sufficiently profound to place it on a sound basis as long as the faith persists. Such experiences carry an important lesson for the student of the psychotherapeutic process.

Psychotherapy and the Process of Conversion

One of the greatest obstacles to psychoanalytic therapy is the fact that we are a stiff-necked people. Every human being wants to be rid of pain; but at the bottom of his heart no human being really wants to change. It is the everyday experience of analysts to be consulted by patients who are in a state of severe mental suffering, but who nonetheless say to the analyst, "I would not mind being analyzed in order to get rid of this suffering, but I do not want to *be* different." Sometimes this desire not to change is conscious; sometimes it is deeply buried; but it is always there. It constitutes one of the most tenacious obstacles to therapy, for the simple reason that neurotic symptoms are always the sparks from the wheel of a disordered personality. It is impossible to get rid of a patient's symptoms if he cannot be led to accept humbly and willingly the fact that he must struggle to become a different kind of person.

This humility, this willingness to change and to become different, is something which sometimes is seen most clearly in the process of religious conversion. Indeed, as psychoanalysts we must say with all humility that a true religious leader can sometimes create in the hearts of his followers a humble need for a different way of life which is often difficult for the analyst to achieve in his patient. It sometimes happens, therefore, that a religious leader will succeed in awakening a need to be different, without having the technical equipment which will enable him to show his "patient" specifically what needs to be changed and in what direction he must change. The psychoanalyst on the other hand has these techniques at his command, but may find it more difficult to evoke in his patient the humble willingness to change which is such an important part of the therapeutic process. It would seem that each could learn something from the other and thus fuse into one healing process the essential elements of the technique of conversion and the essential elements of the technique of psychoanalytic therapy.

Psychoanalysis and Religious Faith

The relationship between science and religious faith has troubled many minds for many years. This is not because the problem itself is intricate, but rather because people often dislike the conclusions to which their own logic brings them and therefore seek philosophic roads to conclusions they prefer. The issues themselves are reasonably simple and clear.

Science is an effort to find approximations of truth about ourselves and the world in which we live. Science depends upon methods of gathering empirical data, methods of testing the degree to which these data conform to external realities, thus establishing approximate "facts," methods of interpreting causal relationships between approximate facts, and, finally, methods of testing the accuracy of these interpretations by efforts to predict future events. Science accepts nothing as valid until it is supported by evidence of this general nature. The essential spirit of science is embodied in the basic principle that truth is always relative, always an approximation to reality, and that its acceptance always waits on evidence.

Religious faith, on the other hand, requires no evidence. For it, truth is established by the act of faith itself, and belief itself is the direct perception of a divinely revealed truth. Faith therefore is not a search, but an acceptance for which no evidence is required. Indeed, dependence upon evidence should logically be regarded as faithless and irreligious. To demand proof of the existence of God would seem to deny Him by implying that He is just a theory like any other, to be tested by evidence. Consequently, whether he realizes it or not, a scientist who has religious faith has consciously or unwittingly divided his universe into two kingdoms: the kingdom of science and the kingdom of faith. In the one he functions as a scientist, accepting nothing without scientific evidence. In the other he functions by faith alone.

Individual scientists vary in their willingness to divide the phenomenological world into these two kingdoms. There are some who hold that the scientific search for truth constitutes in their lives the equivalent of religion. If their philosophical self-scrutiny is mature, they will recognize that they base their life-work on certain tacit assumptions; but if they are consistent in their scientific spirit, they will use these assumptions only as working hypotheses to be tested and discarded whenever contrary evidence comes to light. As a matter of fact, it is precisely this willingness to test and discard one's premises that characterizes the scientific spirit as opposed to the spirit of religious faith. The two attitudes would seem to be mutually exclusive; yet there have always been some scientists who worship in a spirit of true faith. They are found among physicists, chemists, biologists, physicians, psychiatrists, and also among psychoanalysts.

The relationship of psychoanalysis to faith differs in one respect from that of the other sciences. Since psychoanalysis studies all psychological processes, it includes in the scope of its investigations the conscious and unconscious determinants both of faith and of skeptical doubt. For the analyst, faith and doubt, like all other psychological processes, are equally objects of scientific inquiry. They are studied in a broad context of the dynamics of all forms of confidence and the lack of it, of trust and distrust, of credulity and suspiciousness.

In his study of the conscious and unconscious determinants of faith, the analyst traces its genesis and development in the life of the individual. Early in life the small child finds his main security against terror by trusting in parents, whose omnipotence and omniscience he quite unconsciously takes for granted. Subsequently, as this first childish "faith" wanes, he may never again trust anyone to the same degree, or he may for a time endow others with similar powers, temporarily placing his faith in teachers or in other older members of his family, or in mankind in general. At some point, however, he turns with his faith to some remote, unseen, supernatural, superhuman, yet more or less personalized power: witch, fairy, ogre, magician, devil, or God. His identification with his parents and their fears and faiths will play an important role in this. The analyst studies the extent to which this dependence upon external omnipotence is an expression of the child's neurotic anxiety or to what extent it may be the expression of other inner conflicts, such as the child's need for protection against his own destructive impulses. He investigates the form the child's "faith" assumes, to see whether it is a learned pattern or is generated spontaneously. In other words, the analyst studies how each child creates his varying images of heaven and of hell and his different concepts of supernatural powers, who can reward and punish him in his struggle between fear, doubt, and rage, on the one hand, and faith, trust, and love, on the other.

The analyst recognizes, furthermore, that our social structure and in some measure our lives depend upon our ability to accept some things on trust. For instance, we go through each day with a tacit assumption that we will be here tomorrow. These are unnoticed acts of faith, which occur in every man's life, even in those who have no conscious faith in an omnipotent supernatural power; and they are closely related to his balance of unconscious fear and unconscious confidence. Some men trust everything and everyone; some men trust nothing and no one. Most men are mixed. There can be trust and distrust in the integrity and goodwill of other men, trust and distrust in the vulnerability of one's own body, trust and distrust in one's own integrity and goodwill. Viewed as a psychological process, faith in a supernatural omnipotent power and agnosticism are both special forms of the more general processes of faith or doubt. There are individuals who have quiet confidence in their fellow men, but none in any supernatural or omnipotent power; others who have religious faith in an omnipotent supernatural power, but none either in themselves or in human beings around them. Furthermore there are people who are consciously devout but unconscious skeptics and, conversely, others who are consciously agnostic, yet unconsciously extremely devout. Thus doubters and trusters are to be found both among the devout and among the religiously agnostic.

Such clinical facts as these about the varieties of the religious experience challenge the analyst as something he must study with an open mind if he is to understand the religious process in the human spirit. For most analysts this tends necessarily to bring faith under scientific scrutiny to a somewhat greater extent than is true for other scientists. There are a few analysts, however, who segregate religious faith in a separate phenomenological world of its own, placing it quite outside of the realm of scientific inquiry (1963a, 1965b).

Chapter XIX
PSYCHOANALYSIS AND
MORAL RESPONSIBILITY

"You may not be responsible for getting into a mess, not the first time at any rate; but who else is responsible for getting you out, and what's more, for knocking enough sense into your head to keep you out!"

The charge is sometimes brought that in his consistent efforts to explain immoral behavior the psychoanalyst abandons the concept of human responsibility, destroys the distinction between good and evil, and merely gives his patient "an easy out." Those who make these charges frequently call analytic explanations of the mechanisms of antisocial behavior "mere excuses." They point out that in his therapeutic work the psychoanalyst does not chide his patients for misconduct or exhort them to be better, and they cite this as evidence of a supposedly immoral or amoral attitude. Before explaining why the analyst avoids moralizing during treatment, we may point out that those critics overlook the fact that the analyst studies in his patients the genesis of both their moral and their amoral behavior, hoping through these studies to improve our techniques of ethical education. This is an area in which improvements are sorely needed if we

216

are to make moral education more effective than the traditional methods of the past have proved.

Psychoanalysis is, however, changing our concepts of moral responsibility in certain respects. For instance, it recognizes that feelings of guilt or of virtue are by no means synonymous with actual guilt or actual goodness. Many people who should feel guilt feel none and behave as though they were the most moral folk in the world, or else they are indifferent to or unaware of the destructive consequences of their behavior. The analyst tries to help such an individual to bring his buried feelings of guilt out into the light, so as to modify the disturbed behavior which they cause. Conversely, there are people who are haunted by feelings of guilt when they have no actual sins on their records. Every policeman is familiar with the man who gives himself up for a crime he did not commit. Every priest deals with penitents who come to confession weighed down with an inexplicable sense of sin. Here the function of the analyst is to help the patient to find the roots of his unreal and fantastic feelings of guilt. Instead of providing an "easy out," the analyst attempts to bring the feelings of guilt and of moral responsibility into harmony with reality.

Psychoanalysis formulates the concept of moral responsibility in terms appropriate to each phase of human development and in relation to two specific issues: (a) the degree of insight into unconscious psychological forces, and (b) the degree of freedom from compulsive mechanisms. Both of these elements in moral responsibility will be discussed in detail.

The Failure of Repression

One of the tragedies of our civilization arises from the fact that for so long the great religions of the world confused morality with ignorance of ourselves. The more "moral" and "civilized" man has become, the less has he known about himself, and the more urgently has he been taught to bury his primitive drives. What he hides, however, always finds some way of expressing itself in indirect and symbolic patterns of thought, feeling, and behavior. As we have indicated in Chapter IV, symbolic acts never satisfy and consequently must be repeated compulsively.

Analysis has demonstrated that, whether we are dealing with fundamental instinctual needs or with complex compulsive drives built on the fundamental instincts, it is costly and dangerous to attempt to manage such impulses by becoming unaware of their existence, because once they are driven underground, they lead to neurosis or delinquency (1948a, 1956a). From this fact, however, the analyst does not draw the fallacious conclusion so often attributed to him, namely, that all of our drives should be given free rein. Right here, let it be clearly understood that although analysis is against repression as a technique of self-mastery, it does not stand for self-indulgence or unlimited gratification.

On the contrary, psychoanalysts know perhaps better than anyone else that, just as the world could not achieve peace by appeasing Hitler, so too the human being cannot achieve peace by appeasing a neurosis through its unlimited indulgence. Freud pointed out repeatedly that the pleasure principle must be subordinated to the reality principle. But, if this restraint is to lead to health and strength, it must be achieved through conscious mastery and not through repression and unconscious processing. The analyst keeps in mind the fact that asceticism can serve purposes quite as neurotic as those of unlimited or compulsively driven license. He therefore endorses neither extreme.

The relation of insight to moral responsibility must also be considered in terms of age and maturity. It was St. Augustine who pointed out that the so-called innocence of the child is due more to the weakness of his limbs than to the purity of his heart. Thus, even before psychoanalysis existed, the Church had recognized that there are stormy elements in the infant, which, unless they are adequately dealt with, can become a major source of distortions in later ethical and emotional development. The psychoanalyst and the Church both recognize that the child is engaged from his earliest years in a violent ethical struggle with the primitive amoral drives of infancy. Up to this point, Church doctrine and psychoanalytic observation coincide. The Church, however, looks upon this manifestation of infant psychology as an inherited sinfulness that merits punishment even before the age of reason, which the Church usually places at about seven. The infant who dies unbaptized is consigned to limbo for sins he has never committed, but which he might conceivably have committed had he lived.

Under our present system of education, the usual outcome of this struggle is that both the offending drives and the ethical conflicts over them are buried in such a way as to become inaccessible to conscious self-examination. It is this process of dealing with ethical conflicts by means of unconscious processes that is called *repression.* And it is this type of control which does harm because it is imperfect control. Unaided, the infant or child cannot resolve these ethical conflicts. He hardly knows they exist. Unless the child is helped to face his conflicts openly, he automatically buries them where they will persist un-recognized throughout his life, giving rise to many disturbing secondary drives. Moreover, because the sources of the latter have become unconscious, he will have lost his ability to control and guide them or to make them conform to his conscious moral ideals. Thus, from the repressed and unconscious residues of ethical conflicts, both neurotic symptoms and immoral conduct arise, sometimes in an individual who may be wholly devoid of conscious evil intent. The very fact that both the drives and the conflicts over them become unconscious is *prima facie* evidence that the child has been engaged in an ethical struggle.

Psychoanalysis recognizes that, early in the mental life of the infant and child, forces of "original sin" battle with forces of "original virtue" and that this struggle continues throughout life, most of it carried on below the level of conscious and articulate awareness. As an unhappy consequence of this, one whose ethical needs have forced him to repress his primitive drives may in turn be forced by the repressed residues of those conflicts to act automatically against the very conscience that buried them. This is one reason why destructive people are so rarely men of ill will or evil purpose (Kubie and Kubie, 1948). And this is why so many of us are driven to wrongdoing by forces within ourselves of whose existence we are unaware, forces that operate even in the face of an exacting conscience. Hence, analysis stresses a guiding principle that criminal law has also come to recognize—namely, that the boundaries of conscious insight mark the boundaries of moral responsibility. Analysis, however, does not thereby lessen the actual extent of the domain of moral responsibility, since it gives us at the same time a tool which in its ultimate effects broadens this domain by providing us with a method by which man can bring the full light of conscious insight to bear on his unconscious conflicts, thereby giving him the opportunity to deal with them effectively. In spite of the fact that *repression* operates largely at the instigation of ethical feelings, in its ultimate effects it is a force for evil in human life, for it drives amoral forces underground where they remain powerful and out of reach of voluntary control.

Why the Analyst Never Moralizes

The fact that the effectiveness of responsibility depends in part upon insight into causal forces plays a practical role in the course of every therapeutic analysis. It is quite true that the analyst never "moralizes"; and for this there are several simple reasons. In the first place, he wants the patient to develop his own conscience and not a borrowed facsimile of the analyst's. Secondly, he knows that his patients have heard plenty of moralizing all through their lives, from infancy on. The analyst may be quite certain that if moral exhortation could have been effective it would have done its job long before the patient ever came to him for help. Furthermore, if the analyst were to moralize, in the patient's unconscious processes he would at once be identified with those people in the patient's past whose moral authority the patient had long since rejected. Equally automatically, this tendency to reject adult authority would be transplanted into the analysis, so that any naive efforts at moral indoctrination on the part of an analyst would of necessity be spurned. Therefore, the most fundamental task of the analyst is to give the patient insight into the unconscious sources of his antisocial behavior without injecting any moral judgments into the picture. It should be emphasized that this elimination of moral judgment is a specific element in therapeutic technique and has nothing to do with the processes of education, or with the nature of the moral values of analysis or of analysts.

In the early phases of an analysis, the effort to give insight is limited to retrospective insight into past errors. There is again a simple reason for this: it is easier for the patient to face past errors than current ones. Later in the analysis, the patient begins to acquire prospective insight, i.e., insight before action. It is this insight-before-the-act that is the basis of mature responsibility, because full knowledge of one's motives before committing oneself to any course of action requires that one give up the illusory "freedom" to act impulsively, which is the earmark of immaturity and of bondage to one's unconscious.

The analyst sometimes epitomizes this for a patient by reminding him that the chain of events leading to our mistakes begins so early in life, so long before it is reasonable to hold the child responsible, that no one is really responsible for getting into trouble. Every man is responsible, though, for getting out of it again; and this responsibility includes an obligation to learn enough about himself to make it possible to keep out of trouble in the future.

The Fifth Freedom: To Think and Feel without Fear and Guilt

Even within the area of conscious insights analysis makes a distinction between the moral values it places on actions, on the one hand, and on thoughts and

223

feelings, on the other, by hesitating to pass moral judgments on processes as automatic as the latter. Self-deception concerning thoughts and feelings is a first step toward repression. Analysis recognizes that to tell a child or, for that matter, an adult, that his thoughts or feelings are wicked can be a first step in the production of either delinquency or neurosis. To the child, such an accusation implies that if he were a "good" child he would have no ideas or feelings which were "not nice," and that in some mysterious way his "goodness" would control the free play of his own psychological associations and their accompanying feelings. When we demand that thoughts and feelings should not follow freely their own natural laws, the child becomes rebellious at the imposition of so unfair and impossible a task, and equally guilty and fear-ridden. It is this demand for the impossible which is the starting point for the split into conscious and unconscious streams of psychological processes out of which evolve the neurotic process and delinquency (cf. Chapter IV). At times the futile attempt to control thoughts and feelings can make a child fearful that there is something wrong with his very mind; the universal fear of insanity has one of its roots in this imposition of an unfulfillable task.

In this respect, psychoanalysis has been a liberating influence in the continuous stream of cultural evolution. Primitive man felt that thoughts were magical and could work evil or do good directly. Man therefore had to be held as responsible for his thoughts and feelings as for his actions. For instance, the Ten Commandments forbid us to covet, and the Bible warns that "he who looketh after a woman committeth adultery in his heart." The Godhead is thus invoked as a superpsychological force to strengthen the good in man, either by making him pure enough to be free of all amoral impulses or else strong enough to control and suppress even their spontaneous psychological representation in thoughts and feelings.

Psychoanalysis faces this problem with different weapons. Man's spontaneous thoughts and feelings are viewed as independent of moral evaluations, since in and of themselves they do not harm either the thinker or those toward whom they are directed. Neither hate nor envy nor lust can do damage unless they are given some form of expression. If they are consciously recognized, acknowledged, and understood, they can be controlled and limited in their expression and even directed into constructive channels. If, on the other hand, they are buried and rendered unconscious, they will express themselves in masked forms, which become automatic, obsessively repetitive, and destructive. Obsession with amoral fantasies and feelings is no more acceptable to the analyst than to the strictest moralist; this is not because the analyst condemns such an obsession as a sign of immorality, but because he recognizes in it a symptom of illness. An elderly clergyman who had led a blameless life came for help because he had been tortured for years by sudden involuntary eruptions of obscene thoughts during religious services, and by thoughts of irreverent puns and witticisms at funerals. This was a problem in health, not in morals, and was only a compulsively exaggerated version of something that occurs in minor degrees in every child and adult.

For psychoanalysis, moral responsibility implies the validity of the ancient maxim to "know thyself," with the added implication that this must mean self-knowledge in depth. This knowledge must penetrate the barrier between conscious and unconscious levels of the personality, since this is necessary for any effective self-control and self-direction, without which responsibility is an empty concept. The right to self-knowledge in depth becomes man's Fifth Freedom, upon which all other freedoms ultimately depend (1952a, 1954a).

The Relation of Moral Responsibility to Compulsions

The psychoanalytic concept concerning the conditions under which it is legitimate to hold a man morally responsible requires one further specification. As we have said, psychoanalysts hold that man can reasonably be held responsible only for those aspects of his personality of whose major purposes he is conscious. In addition, it is reasonable to hold him accountable only where the possibility of control exists. Clinical experience demonstrates the practical value of this point. As was pointed out in Chapter IV, whenever conduct is determined predominantly by conscious psychological forces, it can respond to moral and spiritual exhortation, to instruction, to rewards and punishments. In short, it can learn from experience. On the other hand, conduct that is determined in major part by unconscious forces is precisely to that extent unalterable by external influences and remains rigidly inflexible until the unconscious forces are brought into the full light of conscious awareness. To hold people responsible for conduct determined by compulsive or, as the law says, "irresistible" forces, is both futile and actually destructive. This is why the law specifically recognizes a special category of "irresistible impulses."

Therefore, in certain situations moral responsibility even for actions must be qualified. There is a difference in responsibility between the man who washes his hands when they are dirty and the man who washes his hands a thousand times a day because he has a hand-washing compulsion. There is a difference in responsibility between the individual who steals because he wants to make money easily and the individual who steals things he does not need and is not going to use or sell, who is under the internal pressure of a compulsive drive, the nature of which he himself does not understand. Subtler and more elaborate compulsive patterns affect many aspects of human life, and in any precise application of the principle of responsibility they must be kept in mind. Where making people feel responsible can help to make their conduct more ethical, the principle of responsibility is valuable both socially and individually. When, however, we try to make anyone feel responsible for something over which he actually has no possibility of control, we merely add a sense of guilt to the complexity of his internal problems, and usually generate rebellious defiance. In fact, there is no surer way to produce delinquents than to give youngsters a sense of shame for conduct over which they have no voluntary control. There is no value in trying to make a child feel responsible for the spots in measles; to make a child feel guilty about a compulsion amounts to the same thing.

It is not possible to offer any simple rule by which one can be guided in the application of this basic principle. In general, however, (as is explained in detail in Chapters IV and V) the distinction hinges on certain simple pragmatic tests of the modifiability of behavior by external experiences, sensible rewards and moderate punishments, arguments, reason, exhorta-tion, and appeals to personal loyalties. Where behavior is resistant to the persistent use of such common-sense influences as these, we may be sure that it is deter-mined predominantly by unconscious forces. Here we are morally responsible chiefly to attempt to under-stand the nature of the unconscious forces that deter-mine such behavior.

Psychoanalysis and the Concept of Altruism

No one will deny that there are actions that aid others and actions that injure; actions that give and actions that take. If altruism is defined pragmatically on the basis of the effects of behavior, any pseudo-philosophical quandary about the existence of altruism would be resolved readily. On the other hand, if its definition must depend on the nature of the psychological processes that determine behavior, the question becomes at the same time extremely complicated and of uncertain significance.

It is clearly impossible to make any evaluation of motives solely from the effects of behavior either upon others or upon ourselves. The forces that produce behavior are by their very nature complex, multiple, and mutually contradictory. Human behavior is never the product of a single impulse, conscious or unconscious. Everything we do represents the confluence of many streams, or better still, the algebraic summation of many opposing forces. In these congeries of conscious, preconscious, and unconscious impulses one will find love and hate, fear and rage, impulses to dominate and impulses to submit, impulses to give and impulses to grab. How can we call this unstable equilibrium of giving and taking either altruistic or selfish when, from the point of view of motivation, it is and always must be both?

It is in the nature of man that his behavior must serve his needs. Otherwise, in the long run, he could not survive. Therefore, the source of the processes that drive the machine must be ego centered. Once launched, however, these forces are guided by many other conflicting considerations, much as a push-ball is forced now in one direction and now in another as one team or another gains a temporary ascendancy. In a similar fashion, within any individual, impulses to take at the expense of others and impulses to give at one's own expense are in a continuous unstable equilibrium, now one predominating and now the other. In some victory will more frequently be on the side of grab-bing, in others more often on the side of giving; but in no individual is it exclusively one or the other. And in the end, to survive both physically and spiritually, gratification must outweigh deprivation. Where this is not the case, sickness is bound to result. From the point of view of the world, it is important only that most men should be so educated that their ego needs will be gratified in part through the service they give to the needs of others.

To the analyst, therefore, altruism and generosity are forms of behavior to which man can be educated, because they meet each man's long-run needs. But to ask that behavior should not in the ultimate analysis be ego-determined is asking water to run uphill, tissues not to require oxygen or water, the body not to need food. It is a fundamental law of life that a man's actions must serve his own needs. But it is an equally fundamental law of society that the service of the needs of the individual and the service of the needs of the group must be harmonized. As long as conscious generosity can screen unconscious selfishness and vice versa, the ancient philosophical issue of selfishness versus unselfishness will remain a battle of words.

Psychoanalysis and the Growth of Conscience

A third contribution of psychoanalysis to the concept of moral responsibility focuses on the question of how we learn to be moral. Ultimately, the greatest contri-bution of psychoanalysis to man's pursuit of the good life may be made in this area. Psychoanalytic studies have shown that automatic patterns of moral behavior are developed, not out of the theoretical and philosophical systems with which we rationalize ethical living, nor out of theological attitudes and beliefs, nor in response to ethical exhortations, but rather out of the deeply buried residues of our earliest emotional relationships to our parents or to other important figures. As a consequence of this, the child of even a socially amoral person may develop firm and unshakable ethical patterns, if that parent is gentle, kind, consistently rewarding, and consistently present to the child. The adult may have taught this child no ethics and no religion, and he himself may have practiced none toward the world at large, yet, out of the quality of the emotional relation between the parent and the child, an ethical adult may develop. Conversely, as is well known, a child of ethical and religious leaders, of parents of the highest degree of social integrity and responsibility, may turn out a criminal. This is not because he has failed to learn *about* religion and morality from his parents, but rather because of some morally destructive component in the relationship between the generations. It is what we are toward our children in the nursery and not what we preach to them that makes them good or bad, because ultimately what they unconsciously feel toward us will determine automatically how they feel unconsciously toward others. It is the quality of these feelings rather than faiths or philosophical systems that in the end determines the ethical level of our lives.

Does this mean that our cultural, ethical, and

religious training is bankrupt and impotent, that it has failed? This question plagues every honest and thoughtful educator, every honest and humble minister of every faith, especially at this juncture in the history of mankind when there is such grave danger that man may destroy himself.

It is no answer to this question to dismiss it by saying, "No, it is *man* who has failed." This is just buck-passing, a defense *in a vacuum*. The goal of all educational, religious, and cultural processes must be to see to it that man does not fail; and if, after thousands of years of effort, man's primitive and destructive drives still remain unaltered in the unconscious depths of his personality, then it is not enough either to bemoan the impotence of cultural influences or to challenge man accusingly. One can say only that to old techniques of human salvation must be added new techniques which can bring out into the open the unconscious aspects of the personality that are the causes of this failure. Blaming is useless, whether it is blaming culture, or religion, or the human being. When an airplane crashes, one saves more lives by learning to understand the laws of gravity than by blaming them. Similarly, the psychoanalyst feels that instead of more exhortation it is the task of culture and of religion to learn enough about man and his nature to be able to bring his unconscious primitive struggles into closer harmony with his conscious ethical aspirations. Conscious good intentions are still the pavements to the road to hell; and conscious good will is not enough, as long as it so often remains a screen for unconscious ill will. This is precisely where psychoanalysis enters the picture. It will play its historic role in the drama of human development by helping man to bring to light those unconscious conflicts that hamper his conscious pursuit of the good life. It can hope ultimately to serve the good life even more effectively by helping us to learn how to bring up our children so that they will not have to spend their lives struggling with the bitter unconscious residues of the ethical conflicts of childhood.

Chapter XX

PSYCHOANALYSIS AND MARRIAGE

The Goal and the Problem

To the *solution* of marital problems, psychoanalysis can sometimes make a significant contribution by uncovering sources of unconscious hostility, guilt, and fear, and by clarifying their disguised influences in the marriage, thereby often lessening or even eliminating their destructive effects. To the *prevention* of marital unhappiness, psychoanalysis may well be able some day to contribute a great deal, but only after young folk have learned that they can never marry themselves out of their neuroses, and that whenever two unhappy young people marry, each adds the problems of his own neuroses to those of the other. From these experiences comes the hard but inescapable conclusion that we must earn our right to marry by solving our individual problems first.

Successful psychoanalytic help for a sick marriage frequently requires conjoint action by the husband and wife. This is one of the reasons why various forms of "family therapy" are now being employed. The fact that excessive and premature claims for it are frequently made should not prejudice us against sober, conscientious efforts to test its usefulness. All too often, however, before husband and wife reach the analyst's office the hostility has become too great for any such mutual effort. The situation is ideal where both come for help, but this is still the exception. More often, one or the other comes secretly, or in fear, or in defiance of the other's wishes. Frequently, patients come to an analyst in a state of concealed panic, without having the slightest idea that their marriages are threatened. Unaware of what they are doing, they may try to strike a secret and unspoken bargain with the psychoanalyst: "You may analyze me, if you will promise not to uncover any trouble in my marriage." Or they may come with an opposite purpose, trying to blame their own neurotic unhappiness on the marriage, and seeking pseudopsychiatric, pseudopsychoanalytic justification for promiscuity or divorce.

At times, someone comes to seek help in a crisis caused largely by the illness of a husband or wife who refuses to acknowledge either the illness itself or any need for treatment. The partner's symptoms may be as obvious as chronic alcoholism, impotence, frank sexual perversions, or sadistic compulsive states; yet he may still refuse to acknowledge his need for help. The partner who comes for advice may have shielded the other for years, so successfully, indeed, that not even their most intimate friends or relatives have been aware of any difficulty until the increasing strain and the incessant threat to the welfare of the children finally compels action. In such situations it is not unusual for the healthier of the pair to ask to be analyzed, hoping that by some trick of superadaptation, some magic of absent treatment, the sick one may be cured without ever submitting to therapy.

Some patients come for analysis resentfully and only under the threat of impending divorce or separation, while others may seek help earnestly, but in the face of bitter resentment and neurotic jealousy on the part of the wife or husband.

These are some of the many and varied snarls the analyst must untangle before he can decide which one of the partners most needs analysis, and which one, if either, can be analyzed. Sometimes, when confronted with a marriage crisis, it is hard for the analyst to decide whether or not to undertake an analysis at all, since, no matter how successful the analysis may be for the one who accepts his own need for treatment, the outcome of the marriage will depend at least in part upon the ultimate attitude of the unanalyzed partner as well as upon that of the patient. Healthy adaptations can never come exclusively from one side.

It is evident, therefore, that marital problems frequently confront the analyst with difficult decisions. He knows that until a neurosis has hurt a patient there is little hope of his seeking therapy. We do not ask to be treated for those of our neurotic traits which hurt someone else while leaving *us* relatively unscathed. Indeed, where a neurosis expresses itself by causing pain in a marriage, the greater the pain it causes the more obstinate may be the self-justifying defenses the potential patient will erect. Frequently, therefore, when an analyst faces a severely threatened and distorted marriage, he may have to clear the air for both himself and his patient by insisting upon a temporary separation before undertaking the analysis. Such a separation, when undertaken for purely technical reasons, can greatly facilitate the progress of an analysis and may actually save a marriage. On the other hand, this cannot always be the outcome. Sometimes the separation makes it possible for each partner to turn his back on his own contribution to the unhappiness of the marriage. The analyst is thus in something of a dilemma. On the one hand, if the couple remains together, the constant interplay of mutual hostility between them is likely to swamp the analysis. On the other hand, separation may bring to each a false peace in which the impulse to search into himself may be completely eliminated. It is impossible for the analyst to be all-wise in resolving this dilemma as he approaches the treatment of either member of such an unhappy marriage. The only thing he can do is try to maintain a *status quo* until he becomes aware of the more important of the unconscious forces playing below the surface.

Occasionally, however, even in situations which at the outset look hopeless, the gradual improvement of one of the partners may lessen the opposition of the other until he finally seeks help for himself as well. If the children have been psychologically injured in the family battle, they too may ultimately need treatment. This spread of psychoanalysis through a family often

arouses cynical comments from onlookers. Nevertheless, to many a family this has meant the difference
between happiness and divorce, between disturbed
children and their harmonious growth and development.

It must be remembered that psychoanalysis is a
medical therapy and, as such, must aim primarily at
the preservation or restoration of mental and emotional health. The psychoanalyst is not a marriage broker,
or a marriage saver, or a marriage wrecker. Whenever
he faces a choice between health or marriage, his
medical duty is at least to present this issue clearly so
that the patient can make his choice in the full awareness of its implications. Happily, such an impasse arises
less frequently than is popularly believed.

Psychoanalysis and Divorce

People in general have an exaggerated impression of
the frequency with which psychoanalysis ends in
divorce. Marital conflicts, like other neurotic symptoms, are usually hidden as long as possible. As a
result, although the caldron may have been boiling
long before it was brought to the psychoanalyst to be
cooled off, no one except the husband and wife may
have any suspicion of the extent of the maladjustment.
And when the couple finally turns to analysis, the
breach may have become too wide for successful
analytic intervention. This is one of the reasons for the
impression that analysis regularly ends in the dis-
ruption of a marriage. Another reason for this im-

pression is that even when the analysis succeeds in resolving marital difficulties, no one may have known that the marriage had been threatened or the husband or wife had undergone treatment. One hears gossip about the analyses which end in divorce, but not about the successful analytic efforts to avert divorce. Divorce has the greater news value.

On the other hand, it is true of course that divorce sometimes is inevitable. This may be due to any of several reasons: (a) Before the problems were brought to a psychoanalyst, the relationship between husband and wife may have been strained for so many years that even the restoration of health may not be enough to free the patients of their bitterness. Divorce may then be chosen in the end, despite the successful analysis of the neuroses that had destroyed the marriage. (b) Many marriages are contracted not on the basis of health, but on a neurotic one. The story is all too familiar of maladjusted young people who try to escape their separate miseries by joining their problems in a marriage. Since marriage never cures a neurosis, it usually ends up being blamed for it; and presently the neurotic angers of both partners are pitted against each other in a merciless battle. Even if this battle can be checked by analysis, the couple may find that with the elimination of the original neurotic reasons for the marriage, no healthy reason remains for continuing together. In such situations separation may be the only healthy solution. (These problems are discussed more fully in other publications [1956c, 1964a, 1964c].)

Divorce cannot be used as an index of the success or failure of an analysis. To do so would be tantamount to claiming that the function of psychoanalysis is not primarily to cure people of their neuroses, but to enable them to put up with all the neurotic mistakes they have ever made. The psychoanalyst aims to save a marriage wherever this is humanly possible; the frequency of his success bears testimony to both his purpose and his ability. Where, however, he must choose between a patient's health and a patient's marriage, this issue must be squarely faced. One cannot leave this topic without looking into the future and asking what would be the effect upon marital happiness and stability if young people had an opportunity to resolve their neuroses before they contracted neurotic alliances. This is a question for the coming decades to answer.

Technical Problems

Of the technical problems arising in the psychoanalytic treatment of marital difficulties, only two require elucidation here. The first is the problem of the concurrent analysis of husband and wife. This may be of great value, especially if the two analyses are conducted independently by two psychoanalysts; but experienced psychoanalysts have generally regarded as unwise the simultaneous treatment of both husband and wife by one analyst. In recent years this has been done more frequently and more freely. It seems to make no difficulty for the analyst; but, contrary to usual expectations, it may make the task of both patients harder. In the end, one or the other is likely to lose his confidence in the impartiality of the analyst, and the analysis of this patient will suffer accordingly. Since it is usually wise not to postpone the analysis of one until after the other is finished, it is well to send the second patient to another psychoanalyst as soon as possible (cf. Chapters XI, XII, and XIII). An exception to this is "family therapy" in which the husband and wife, and sometimes the children as well, are treated as a group in conjoint sessions.

Certainly in the preparatory antechamber to the analysis, or in cases of marital maladjustment which are not to be psychoanalyzed, both patients can sometimes be handled effectively by the same physician. Yet, even here, if the currents of hostile feeling run strong, it may be advantageous to seek the help of two physicians instead of one.

In the analysis of marital problems, one other technical problem is of practical importance to other than psychoanalysts, namely, the problem that arises whenever a patient has to work out both a severe personal neurotic problem and a complicated marital conflict. In such circumstances it may be extremely difficult to make headway without separating the two problems. In order to do this, it is sometimes necessary to arrange for a temporary separation so that the individual's neurotic difficulties can be clarified in some measure before tackling the problems of mutual adjustment. In any analysis, there may be periods

241

during which neurotic rage is stirred up, and it is almost inevitable that this rage will be vented on the marital partner. A technical separation during part of an analysis may spare a marriage stresses and strains that might otherwise do final and irreparable damage to it.

Chapter XXI

PSYCHOANALYSIS IN RELATION TO SOCIAL, ECONOMIC, AND POLITICAL CHANGE

"The Truth Shall Make You Free," *John*, 8:32.

There is so much misunderstanding and misinterpretation of this topic that it is necessary to dispose of the misconceptions before one can discuss profitably the potential contributions of psychoanalysis to the evaluation of the forms and structure of human society.

In the first place, psychoanalysis is not a philosophy of passive submission to the status quo. Its therapeutic goal is not to enable people to put up with the imperfections of our social organization. The analytic ideal of adjustment is rather to enable a man both to acknowledge his own suffering and to identify with that of others without becoming obsessively preoccupied with pain alone. At the same time it aims to give him courage and clarity in his efforts to correct those defects of society that exist all around us. For reasons that will be discussed below, this clarity must include an understanding of many subtle unconscious forces.

In the second place, psychoanalysts as a group adhere to no one political or social or economic philosophy. The most one can say is that like other intellectuals they are thoughtfully concerned with social issues, aware of their complexity and of the limitations of their own technical knowledge in these fields. Politically, most analysts are liberal in their sympathies, some tending more to the left and others more to the right, largely on the basis of temperamental differences. In his approach to social issues, the only attitude that sets the analyst apart from other intellectuals is a wary search for the influence of unconscious forces, warping man's judgment on social as on other problems, inflating the passion of his convictions, and determining the methods he chooses. Because of his suspicion of violence, the analyst is rarely extreme about social issues. He is rarely blindly reactionary, or impatiently revolutionary. Let us repeat that nevertheless his goal, both for himself and for his patients, is not to be a fence-sitter but to achieve freedom for dynamic and effective action, freedom that comes from a clear understanding of the role of unconscious processes in human judgments about all external issues (1968a).

It is no accident that so many contradictory accusations are made about the role of analysis and of the analyst in social issues. All extremists tend to be afraid of analysis. Reactionaries, whether in politics or in religion, call it a radical influence. Radicals call it reactionary, both sides advancing arguments that are full of internal contradictions. Some critics of analysis claim that all neuroses are due to idleness, a mere luxury of the leisure class. Some even go so far as to state that if wealth, economic inequity, and the profit motive were eliminated, all neuroses would automatically disappear. The same critics will in the next breath assert that neuroses are due not to idleness and wealth but to poverty and want and external insecurity and overwork—failing to realize that the two statements are mutually so contradictory as to nullify each other. A man may make both accusations because they express his preconceived hope and faith that economic and political reforms can cure all human suffering.

The analyst points out that none of the assumptions underlying any such conclusions are true. In the first place, identical neuroses are found in approximately the same incidence up and down the entire social scale, in all economic classes, in the city and in the country, in highly sophisticated urban circles and on the frontiers of society. Statistical inquiries into the incidence of neurotic difficulties in draftees demonstrated only one clear social factor—namely, that the largest number of rejections for neuropsychiatric disabilities came from those urban districts where the population density was highest.

Clinical experience, therefore, forces the analyst to reject any oversimplified hypothesis that the neurotic process is due to economic inequity. This does not mean that the analyst is complacent about poverty. Here again, not all analysts are cut from the same cloth. They bring to their profession as wide a range of political and economic leanings as is found among lawyers, stockbrokers, school teachers, clergymen, chemists, engineers, and housewives. There are, moreover, some who concern themselves exclusively with scientific problems. This is entirely legitimate, since some men can make their greatest contributions to human welfare by an exclusive absorption in science. Except for the fact that analysts practice all day and teach all night (cf. Chapter XXIII), and consequently have little time for other interests, there is nothing in analysis as such that would force all analysts into either a scientific ivory tower or the market place. Like other scientific disciplines, analysis allows the individual analyst freedom to express his social and political interests in his own way.

There is one further reason, however, for the persistent notion that analysts isolate themselves from the economic, social, and political problems of the world around them. However deeply concerned about such issues an analyst may be, he soon finds that once he begins to devote much time and attention to them he is in danger of short-changing his patients. At first this will be negligible in its effects; but as time goes on their analyses suffer seriously. More important than the time and energy absorbed by extra-analytic activities is the shift of the analyst's own interest and feeling from the exacting work of analyzing to the emotionally less taxing and somewhat more spectacular field of social reform. It is like looking up from a microscope to admire a view. For an analyst with a conscience, a good fight in a worthy cause is a powerful magnet, luring his attention from the subtler task of analysis; but any analyst who has checked himself closely must admit that during periods in which he has become involved in worthy nonanalytical activities he has found it more difficult to keep his attention focused on his patients sufficiently to enable his own thoughts to play spontaneously, freely, and imaginatively with the patient's material.

Analysis is a lonely task, and one requiring of the analyst that all of his conscious and unconscious angers must be drained off into channels that will not endanger the analysis. Social and political reforms, or fights about the organization of analytic education and about analytic theory or technique, drain off these feelings and lessen the analyst's loneliness. This is on the credit side. On the debit side is the danger of draining off the creative as well as the destructive energies of the analyst from the work of analyzing. That is why some analysts say half-jokingly that in order to do the finest analytic work humanly possible, the analyst should be a reformed rake living in a monastery on top of a mountain.

Evidently, in this matter the analyst faces a dilemma. On the one hand, if all analysts were to retreat into isolation, analysis as such would lose much of its social value and cultural significance. On the other hand, active participation in social problems jeopardizes in some measure the individual analyst's value to the patients for whose treatment he has assumed a deep moral responsibility. Before he undertakes any activity outside of his analytical work, he must satisfy his conscience: (a) that this activity is so essential that he is justified in allowing it to break into his analytic schedule; and (b) that he is the only person, or the best person, or the essential person to do that particular task (1950, 1951c, 1968b).

It is important for society and for analysts themselves to be clear about this, because as analysis grows in popularity, the counsel and advice of analysts are sought on public issues and their participation is valued in many communal activities. Some analysts are particularly gifted and effective in such work and consequently are likely to be drawn into many worthy "causes." The more successful they are, the stronger is the pressure on them to take on more and more of such activities. The analyst who yields to this seduction tends to turn away from analysis. He may then rationalize this by belittling the importance of analytic work with the individual patient, forgetting that this has been and will continue to be the source of almost everything analysts can contribute to an understanding of public affairs. Under these circumstances, there is some danger that the patient would become the forgotten man of analysis (1970b). How psychoanalysts will ultimately resolve this dilemma is not yet clear. We may be sure that the same individual cannot perform both functions, except at the expense of his patients. On the other hand, if one group of analysts sticks to the clinical grindstone and another group gambols over the fields of social reform, mutual distrust and suspicion are likely to arise. The clinicians may turn their backs on world forces, while the reformers are likely to lose contact with the subtle complexities of the clinic. The contributions psychoanalysts can make to social problems are so great that some solution for this dilemma must be found. We must watch carefully, however, to make sure that in expanding into the social fields we do not sacrifice technical precision or theoretical clarity about the individual human being, his unconscious, and about the interrelation of conscious and unconscious processes. Without technical precision and theoretical clarity, psychoanalysis would have nothing to offer to human progress.

A more specific accusation, i.e., that the analyst is unconcerned with the welfare of the poor, arises in part from those anomalies in the economics of analytic practice discussed in detail in Chapter XVII. The wholly erroneous impression that the analyst deals only with the wealthy leads to the further assumption that his social and economic attitudes will be colored by this hypothetical clientele. None of this is true; but even if it were, it would concern only the facts of psychoanalytic practice in our present economic system, and would have nothing to do with the bearing of psychoanalytic theory on economic and social reform.

The spirit of scientific skepticism and inquiry that psychoanalysis brings to bear on the human spirit also has something to do with the suspiciousness with which both sides of the political fence view analysis. Neither side wants its own unconscious motives examined, but the analyst is equally suspicious of the drive to maintain the status quo and of the drive to change everything. The analyst deals constantly with the disguised derivatives of the primitive and unconscious cruelty hidden behind our civilized mask, and his knowledge of unconscious conflicts makes him fearful of irresponsible power, even in the hands of consciously well-meaning people. He is acutely aware of how essential it is to limit and restrict power, to hold responsible those who wield it, and to buffer people against its direct manifestations. Above all else he fears any struggle for naked and irresponsible power, whether in industry or in government.

Indeed some analysts feel that the rivalry for property, for purchasing power, and for display, may be less brutally inhuman in its effects than the primitive rivalries and brutalities of totalitarian power politics. As deeply as anyone else, analysts deplore the abuses of the struggle for money, but inasmuch as the neurotic process starts long before the infant deals with any medium of exchange, few analysts regard money as a causal factor in the origin of the neurotic process. That money can influence its evolution and become one of its symptomatic expressions is obvious. Many analysts wonder whether the human race will be ready to do without this shock absorber of human aggressions until it has learned to resolve in early childhood the angry struggles that are the unconscious and insatiable origins of adult rivalry and envy.

Analysts vary widely in their convictions on such issues as these. What is important is that these are not issues about which psychoanalysis per se demands any single conviction. It is essential that the layman, whatever his political persuasion, be clear about this, because among some of the more naive deviant groups there has been a revolt against the Freudian concept of the biological basis of neurotic behavior, which parallels closely the Russian revolt against certain basic elements in the concepts of heredity. Just as the Russian political ideology rejected heredity because it seemed to them to limit the power of economic reform to cure all human ills, so these so-called "analysts" reject biogenetic factors because they want to attribute to social forces a curative power that can overcome any disturbing psychological force. Out of this bias they have brewed an intellectually incompetent and indigestible mixture of reactionary science and economic radicalism. They have used this, in turn, as a platform from which to attack psychoanalysis, as though the latter stood for accepting the status quo supinely and at any cost, which is demonstrably untrue. As we have said, the goal of analysis is to develop a maximum degree of conscious dynamic adaptability and flexibility in every individual, while creating and preserving an active need to eliminate the abuses in human life, coupled with clarity about both the reforming drive and the abuses that demand reform.

The accusation that the goal of adjustment is to make human beings submit meekly to all of the inequalities and abuses of life has a familiar ring. We have heard it often in the past, in connection with every effort to help man to adjust to the realities of life. It has often been leveled at religion. It is true of course that, in the history of the world, religion has frequently been exploited for this purpose by vested interests. Yet many deeply religious people have been revolutionary in their attitude toward economic, social, and political wrongs, proving that a passive and uncomplaining acceptance of evil is certainly not an essential part of religion. The accusation is equally invalid when it is leveled against the essential goal and purpose of psychoanalysis.

In clarifying this misunderstanding, it may be helpful to consider one further reason why these accusations are made. It is to be found in the psychology of the reformer. Most reformers hope that alterations in the form and organization of human life will eliminate human misery and discontent. They naturally resent anyone who points out the complexities of the process of human progress, because an acknowledgment of complexity frustrates their need for simple solutions. Furthermore, just as the stand-patter may be moved by his unconscious anger to exploit and oppress and exclude, so, too, the need for change at any cost may be driven by a secret rage, which finds a legitimized expression in the reforming impulse. The furious and prurient obscenity of some of the advocates of purity is a well-known and gross example of this, but it is difficult for men of more genuine good will to recognize in their own activities subtler versions of the same paradox.

In his approach to social reform, the psychoanalyst is impressed by the many examples of confused thinking arising out of the unconscious residues of the early struggle against parental authority. This struggle begins in the small child's impotent struggle against the power and authority of adults, and in his rivalry with other children. In every individual, this gives rise to an internal conflict between impulses to submit and impulses to rebel, a struggle that usually becomes so violent it has to be repressed. Years later, this hidden conflict reappears, displaced against social institutions or various substitute figures. The man who as a child could not acknowledge his patricidal rage against his own father may rebel with an inappropriate murderous anger against the army, against his foreman or his boss, or against society as a whole. Another may repress the same conflict so deeply that he will submit to anything. Sometimes both of these contradictory components of a child's feelings may be expressed separately in the same adult. Thus, one man may accept irresponsible power in his own country without objection, while railing against absolute power in some distant land, i.e., at a safe distance. Another man may protest violently against the least flaw in civil or economic liberty at home, but will praise totalitarian power thousands of miles away as though it were a blessing. In neither of these instances does analysis aim to make submissive children out of adult men. It aims

rather to clarify confusions and to eliminate paradoxical inconsistencies by enabling men to deal objectively with problems of authority. The analyst wants
men to seek emancipation with open eyes, free from
concealed neurotic distortions.

Because the analyst deals every day with the adult
manifestations of the residues of childhood fear, hatred, jealousy, and greed, he knows that these infantile
emotions occur even when no external deprivation
exists. In the most inclusive sense of the word, therefore, the goal of analysis is freedom. By freedom,
however, the analyst means freedom from the tyranny
of unconscious psychological forces quite as much as
freedom from external tyranny. The goal of analysis is
the freedom to change (1968a). The struggle for external freedom has produced the evolution of political democracy, which now is moving slowly and painfully
toward economic democracy. Analysis recognizes the
fact that to make democracy work requires emotional
as well as intellectual maturity, a maturity that implies
freedom from the grip of those unconscious inner
forces which are the residues of our infancy and
childhood. In the analyst's experience internal slavery
proves to be quite as destructive of human happiness as
political and economic slavery can be of human life.
The analyst knows that in order to succeed, basic
changes in the organization of human life must be
paralleled by an internal and spiritual evolution. As he
strives for this goal with each analytic patient, he views
their joint endeavor as part of the great human
struggle for freedom.

In the long view the analyst is a revolutionary who seeks revolution by evolution, and who resorts to violent revolutionary techniques only reluctantly and as a last resort. Once he has become convinced that revolution is the only method by which progress can be achieved, he will not flinch from it, although he will take no joy in it. It is the difference between the soldier who fights well although he hates war and the psychopath who wins Congressional Medals for bravery because combat gives him a legitimate way of expressing his antisocial, amoral destructive impulses. It is this kind of soldier whose influence the analyst would attempt to eliminate from the battle for social, economic, and political reforms.[1]

[1]Those who are particularly interested in this problem can be referred to an article by Judson T. Stone on "The Theory and Practice of Psychoanalysis," which appeared in *Science and Society* in 1946, Vol. 10, No. 1, pp. 54-79. This with a few reservations is an excellent introduction to certain theoretical aspects of the topic, and also to the literature. Others may be interested in Lenin's caustic criticism of certain types of blind radicalism in *'Left-Wing' Communism, an Infantile Disorder*, V. I. Lenin, The International Publishers, 381 Fourth Avenue, New York 16, N.Y.

Chapter XXII

A RECAPITULATION OF CERTAIN COMMON MISCONCEPTIONS ABOUT PSYCHOANALYSIS

It is natural that a young science should be misunderstood. It passes through periods of conflicting theories. New concepts develop and new terms are coined which overlap with earlier terms and concepts and with one another. Theories are advanced simultaneously in different countries and in different languages; imperfect translations result in confusion over the mere meaning of terms. Gradually, however, as a science comes of age, its language is pruned and its garden of concepts weeded. In psychoanalysis the pruning and weeding has barely begun.

In time these natural sources of early misunderstanding all yield to clearer thinking and simpler language. Sometimes, however, misunderstandings persist in spite of all explanations. When this happens it is due, not to confusions within the growing science, but to the fact that deeply entrenched biases, both conscious and unconscious, have been challenged. Witness the violent attacks made by supposedly learned men against those who first insisted that the world was round rather than flat, and against the discoverers of the theory of evolution. Such attacks are often filled with misrepresentations which are hard to correct. This happened to Darwin, Huxley, Pasteur, and, more recently, to Freud.

In spite of many careful explanations, psychoanalysis continues to be subjected to gross misrepresentations, almost as though its critics need to make it appear foolish or obscene, want it not to make sense, want it to seem immoral, and therefore never read the many published explanations that could dispel their misconceptions. Striking examples of this have recently been broadcast to the public both from the pulpit and in popular periodicals. Therefore, once again, one sets about the slow task of undoing the mischief (1947d, 1962c, 1966a).

There are many such misconceptions, some of which have already been dealt with.

(1) Does analysis, as opposed to something called "synthesis", destroy the personality? (2) Does psychoanalysis deliberately cultivate a love relationship between the patient and the analyst through what is called the "transference"? (3) Does psychoanalysis deny moral responsibility and sanction sin? Connected with this is the question of the relationship of analysis to the confession. (4) Does psychoanalysis advocate the unlimited pursuit of pleasure and of self-indulgence? (5) Why is the cost of psychoanalysis high; is it prohibitive; and if so, what can be done about it?

1. One frequently hears that analysis is a disinte-

grating experience. To anyone who understands the processes by which neuroses form and by which they are cured, this statement is so naive as to be meaningless. In the psychological apparatus of every human being, sick or well, there is an incessant interplay between synthetic forces and dissociative or disintegrative forces (1945). Neuroses form when the balance moves in the latter direction; and when the balance moves in the former direction the process of healing is at work. This can happen only when disintegrative and dissociative forces are eliminated; their elimination is precisely the goal and technique of analysis. When this occurs, spontaneous synthetic processes are freed, and nature takes care of the rest. The protest that analysis is disruptive is as meaningless as it would be to say to a surgeon who removes a tumor that what we need is healing not cutting. Just as health is the goal of medicine but not a technique of treatment, so synthesis is the goal of psychoanalysis, as of all psychotherapy, but not a technique for getting well. In psychological matters as in the tissues, once the causes of dissociation have been removed, synthesis occurs spontaneously. (See Chapters IV, V, and XVI.)

2. The answer to the second question has already been given in Chapter IX.

3. Another widely held misconception is that psychoanalysis is "an easy way out", a slick device for dodging responsibility for our mistakes, a method of explaining everything away so as to avoid paying the piper. This again is far from true. It is obvious that

actual guilt and fantasies of guilt are not identical. Every psychiatrist knows the blameless patient who is haunted by feelings of guilt, and who goes around wringing his hands and saying, "There is something I am guilty of, but I don't know what it is." Every police officer and every priest knows that men give themselves up for crimes they could not possibly have committed. Every juvenile court officer knows how many youngsters actually set out to get caught, so as to be punished for minor crimes, in order to hide their guilt over impulses about which they feel more guilty than about any act (Healy, 1917). And every analyst knows that many men and women wear masks of innocence while hiding from themselves the most profound and devastating unconscious convictions of sin. It is the job of the analyst to attempt to bring order out of this chaos. This he does by bringing to light the unconscious feelings which may hide behind conscious feelings of either guilt or innocence and by making it clear how, in some instances, we bribe our consciences into silence, and in others torture and flagellate ourselves with fantastic feelings of guilt. Certainly, there is wisdom in the old saw that honest confession is good for the soul; but analysis has made us realize how subtle and elusive an honest confession may be. Confession, like everything else in human life, may be misused for neurotic purposes (cf. Chapter XIX).

I would like to quote from *Mind, Medicine and Man*, by Gregory Zilboorg (1943): "Psychoanalysis is not confession, nor is it like confession. Confession is a conscious act of repentance, and a ritual. Man can confess only that which he consciously knows, that which makes him consciously guilty. As a result of confession and the officially given absolution, man feels relieved, and he is admonished and inspired not to sin anymore. In psychoanalysis the patient cannot confess in the usual sense of the word. The patient gradually reveals the unconscious sense of guilt of which he has been unaware; he is not given absolution, nor does the psychoanalyst have any means at his disposal to relieve the patient of this guilt. What the psychoanalyst does do is listen and watch how the patient learns, gradually and almost imperceptibly, to differentiate fantasy from reality, infantile from adult impulses. The patient then obtains relief from feeling guilty about things of which he is not guilty at all, and he continues to feel guilty about those things of which one usually does and should feel guilty."

Psychoanalysis recognizes that from our early years many streams converge to make us behave as we do, and that many of these streams started at so early an age that we can hardly be said to have been responsible for them, in an adult sense. Consequently, no individual alone and of himself is responsible for landing himself in a mess. The very existence of analysis as a joint undertaking of patient and analyst is an acknowledgment of the fact that, whether or not we are responsible for getting ourselves out of trouble, the responsibility for getting ourselves out of trouble rests with each one of us. This is true ethical responsibility because it implies that it is our job to repair even those psychological damages which we have not brought upon ourselves. To analysis, payment in kind is not enough. Self-flagellation is not enough. Penance and confession alone are not enough. The sick human being can misuse all such ethical devices and still "sin" again. To these time-honored ways of dealing with the primitive components of human nature, analysis adds an insight into the unconscious as well as the conscious roots of conduct; it is specifically this insight which gives human beings their first real chance to rise to new levels of emotional and ethical maturity.

Perhaps it is accurate to say that all modern theologies use the feelings of guilt and anxiety as forces by which the sinner may be led to repent and to turn to faith as a divine mercy. At times every psychiatrist sees patients in whom the resulting burden of guilt and anxiety is inflated to a destructive extent by unconscious fantasies. This is especially true when rigid ethical standards are exacted not merely for acts, but also for thoughts and feelings. The expansion of the ethical code to include responsibility and accountability not merely for deeds, but also for thoughts, feelings, and desires was a momentous step in human culture. But it placed an unfair and sometimes crushing burden on the human spirit because, before the discoveries of psychoanalysis, nothing was understood of the role of unconscious forces in determining conscious levels of thought and feeling. Any system of ethics that demands something which is psychologically impossible must inevitably create a pathological anxiety and pathological guilt, and these substitute obsessional struggles over scruples and rituals for normal ethical goals. The outcome of this is to divide men into two groups: neurotic slaves to rigid systems of ethics, and neurotic rebels against them.

Once this is clearly understood, it becomes evident that in a quite specific way psychoanalysis is an essential supplement to the cultural advances of modern religion, for it gives us a weapon with which to alter the primitive and savage unconscious levels that form the core of our major ethical struggles.

4. Another frequent misconception about psychoanalysis is the idea that it advocates an undisciplined pursuit of self-indulgence; or as one critic recently put it, "materialism, hedonism, infantilism and eroticism." This is especially untrue. The Freudian concept of the human struggle actually has its roots in sober and time-tested theological formulations. Like the theologian, the analyst sees man as struggling up from childhood between primitive destructive and erotic instincts on the one hand, and his conscience and his ideal aspirations on the other. What psychoanalysis has added, however, is the knowledge that a large part of this struggle takes place below the level of consciousness, and that the unconscious protagonists in this conflict must be mastered, as well as the conscious. Out of this psychoanalytic discovery has come the beginning of a technique, faltering and imperfect though it still is, by which human beings can bring their primitive uncon-

scious drives to the surface where they can be controlled and directed.

It is fair to remind ourselves that, before this discovery, man's progress had in fact been blocked for centuries. Even prior to the Christian era, man could formulate his goals; religion indeed did so, beautifully and movingly in religion, in literature, and in the arts. But experience has taught that to describe these goals or to seek them with exhortation and prayer fails to bring us much closer to them. As long as they remain hidden, our concealed inner drives continue to force us to live in ways that run counter to our highest aims. Only by the mastery of these buried forces can man win the freedom to attain his ideals. Many have described the shining city at the end of the road. It is the grubby function of the analyst to learn how to roll out of the path the internal boulders that make progress so difficult. This is hardly a picture of the idle, frivolous, hedonistic, pleasure-loving philosophy so erroneously attributed to the psychoanalyst.

Nor is it true to say that psychoanalysis advocates unlimited self-indulgence of any kind. Freud, himself, a strict and almost ascetic figure in his personal life, never said that the control of instincts was to be abandoned in favor of unbridled pleasure-seeking. Quite the contrary, he repeatedly described how the pursuit of pleasure (the "pleasure principle") must even in infancy be tempered by the "reality principle." Here again Freud added two discoveries, both of which are often misrepresented: (a) that conscience itself, like the instincts of man, can serve unconscious neurotic processes which we must learn to understand; (b) that whereas conscious mastery and control of instincts leads to health and strength, unconscious suppression (i.e., repression) leads almost regularly to illness. This distinction is so elementary and has been explained so often that it is hard to understand how it can still be misunderstood and misrepresented.

The notion that analysis advocates the unchecked and self-indulgent expression of every impulse arises not only from a misunderstanding about the difference between conscious and unconscious control, but also from a failure to realize the difference between therapy on the one hand and education or child training on the other. It is true that, for technical reasons in treatment, as a temporary device one sometimes has to relax many of the ordinary controls. In the early days of psychoanalysis, what was then called "progressive education" made the natural mistake of thinking that this therapeutic device should apply to schools and to the training of children in the home. Therefore, we passed through a somewhat grotesque period in which the so-called "modern" school or "modern" home encouraged children in all kinds of unwise extravagences of speech and behavior. Happily, this period has long since passed, but the popular misunderstanding persists.

5. Finally, what of the frequent accusation that psychoanalysis is only for the wealthy? Even in the pioneering period which is ending, many more analy-

ses were performed without charge, or for token payments, than has been realized. Whenever in the history of medicine a new technique has first to be tried out in private practice, it is unavoidable that there will be a period during which its use is limited to a relatively small group among all who need it. During this phase the rich are the proving ground for the poor; and it is only as the new techniques become well established, and as many physicians are trained in their use, that it becomes possible to distribute their benefits widely. Psychoanalysis is at present emerging from this initial phase of predominantly private practice, to one of broader social applications in many fields. The practical problems with which such a program is confronted are described in Chapters XVII and XVIII.

In order to place psychoanalytic knowledge at the service of larger segments of the population, it will be necessary to provide funds and an organization for the training of more psychiatrists in psychoanalysis, and various new types of treatment facilities in which psychoanalytic psychiatry can be used: e.g., in outpatient clinics for the treatment of the neuroses, in the treatment of psychosomatic problems in general hospitals, in the rehabilitation of workers in industry, in family counseling, at all levels of schooling, and in courts and social agencies. The number of individuals to be helped is enormous; the number of those who are adequately trained to give such help is pitifully small. This is the bottleneck, and it can be broken only by endowing teachers and students alike. A few years of generous policies in this matter, making use of both private philanthropy and public funds, would be repaid many times over. Such organizations as psychoanalytic institutes are even now attempting to raise large endowment funds and are giving free and low-cost therapeutic services.

Thus, there is good reason to believe that psychoanalysis stands on the threshold of a new era; and that what has been learned during its first seventy-five years will make wider applications possible both in prevention and in therapy. To reach these goals, however, requires the understanding cooperation of the community in which we live and work, and especially of all those institutions and instruments of popular instruction which form and influence public opinion. That is why from the point of view of the community and its needs it is worthwhile to attempt once more to dispel some of the more frequent misconceptions about analysis.

Chapter XXIII
PSYCHOANALYTIC TRAINING

The Name

There is no copyright on the name "psychoanalyst," and it is in the interest of the public and of the medical profession in general to define a psychoanalyst as one who is a member in good standing of any psychoanalytic society affiliated with the American or the International Psychoanalytic Association. Such membership is equivalent to certification as a specialist, and it is a sound medical practice to deny the name of psychoanalyst to anyone lacking such training. Therefore, it is a useful precaution to find out whether any man calling himself an analyst belongs to such a society or is sponsored by a training institute (e.g., an advanced student) before accepting him as an adequate representative of the method he claims to use.

Historical Development of Psychoanalytic Training

When psychoanalysis was young, anyone who was interested could join a psychoanalytic society, whose members met to discuss the new science and to listen to lectures on the subject; and any member could practice something he called "psychoanalysis." Thereafter, his further growth was determined by his own clinical experience, his study of the writings of others, his

267

inherent gifts, and his integrity. Many able and courageous pioneers grew up under this system, but the going was hard. Because they faced bitter and scornful criticism, and material rewards were limited, for many years no opportunist was tempted to exploit the new technique or its name and fame.

As the popularity of psychoanalysis grew, however, this informality and lack of well-defined standards of training led to abuses. Many people began to call themselves psychoanalysts who by no process of self-instruction or self-discipline had achieved any understanding of the principles and methods of what they claimed to practice. There still are such men whose methods are at variance with the essence of psychoanalytic technique, but who nonetheless are regarded as psychoanalysts by the laity, and even by some uninformed members of the medical profession. Some of these were in the field so early that they have been members of some psychoanalytic society for many years; but only a few of them are left. Fresh abuses still occur. Recently, a sign in a window claimed that the man within was a "Chiropractor and Psychoanalyst." Another man boasted that he could "analyze" his patients in an hour. A glib physician, totally without training in either psychiatry or psychoanalysis, talked of "working the transference on" his patients. A woman thought she was being analyzed when she was seeing her physician for half an hour once a week over a period of a few weeks.

A more respectable source of confusion remains,

which can be stamped out only with the full cooperation and help of the laity and of the medical profession. This is the unwitting misuse of the term "psychoanalysis" by physicians who may be well trained in other fields of medicine or surgery. Every physician is likely to be called upon by his patients to advise them on their emotional problems. Some physicians have a special aptitude for this work, and before long the word goes around that they are "analyzing" their patients. The physician may or may not be responsible for this confusion. Sometimes he himself does not understand the difference between analysis and what he is doing. There is no consultant in the field of psychiatry and psychoanalysis who has not had to repair the damage which these well-intended but untrained efforts can cause.

Some of these physicians may sincerely believe that a "flair" for human contacts is the equivalent of training in psychiatry and psychoanalysis, as though a man's manual dexterity were the equivalent of a thorough apprenticeship in surgery. On the basis of an interest in the problems of human nature, they offer the public their personally blended version of psychotherapy, in which some features of psychoanalysis may be included. To analytic colleagues, these men will carefully explain that what they practice is *not* psychoanalysis; but to their patients or in the presence of a more naive group they maintain with equal vigor that it is, and rationalize their lack of training by attacking analytic training as rigid and "orthodox." *It is true, of course, that formal training in any field has to guard constantly against rigid traditionalism; but this is hardly a valid excuse for rejecting training in toto.* Sometimes this rejection is sincere; sometimes it is a product of a physician's megalomanic neurosis; sometimes it is a flagrant opportunism. But it is well for the medical profession and public to remember that there is no royal road to analytic skill through guess and intuition alone.

Occasionally under the pressure of the difficulties into which they flounder, these medical or surgical colleagues apply to the nearest psychoanalytic institute for admission as regular students. If they agree to accept the jurisdiction of the school, to fill in the basic gaps in their psychiatric education, and to put themselves through the further training which is required of all students, such applications are welcome. The sacrifices this involves are heavy, however, and include the abandonment of the pseudoanalytical practice on which the applicant has probably come to depend for his very living. When they find out how great a sacrifice is involved and how exacting is the discipline, some of these applicants change their minds and fail to start; of those who start, some fail to finish. Some, however, have completed their belated training, and their courage and integrity have been rewarded by the acquisition of an exceptional skill.

It has been for the purpose of training competent specialists that institutes were organized in which to educate those who wish to master this particular branch of psychotherapy. The training given by a recognized psychoanalytic institute constitutes the best evidence of a physician's right to call himself a psychoanalyst and to call what he practices psychoanalysis.

The International Psychoanalytic Association

This training developed first under the supervision of the International Psychoanalytic Association. Before World War II this consisted of societies in many lands whose individual members made up the membership of the international body. The International Psychoanalytic Association was thus a federation of local scientific societies, and membership in it was automatic upon election to any one of the local societies recognized by the international body. Under the guidance of an International Training Commission the local societies organized training institutes. Thereafter, no one could be elected to membership in any society who had not graduated from such an institution. All training was based on certain general principles laid down by the Training Commission of the International Association.

In the early days of psychoanalysis this centralized control made it possible for responsible leaders of psychoanalysis to establish and maintain high standards everywhere; but it entailed the risk of becoming too authoritarian and too tradition-bound in theory and technique. Consequently, the organization that was formed to preserve standards led to the splitting-off of some rebellious groups, amid angry accusations that the Training Commission was stifling free scientific thought. This, though a source of confusion to laymen and physicians alike, has been a natural and transitory difficulty. In the main, whatever was valid in these rebellions was absorbed into the theories and techniques of the parent group and consequently their effect was healthy and stimulating. With the vigorous scientific development of psychoanalysis and its wide dispersion over the world, the authority of the Central Executive and of the Training Commission of the International Association has lessened steadily, and the whole structure is now in the process of being decentralized.

The American Psychoanalytic Association

In America for many years there has been an organization known as the American Psychoanalytic Association. During its early years its members varied widely in their technical methods and aims since, at the beginning, membership in the Association did not rest upon any prerequisite training. In the early nineteen-thirties this organization was converted into a federation of local American societies. In 1937 a group of training institutes was recognized by the national body and, by mutual agreement, minimal standards were established which now govern their activities and those of any new training groups applying for recognition. This agreement is revised periodically to keep up with changing and developing experience.

By 1947 the local societies making up the federation and the local training institutes which had been recognized by the national body had multiplied in numbers and grown in strength to a point where many of the functions of the central body could be handed over to the local societies and institutes. Thus, in the development of the American Psychoanalytic Association as in the development of the International, there has been a healthy diffusion of authority to the local groups. The American Psychoanalytic Association has become a direct membership society, a forum for scientific discussions, a guardian of standards, and an adviser on educational issues, but it retains little or no executive authority.

The Training Institutes and Centers

Not all the societies affiliated with the American Psychoanalytic Association are large enough to organize their own training institutes, although each group assumes the responsibility for training psychiatrists in psychoanalysis. Originally all training institutes developed as part of psychoanalytic societies. Some institutes have recently formed independent of any society, some of them as special subdivisions of the department of psychiatry of a medical school (1952b).

Because much of the instruction is on an individual basis, the ratio of teachers to students in psychoanalytic institutes must be high. Another peculiar feature of psychoanalytic education is the one-to-one relationship of teacher to student both in the preparatory analysis and again in supervision. This creates a bottleneck at the initial and final stages of training.

It is important for each student to have contact with

many analysts so that his preparatory analysis, his seminars, his theoretical lectures, his technical lectures, and his supervised clinical work should not all be given by one small group of teachers. Any lack of balance in the presentation of theory and technique that may arise out of personal biases can be turned to advantage if the influence of any one teacher is balanced by contacts with many other viewpoints. This means that training units in psychoanalysis are most effective if they are large. But even those medical schools which are most hospitable to psychiatry and to psychoanalysis can appoint only small numbers of psychiatrists and psychoanalysts to their staffs, so that whether this is desirable or not, for a considerable time to come, most psychoanalytic training will probably be given in institutes that are independent of universities.

The independent institute has certain other advantages. In the first place it is able to provide postgraduate training for members of the departments of psychiatry of all medical schools in its general neighborhood. As an example, a statistical survey indicated that in 1950 ninety per cent of the men teaching on the faculties of psychiatry of the medical schools in and around greater New York either were at that time or had been students at the New York Psychoanalytic Institute. At one time, the same institute was providing instruction to members of the faculties of medical schools in New Haven, Montreal, Toronto, Boston, Philadelphia, California, Denmark, Norway, Holland, and various South American countries, and to our own

274

armed forces as well. Thus the concentration of available teaching personnel in the well-organized curriculum of a single institute can be an economy for all of the medical schools served by that institute, making it possible at the same time to give the students a broader and more varied interpretation of analysis than could be provided by a small psychoanalytic unit in any one medical school. Size automatically saves an institute from becoming the unbalanced expression of any one viewpoint or a factional representative of either "orthodoxy" or "heterodoxy."

On the other hand, the independent institute also has certain disadvantages. Because of their many and varied outside responsibilities and allegiances, the students at such an institute are not as easy to supervise as they would be if all of their activities were concentrated in one organization which had behind it the authority and prestige of a medical school. Similarly, it is more difficult for the unattached institute to select patients and to match them to the students according to their development and training. For this, clinical facilities are essential, and the unattached institute finds it difficult to assemble, sort, and distribute such clinical material. As a result, many institutes are developing their own clinical facilities in the form of low-cost or no-cost outpatient clinics. Another disadvantage is that, for certain types of research work, hospital facilities with at least a few beds are essential. Finally, it is difficult to finance independent institutes. All such institutes have discovered that foundations and even many individuals do not recognize that these institutes are equivalent to a university department in a post-graduate medical school, and they often refuse grants to psychoanalytic institutes, even while they provide funds for the medical schools whose psychiatrists these same institutes are training. This makes it difficult for institutes to create part-time fellowships and part-time jobs for students, to accumulate funds with which to place their faculties on part-time salaries, or to finance clinical facilities and research.

These considerations lead to the conclusion that a formal liaison should be worked out between existing independent institutes and medical schools so as to integrate training in psychoanalysis with various phases of medical and psychiatric education.

The Organization of Training

In all institutes and training centers, responsibility is placed in the hands of an educational committee which selects students from among the physicians who apply, organizes courses, appoints the faculty, supervises training, and recommends students for graduation.

In many ways the selection of students is the most difficult task of all. It is easy to ascertain the general intellectual caliber and the academic record of the applicant and whether he can fulfill the formal training requirements. These include graduation from a Grade-A medical school, a general medical internship, a thorough grounding in hospital psychiatry, or an equivalent postdoctoral training in clinical and medical psychology, and an adequate training in the fundamentals of neurology and neurophysiology.

What is more difficult to ascertain is his aptitude for psychological work (Chapter XXV) or the presence of subtly masked neurotic difficulties, which may affect both the quality of his work as an analyst and his vulnerability to the emotional stresses of the analyst's life. Each applicant is carefully scrutinized with this in mind by a special subcommittee of the educational committee. Different institutes are experimenting with many different procedures.

The cost of psychoanalytic education is high both for the student and for the institute, and its duration long. From a practical viewpoint alone, it is therefore of the utmost importance to the applicant and to the institute to rule out as many unsuitable applicants as possible. From a scientific and social point of view, the value of eliminating those who might exploit analysis or become ill themselves is of obvious importance. This is why so much stress is laid on the process of selection.

(a) *The Curriculum*

Psychoanlytic education can be subdivided into five components: (1) the development of psychoanalytic insight into oneself, through the personal analysis; (2) training in the history of psychoanalytic concepts and theories; (3) education in the principles of psychoanalytic technique; (4) the theoretical application of psychoanalytic principles and techniques by participation in clinical seminars; and (5) finally, the practical experience of conducting the psychoanalytic treatment of selected patients under supervision.

Each student is usually required to pledge himself not to start psychoanalytic practice until his preparatory analysis is approved by the educational committee. Thereafter, his first step in training is to become a patient in a training analysis, variously called the "didactic" or "preparatory" analysis. This analysis is conducted by a psychoanalyst who is on the faculty of the institute. The duration of the training analysis varies considerably—the factors determining its length being for the most part technical. Training analyses never last less than a year, however, and usually longer. It is generally believed that a training analysis must be at least as thorough and as deep as the therapeutic analyses the candidate will ultimately conduct. Actually, the aim of every preparatory analysis is also therapeutic. This therapeutic goal is often elusive, since in the training analysis one is aiming at the illumination of subtly disguised and well-compensated personality weaknesses, trying not only to achieve intellectual clarity but also to strengthen the future analyst to withstand the severe emotional stresses to which he will be subjected throughout his future professional life.

After a certain point has been reached in the course of the preparatory analysis, the student is allowed to attend theoretical and technical lectures, practical case discussions, reading courses, and the like. This is his first formal contact with the teaching activities of the institute, and it includes an opportunity to participate in the discussion of the progress of patients who are under analytic treatment with experienced instructors and advanced students. In such discussions the identity of the patient is never revealed.

As the student builds up his knowledge of theory and technique, selected patients are assigned to him for analysis. This analysis is conducted under the supervision of an experienced training analyst who is a member of the faculty. The student brings the supervisor the material of his work with the patient, usually at least once a week, for review, criticism, and suggestions.

After the successful conclusion of several such supervised analyses, the student's status is again reviewed by the educational committee, with reference to his preanalytic experience and training, any additional formal training in psychiatry that may have been required during the intervening years since his original application, the quality of his work in seminars and case discussions, and his work both as a patient during his own preparatory analysis and as a psychoanalyst during the conduct of his supervised analyses, his grasp of theory and technique as evidenced in his reports on the analyses he has conducted under supervision, and, finally, his general grasp as evidenced during a searching oral examination by a faculty committee.

In 1960 the whole spectrum of psychoanalytic education in this country was surveyed for the American

Psychoanalytic Association and the findings published (Lewin and Ross, 1960).

The Training Institute as a Guild and as a Moral Influence

Most institutes are chartered in their respective states as recognized educational bodies. This gives them no legal power to enforce their exacting standards, but their moral influence is making itself felt increasingly. For many years training institutes have been conducted by psychoanalysts at the cost of much time, for which the faculty has not been remunerated. Nor does the faculty in most institutes receive a salary. Running expenses have been met by dues paid by the analysts themselves and in a small part by tuition fees. Recently, limited outside funds have become available to assist the work of a few of the institutes.

The institutes exist, not to limit the number of "competitors," but to train more young colleagues to become competent practitioners of psychoanalysis. The ultimate influence of the societies and of the institutes depends upon the support given them by physicians in general and by the public, a support which will be most effective if it takes the form of making sure that any man who claims to be a psychoanalyst is associated with one of the psychoanalytic societies and institutes recognized by the American Psychoanalytic Association. Psychoanalytic institutes have the further purpose of providing advanced training for members, for whose benefit advanced courses and advanced technical seminars are given in which new developments and research problems are discussed.

The Economics of Psychoanalytic Training

Four basic factors determine the economics of psychoanalytic education and, indirectly, of psychoanalytic practice (cf. Chapter XVII). One is its duration. The second is that the prerequisites for psychoanalytic training take so many years to acquire that by the time a student is ready to start his analytic training he is usually in his thirties, married, and has a family to support. The third is that there are at present almost no endowments out of which to pay salaries to the faculty or fellowships to the students. The fourth is that there are few part-time jobs for the students which would enable them to earn a living and still keep part of each day free for study.

As a consequence, with few exceptions, psychoanalytic training is carried on at night. The instructors spend their days in the practice of psychoanalysis. The students spend theirs in general psychiatric practice, either privately or in psychiatric hospitals or outpatient clinics. Obviously, it is impossible for work of the highest caliber to be done under these circumstances. Funds are needed to provide salaries for instructors, and fellowships and part-time jobs for students, to make training possible during the day. Everyone recognizes the urgency of this need, since the shortage of trained personnel is the bottleneck in any plan to make psychoanalytic therapy available to more people.

Many institutes have nonetheless found it extremely difficult to raise money for this essential purpose, and so, for the present, our institutes for postgraduate medical training in psychoanalysis are forced to operate largely as night schools.

The duration of training is longer than is ordinarily realized. The minimal duration of the course is three years; it usually takes four to five. This depends in part on the duration of the preparatory analysis, and in part on difficulties the student may encounter as he undertakes his supervised work, or in his advanced theoretical courses. This follows four years of medical school, or postdoctoral training, an additional three to four years of internships and residencies in general medicine and in psychiatry, a variable period of work in outpatient clinics, child-guidance clinics, and, if possible, work with the psychiatric problems of medical and surgical wards. The beginning of psychoanalytic training can be introduced into this sequence after two years in a psychiatric hospital. If the young physician knows from the start what he wants to do and begins his program immediately after graduation from medical school, the full further training will still take anywhere between eight and ten years. If, as often happens, the young physician experiments for two or three years before he makes his final choice of a career, the full period of training will take that much longer. As a result, before the war the average age of a hundred consecutive physician-students on admission to the New York Psychoanalytic Institute was thirty-six years, their average age on graduation close to forty.

This creates a serious problem for society as a whole. It means that the trained analyst has relatively few years in which to practice the technique it has taken him so many years to master. This automatically limits the supply of trained analysts. As has been said earlier, it also creates a serious economic problem for the analyst himself, because he has few years in which to earn security for his old age and an education for his children. This is one reason for the relatively high cost of psychoanalysis. From the point of view of the community, it is one more reason why subsidies are needed to facilitate the training of more analysts, and why it is important to find some way in which the training can begin earlier without sacrificing either maturity or ability.

During the training period, the heaviest expenses for the student are his long years of low earning capacity and the cost of his preparatory analysis. Because the faculties of most institutes give their services without remuneration, the charges which the institutes make to their students are relatively low when compared to those of other academic organizations.

This program constitutes a heavy drain on the time, energy, and financial resources of the faculty. The individual instructor conducts most preparatory analyses at reduced fees. As he becomes older and more experienced, more students seek to be trained by him; but with advancing age the instructor cannot work the long hours which this imposes on him, since he usually must take the student into training in addition to his schedule of patients and not in place of a patient. As the demand for psychoanalytic training grows, it will become necessary to find some means whereby the training analyst can be adequately compensated, if the whole system is not to break down.

The one important criticism which may justly be leveled against the existing system of training students is that it is not free from the dangers of rigidity and traditionalism. One cannot brush aside this criticism. Nevertheless, in this particular field of work, where the danger of untrained practice is great, the individual patient runs a lesser risk by turning to the carefully trained man, even if this long and difficult training costs the analyst some of his freedom and spontaneity and science loses some of its momentum of change. In the long run, well-educated men do not remain slaves to any theoretical system. The existence of a normal amount of free growth and development within the psychoanalytic point of view is shown by the frequency with which it has been accused of inconsistencies that have arisen out of changes in theory and technique over the course of the years.

Training in Non-Freudian Psychoanalysis

None of the earlier divergent schools of analytic thought, i.e., those of Adler, Jung, Rank, Stekel, etc., developed an organized plan of training. Some more recently organized groups have copied the general outlines of the plan described above.

This is not the place for a discussion of the differences between the theories of the Jungians, the Adlerians, the Burrows group, Stekel, the Rankians, Horney, Klein, etc. No one group can lay claim to a monopoly on truth. Certainly the psychoanalytic societies and institutes that are recognized by the American or International bodies, with their Freudian approach, can set up no claims to omniscience. They can justly claim, however, that their training regulations are fair and thorough, that any honest, healthy, non-neurotic, well-prepared, and intelligent physician can go through this apprenticeship, and that, subsequently, on the basis of this fundamental discipline, he can develop his own ideas and test his own theories freely.

In this singularly confidential field of medical practice it is only by working in such institutes as these that a physician can be given an opportunity to subject his work to the scrutiny and criticism of his colleagues. More than any other branch of medicine, psychotherapy has to be conducted in privacy. This makes it particularly difficult to know just how a colleague works. The best way to increase one's own skill by study of the techniques of others is through the apprenticeship of the institute. This is a further reason why it is sound to insist that experiments with modifications in technique must rest upon a mastery of existing techniques.

Finally, it should be borne in mind that from the viewpoint of patients the only important part of the struggle over so-called Freudian "orthodoxy" is concerned not with matters of theory, but with the problems of technique. No one accuses a surgeon of being too orthodox because he subjects himself to the rigid discipline of aseptic surgery. No one accuses an experimenter of being too orthodox if he scrupulously avoids introducing unknown variables into a complex experimental situation. Similarly, everything that is rigid and formal in psychoanalytic method has grown out of the necessity to carry on psychotherapy in a situation in which external variables are reduced to a minimum, since it is only in this way that the production of psychological data can be free, unguided, and undistorted. Without a technique to maintain constancy in the therapeutic situation, there can be no such thing as psychoanalysis. Important though the inner gift may be for the student of psychology, it is no adequate substitute for discipline and training in the use of a highly complex instrument.

In certain instances, either the theories or the practices of the various divergent groups, or both, are diametrically opposed to some aspect of the Freudian approach. In other instances a single concept is given undue emphasis and is regarded as an adequate substitute for what is omitted or rejected. It is significant that the early dissenting group gave up the use of the word "psychoanalysis" in order to disassociate themselves from Freud, and referred to their position as "anti-Freudian," whereas all the more recent deviants insist that they are analysts and that they are not *anti-*, but only *neo-*Freudian. This ferment is healthy, as long as it does not lead to any reduction in the standards of a fundamental and inclusive basic training. Our position is that the fundamental training should be the same for all, and that experiments leading to the modifications of theory and technique should be conducted by men who have been thoroughly schooled and experienced in existing theory and technique. New "schools" of theory and technique should not be proclaimed as great new revelations; nor should they be broadcast to the laity in popular books or taught in "unorthodox" institutes before they have been carefully and thoroughly tested before a jury of fellow-scientists. This is the way all medical science progresses.

Chapter XXIV
THE PROBLEM OF THE NONMEDICAL PSYCHOANALYST

Few psychoanalytic controversies have been more heated or more confused than those which have centered around the question of whether it is wise to train nonmedical men to give psychoanalytic treatments, and especially whether laymen so trained should be allowed to treat people who are psychologically ill. No one questions the advisability of allowing nonmedical scientists to use psychoanalysis for investigative purposes.

The issue arose originally because of events that occurred during the early days of psychoanalysis. In Vienna, for many years the opposition to psychoanalysis on the part of the medical profession was intransigent. The medical schools fostered this attitude in young physicians, so that their minds were closed to the newly developing system of psychological theories and techniques. In time this embittered Freud, and his early followers naturally banded together for mutual encouragement and moral support against the hostile medical world. These early students of psychoanalysis came from many disciplines and many backgrounds. Among them were artists, writers, psychologists, educators, parents, religious leaders, lawyers, journalists, anthropologists, and a scattering of psychiatrists. Since at that time there was no academic recognition of the value of studying Freud's work, most of those who came to him came either out of a need for personal therapy, or, as in the case of the few psychiatrists and other scientists, because their interest had been kindled in the new psychological world which psychoanalytic literature described. Thus, many of the laymen were "lay," not merely in their lack of medical training, but also in the absence of any general scientific background, and especially in their lack of a fundamental training in scientific methodology. Nevertheless, many showed considerable psychological aptitude, and of these some decided to professionalize their interest in psychoanalysis by undertaking to practice psychoanalysis in the treatment of others. In certain instances, the lack of a general scientific training permitted uncontrolled speculations to pose as scientific hypotheses. The difference between such speculations and the responsible formulation of verifiable hypotheses was not always clear to some of them. It is possible to say that, in balance, the positive contribution of the more gifted and intellectually meticulous of these nonmedical analysts far outweighed the confusion caused by others who were less scrupulous and less meticulous in their self-criticisms.

As psychoanalysis has come to occupy an increasingly important place in psychiatric education, the role of the nonmedical scientist in psychoanalysis has become a controversial issue. There are those who feel that he should play no role at all in psychoanalytic therapy and that his psychoanalytic activities should be restricted to its applications to anthropology, art, sociology, education, and research. The arguments of these opponents of lay analysis must not be brushed aside lightly. They point to the fact that American medicine has been more open-minded and hospitable to psychoanalysis than was true in Europe, and they are afraid of jeopardizing the close integration of psychoanalytic psychiatry into American medicine in general. They feel that, irrespective of the merits of the case, for the time being at any rate, it would be strategically unwise to allow laymen to play any role in therapy lest this widen again the old breach between the psychological and the organic aspects of medical therapy, precisely at a time when a harmonious relation between them is being established.

These critics also point to certain deficiencies the layman not infrequently brings to therapeutic procedures. There is the danger that, in his eager search for psychological causes that can be reached by psychological methods and because he does not understand the nature of organic illness, the lay analyst may overlook early warning symptoms of physical disease. Some lay analysts become defensive with regard to organic medicine, which may lead them to neglect adequate checks. Others overcompensate by sending patients for superfluous physical checkups, thus playing into a patient's hypochondriacal tendencies. The critics of lay analysis are afraid also of the layman's naive enthusiasm for therapy, an enthusiasm which centuries of lessons learned painfully at the autopsy table have taught physicians to curb with rigid skepticism and self-criticism. They are afraid of the layman's lack of a fully developed sense of therapeutic responsibility and of his lack of that basic scientific training which is needed if the therapist is to use sound critique in evaluating his results. The further argument is advanced that especially in psychotherapy the interplay of physical and psychological factors must be watched carefully at all times. Physical disturbances can be superimposed on psychological illness and vice versa, and sometimes it is far from easy to demarcate the boundary between the two. It is fair to assume that in such cases the medically trained psychoanalyst will approach such problems with less danger of underestimating the hints of organic illness or of exaggerating them.

On the other hand, the supporters of the analytically trained lay therapist believe, with this writer, that an adequate curriculum could and should be established by law that would provide fundamental training in the basic sciences and in the self-critical methods of scientific work, specific training in physiology and psychology, both normal and abnormal, and, finally, in all psychotherapeutic techniques and especially in psychoanalysis. Such a man could be given a Doctorate in Medical Psychology and licensed specifically to practice psychotherapy and psychoanalysis. His patients could be protected by two further safeguards: (a) he could be licensed to accept patients for treatment only *after* a thorough medical and psychiatric examination; and (b) he could be enjoined by law to send all patients for medical re-examination periodically throughout the course of the treatment. Theoretically, therefore, if the lay analyst had adequate training and if his right to practice were safeguarded by adequate legally specified restrictions, it should be possible to protect any patient who is being analyzed by a trained layman against the dangers that the nonmedical therapist would overlook organic disease or make mountains out of organic molehills.

Possible Gains vs. Immediate Dangers

It may well be asked whether there are any advantages to be derived from the therapeutic practice of psychoanalysis by people who are not trained in medicine. This question is difficult to answer in general terms. From the point of view of psychoanalysis as a science, much can be contributed by men who are trained in such fields as anthropology, ethology, philology, mythology, education, psychology, sociology, the law, and the like. Psychoanalysis needs their special knowledge and experience. Nor is it humanly possible for any one physician to master these allied fields in addition to the medical disciplines and psychoanalysis. If representatives of these allied disciplines are to make as full a contribution as possible, they must have a thorough training in psychoanalysis; and if this training is to be inclusive, it should include at least some measure of experience in its therapeutic application.

It is impossible, therefore, to make any general rule regarding the best policy to pursue; and in different countries psychoanalytic institutes have different rules about training nonmedical students. For many years, American medicine has had to carry on a fight to rid the American scene of untrained and unscrupulous charlatans and of many therapeutic cults. With this long struggle in mind, physicians are reluctant to open the door to the practice of any form of therapy by medically untrained people, however upright their motives and however skillful their personal techniques. They fear that a lowering of the barriers against nonmedical therapy in any direction might result in a lowering of the barriers in other directions as well.

Hence, this is one of those issues in which long-term scientific advantages must be balanced against immediate social considerations, since under certain circumstances even considerable scientific gains can be socially ill-advised or ill-timed.

At present the official policy of the American Psychoanalytic Association and all the institutes it recognizes is opposed to the training of nonphysicians in the therapeutic applications of psychoanalysis.

To many people, however, it seems that if it is ever safe to make an exception to the general rule against nonmedical therapists, it is in the field of psychoanalytic psychotherapy. Where no struggle against charlatans has had to be waged, or where it has been successfully won many years before, a community may safely adopt a broader policy toward the training of laymen for the therapeutic practice of psychoanalysis, always provided, of course, that the lay practitioner will subject himself to training requirements as rigid and exacting as those to which psychoanalytic institutes now subject the physician who comes to them for training.

One cannot, however, evaluate this problem solely in terms of theoretical scientific values. There are in addition some important practical and cultural implications of the participation of laymen in psychotherapy, and certain implications for medical education in general. Here we are confronted with some basic facts. First among these is that the ordinary physician is as untrained in psychotherapy as is the ordinary layman. Through failure to understand fundamental principles of psychotherapy, he is capable of doing as much harm as the lay analyst may do through ignorance of the fundamental principles of bodily disease. Second, we must face the fact that for many years clergymen who are interested in pastoral counseling, clinical psychologists, educators, and social workers have all been practicing psychotherapy, and not infrequently analytical psychotherapy or even full-fledged psychoanalysis. Third, anyone who considers objectively the overall picture of medical education in this country will realize that our existing facilities will never be able to train enough physicians, either in general psychotherapy or in psychoanalysis, to meet community needs. These needs include psychiatric service in schools from kindergarten through college, in courts, in social agencies, in industry, in general hospitals, and a more adequate staffing of outpatient psychiatric clinics and psychiatric hospitals, not to mention the needs of private psychiatric practice.

Some medical educators are convinced that we must evolve, under the auspices of our medical schools and teaching hospitals, a new therapeutic discipline, i.e., a doctorate in medical psychology. They feel that laymen should be trained specifically for psychotherapy in medical schools and in teaching hospitals, where they will have an opportunity to acquire broad clinical experience and certain important habits of the medical mind, namely, the dedication to therapeutic responsibility, the respect for the patient's right to privacy and anonymity, a familiarity with the phenomena of organic disease, the objective skepticism which the well-trained physician feels for all overenthusiastic therapeutic claims, etc. The advocates of such a doctorate in medical psychology also argue that certain parts of the medical curriculum could be eliminated from the curriculum of the new discipline, with the result that, instead of taking twelve to fifteen years after college (the time needed to complete the training of a psychiatrist in psychotherapeutic techniques), the doctor in medical psychology could be thoroughly trained in six to eight years after college.

This plan would have many advantages: (a) a nonmedical psychotherapist who was trained in this way would not be a layman, but a well-trained and well-rounded scientist in clinical and therapeutic psychology; (b) he would have acquired a medical viewpoint and habit of mind through being trained in a medical atmosphere; (c) he would understand the essentials of normal and pathological human physiology; (d) he would have had the invaluable experience of working psychologically with patients who suffer from organic as well as psychological illnesses; (e) he would be trained in all psychological techniques far more fully than is the average young psychiatrist; (f) finally, instead of finishing his training between the ages of thirty-five and forty, he would finish it somewhere between the ages of thirty and thirty-five, and would have that many more years before him in which to use his skills in the service of the community. Under such a plan, the same educational facilities could train twice as many therapists in the same length of time, and treatment services would consequently become available to the community in greater abundance and at lower cost. Finally, with adequate legal safeguards there need be no loss of security from the point of view of the organic welfare of the patient.

The problem is complicated, and there are many things to be said on both sides of it. It is the subject of investigation and discussion today by many thoughtful medical educators, and by many foundations interested in the improvement of medical education (Freud, 1927; Kubie, 1947a, 1948b, 1954c, 1957, 1964e, 1967a, 1967b, 1968c, 1970a).

Chapter XXV
THE APTITUDE FOR
PSYCHOLOGICAL WORK

Psychoanalysis focuses its attention on the investigation and relief of many forms of human suffering and discontent. From these studies it has learned that most psychic pain is the product of subtly disguised neurotic processes which are at work in the lives of every "normal" human being. This finding has forced us to face the sorry fact that we do not yet know how to bring up our children free from transient neurotic episodes that leave scars for which in adult years we pay a high price. It is therefore not strange that among those who become interested in psychiatry and psychoanalysis are many drawn to it by their own struggles with unhappiness. The influence of personal unhappiness and maladjustment on the effectiveness of the future analyst depends on several factors, some of which are grouped together under the general heading of "psychological aptitudes."

Psychological aptitude is one of those human attributes which is more easily recognized than measured or defined or analyzed into its components. Indeed, institutes for the training of psychoanalysts are currently making extensive investigations into its nature, because an evaluation of potential psychological aptitude is of major importance in the screening of applicants. Presumably this gift must have its roots in subjective experiences of emotional stress and strain that have been frankly faced and out of which develops the capacity to identify with the pains and joys of others. This is what enables one man to sense what others are going through and to relate it in some degree to his own experiences. Psychological aptitude probably requires, too, some degree of confidence in one's ability to recognize and appraise intuitively the expressions, gestures, and intonations of others and the sequences of mood and content in their speech. Something of all this must go into this elusive and subtle talent, but its exact make-up and its precise sources have never been ascertained. Not even its relationship to suffering is entirely clear.

There is a widespread belief that all sufferers from neuroses are "introverts" and that all "extraverts" are neurosis-free. This is entirely false. Although certain types of neuroses force their victims to attend closely to their own feelings, other neuroses serve as an effective defense against self-awareness. Among those who suffer from frank neuroses, one patient will constantly feel his own emotional pulse, while the next never stops to ask whether he has any emotions. It would therefore not be true to say that all sufferers from neuroses are overemotional or that all individuals who are preoccupied with their own emotional difficulties are necessarily more neurotic than those who seem to have none, or that either group has problems which are more difficult or less readily soluble than those of the other. These are merely two quite automatic ways of handling neurotic problems. The self-aware individual, however, *is* likely to have more psychological aptitude than the other.

Another factor seems to be related to the age at which the individual first becomes aware. No human beings go through life without periods of turmoil. There are some whose neurotic mechanisms manifest themselves early, but who compensate and whose symptoms subside quickly; there are others whose neuroses appear early and never subside; and there is still a third group who to the casual observer seem more stable at the start of life, but whose hidden problems become manifest as neurotic symptoms only in the thirties or forties. Many "campus heroes" come to neurotic grief in these years, and it is a fallacy to think of the pseudonormality of their early years as a standard of healthy adjustment. Again, such differences in timing are not differences in kind; but their effects on life and consequently on the consciousness of suffering vary widely. One may say that in general those who put on a bold front through early maturity tend all through life to hide from their own emotions and from those of others and therefore have a limited ability to understand and sympathize with psychological problems. This is what primarily accounts for the supercilious contempt with which people who have been able to hide from their own pain look down on those who acknowledge suffering more humbly and frankly. They could not face with tolerance and sympathy the pain of others without being forced to face and accept their own.

For the sake of man's understanding of his own nature, it is fortunate that there are always some men who early in life are forced to ponder on their own capacity for happiness and unhappiness, men who, with Thoreau, wonder why it is that "all men lead lives of quiet desperation." These individuals tend to become what is called "psychologically minded"; and it is quite inevitable that those who make it their profession to study the problem of human discontent should come largely from this group.

Many factors determine when in life an individual will first be forced to face his emotional problems. For all alike, the struggle begins in infancy over the feelings of helplessness and inadequacy at the frustration of unattainable yearnings, a frustration that in time generates impotent rage and fear. This starts long before there is any conscious awareness of variations in the outer circumstances of life. In the later management of that struggle, however, the feelings which are emphasized and confirmed by the circumstances of life acquire increasing power and significance. Advantageous and reassuring circumstances, such as wealth, membership in a dominant group, unusual athletic prowess, great beauty, special talents, tend frequently, though not always, to obscure the subtler inner conflicts. Conversely, disadvantageous circumstances during the developmental years accentuate the inner doubts, and focus the sufferer's attention on them. This is especially true when the external situation seems to single out a child for scorn for reasons which are beyond his control, as for instance because of his origins or the color of his skin. Indeed, for every man his origins can be a particularly important source of either reassurance or self-depreciation. To come from "important people," to belong to a "great" nation, to have an illustrious ancestor, becomes in most instances a prop to a child, whereas to come from a group that is scorned feeds the fires of self-doubt smouldering in everyone.

That is why members of all alien minorities find that even where they are subjected to merely petty social discriminations, these exaggerate the feelings of insecurity of the young. Consequently, children from minority groups soon tend to become either over-aggressive, or oversensitive, and live with a frank awareness of insecurity and self-doubt. These circumstances increase their emotional vulnerability. When this is directed into productive channels, it can serve as a spur to intellectual, artistic, and economic productivity. This accounts in part for the disproportionate role that artists of continental origin have played in all Anglo-Saxon cultures. It also accounts for the extraordinary interest in psychiatry and psychoanalysis on the part of members of minority groups.

Although discrimination affects all minority groups, it exercises a special influence on the Jew. This, together with the fact that Freud himself was a Jew, has led some critics to ask whether or not psychoanalysis should be looked upon as a "Jewish science," i.e., a system of ideas which bears the stamp of a particular theological system or of a particular emotional attitude to life and its problems. The question itself could scarcely be asked seriously about any other scientific theory. The theory of relativity is not "Jewish," because Einstein was a Jew. If a Christian mathematician uses the theory in computing the answer to some problem, his answer is not therefore a "Jewish" answer. Obviously, psychoanalysis is not "Jewish" merely because Freud was a Jew. Furthermore, psychoanalysis uses as its chief implement the method of free association, which was derived from the earlier work of a German Protestant, and which was subsequently investigated in many other connections by psychologists of many lands and many faiths.

Of even greater moment, however, is the fact that the essence of psychoanalysis is not a body of doctrines, but a technique that is applied by many and varied human beings to the study and treatment of the problems of other human beings. Catholic psychoanalysts treat Jewish or Protestant patients and vice versa. The majority of analysts and of analytical patients do not come from any one religious faith or from any one national or racial group.

As we have already indicated (cf. Chapter XXIII), the relation of psychological aptitude to neuroses, healed and unhealed, is an important practical problem for every training institute and cannot be fully dealt with here. The fact that early in his life the analyst may have had to deal with some type of neurotic disturbance in his own personality can be a positive asset to him in his later work. Indeed, even analysts who have been quite sick psychologically, and in whom a not inconsiderable amount of illness persists, may possess great theoretical brilliance. This does not mean that the analyst must remain sick in order to retain his psychological aptitudes. Such sensitivity is never lost in the healing process; and in the training of the analyst a major emphasis is laid on the therapeutic effect of the training analysis, without fear that the student will thereby lose his ability to estimate the moods and feelings of others.

There is no general agreement on the forms of neurosis in childhood and adolescence that may leave advantageous residues in the make-up of the future analyst, or what forms should constitute grounds for turning down the application of a would-be student. This is a matter that is being subjected to investigation. It has been found that in the training of the young analyst the process of therapy can at times present special difficulties, and, in spite of the therapeutic purpose of the training analysis, its therapeutic leverage is not as great as that of the analytic process when it deals with patients. Perhaps it is fair to say that in training we often start with an individual who is more than usually vulnerable to emotional stress and try to make him less vulnerable than the average so as to enable him to withstand a life full of exceptionally severe emotional strains. It is not surprising that the training process does not always attain this goal or that, in their personalities and in their lives, even mature and able analysts may show that they are not free from internal conflicts and stresses. From the point of view of the patient, however, it is essential only that these residues of earlier neurotic difficulties shall not under any circumstances interfere with the analyst's objective attitude toward his patient's problems or with his therapeutic relationship to the patient himself.

Section II

Chapter XXVI
CONTROVERSIES AND FRONTIERS

Controversies in psychoanalysis fall into two major areas: controversies over psychoanalytic theory and controversies over psychoanalytic technique. These are related of course, but frequently they have started independently and can most easily be described separately.

Controversies over Theory

Early theoretical controversies revolved around the role of sex in the conflicts that produce neuroses. The dissenters moved in various directions. Breuer, Freud's first co-worker, could not accept Freud's evidence that unrecognized erotic impulses could invade even the patient-doctor relationship and had therefore to be dealt with in therapy in such a way as to clarify the patient's understanding of this aspect of his life. Some years later Adler also turned his back on sexual conflict, substituting an almost exclusive emphasis on a blind drive for power and on the tendency to overcompensate for bodily weakness, whether real or fancied, with hostility and aggressiveness (Adler is responsible for that overworked cliche, "inferiority complex"). Unfortunately, in his effort to prove that sexual conflicts were unimportant in the genesis of the neurosis, Adler went so far as to look upon the sexual drives themselves as largely a competitive struggle with the outside world. For reasons that are not entirely clear, Adler not only minimized the importance of guilt and fear over sexual conflicts, but also paid little attention to the difference between the effects of conscious and unconscious conflicts. Little remains today of Adler's teachings, except those parts that early on were incorporated into Freudian theory and technique.

As might have been expected, Adler's effort to prove that sex was of little importance was soon balanced by Stekel's attempt to prove that it was all important, an effort paralleled in a curious and distorted fashion by the fantastic speculations of the late Wilhelm Reich, to which no analyst of any school subscribes.

The next effort to dispose of sex as a source of significant neurotic difficulty was made by Carl G. Jung of Zurich. By stages, Jung came to substitute for the individual's struggles with his own developmental processes the notion that the source of the neurosis was to be found in a struggle with a quasi-mystical, universal or "collective" unconscious. In that Freud, too, was concerned with the possibility that unconscious thought and feeling might be more or less universal and relatively independent of individual experience, there was at the start some overlap between the Freudian and Jungian concepts. To Freud, however, the idea of a collective unconscious always remained an accessory one, whose existence and possible influence he was forced to consider seriously, since it might supplement and complicate the effects of experience. The existence of inherited patterns of unconscious conflict never became a cornerstone in Freud's concept of the unconscious, as it did for Jung; and never did inherited patterns seem to Freud to operate as a collective mystical force, apart from their manifestations, both conscious and unconscious, in each human being. Jung's almost mystical concept of a collective unconscious took a malignant turn during World War II, when he used it as a pseudorational excuse for his outspoken flirtation with the Nazis and Nazi ideology. Jungians in America are few and are decreasing in number, except in certain centers where they have become Freudian in all but name. American Jungians vary widely in the degree to which they accept Jung's formulation in all its implications and, consequently, in the degree to which they follow his rejection of the simple earthy struggles over unconscious loves and hates on which Freudian theory and therapy are based.

After Jung, there were for some years no further disagreements about the role of sex or of aggression in the genesis of the neurotic process. In time, however, Horney and her adherents returned to a new version of this ancient issue, offering the pressure of modern cultural and environmental stresses as a timely alternative to the struggle with instinctual processes. She writes of the neurotic problems "of our times," overlooking the fact that there is no evidence that the neuroses of today differ in any but their superficial symptomatology from the neuroses of our ancestors. In Horney's confused theoretical structure there is the further implication that environmental stresses can operate apart from the instinctual forces in individual development. Horney and her followers minimize the importance of what they call the "genetic" or instinctual struggles and of the unconscious residues of early troubles, attributing neurotic difficulties largely to current situational problems and to certain neurotic "trends" which the individual's past has engraved on his personality. This is indeed a perplexing paradox, since the neurotic distortion of the personality is itself the most important product of the neurotic process rather than its cause.

In terms of simple common sense these ideas would seem to be the strangest and least psychological of the various deviations. The superficial forms of the neuroses have varied from culture to culture and from age to age, but the neurotic process as such is not a product of modern times, and there is not one shred of statistical evidence to show that there has been any percentage increase in the incidence of the neurotic process in modern man. The most that can be claimed is that the price man pays for his neurotic infirmities has changed, and that in certain respects it has increased. This makes a significant difference in the fate of the neurotic process, but has nothing to do with its genesis.

By implication, another theoretical controversy arises out of this "cultural" viewpoint, a controversy that has cropped up repeatedly and in changing forms during the short history of psychoanalysis. This is over the question of how early in the life of an individual one can find the roots of neurotic trouble. Freud first looked for the origins of the neurosis in some upsetting experiences, usually during puberty or early adolescence. Clinical experience soon proved, however, that many of these "events" were either wholly imaginary or else largely embellished with unconscious childish fantasies, and that even where there had been a real traumatic experience, the event itself was only a small part of the total psychological experience. As Freud came to recognize the role of fantasy in these traumatic experiences, it also became clear to him that the earlier these happened the more important they were. In the course of time, his emphasis shifted from single or even repeated traumatic events to those continuing stressful situations that are an integral part of family life and of the process of growth (see Chapter IV). With these shifting and evolving emphases, there have been recurring disagreements about how early such situations exercise their destructive influences. Freud's major concern was always with the years between two or three and puberty. Various deviants have gone in the only two directions possible, some emphasizing earlier years, some later.

Otto Rank first went everybody else one better and, for a time, attributed all of man's difficulties to the initial traumatic experience of being born. This was a notion Freud never accepted and that Rank himself

311

subsequently abandoned. Unfortunately, there still have been no adequate studies of the long-run effects of different kinds of labor and delivery on subsequent psychological development. More recently, Melanie Klein and her followers have taken a position almost as extreme as Rank's. They believe they can recognize in the events of the first six months of life a psychological impact that can be either critically formative or destructive for an entire lifetime. At the other extreme is Horney, who minimizes the importance of early years and emphasizes the current poblem, as Adler had done before her, and also Rank, in his later thinking.

This preoccupation with the age at which trouble starts has taken several forms. Freud gradually came to emphasize a somewhat rigid series of phases in the development of the sexual and aggressive instincts. This viewpoint has come to be called the *Instinct* or *Libido Theory* and has led to various attempts to derive personality traits and different constellations of neurotic symptoms from a constitutional overactivity of some particular phase of instinctual development, or from a fixation at that phase by a traumatic experience or external stresses that happened to occur as the child was passing through that period of his life. This working hypothesis still governs the thinking of many analysts, but evidence regarding the limits of its validity is far from complete. The theory itself has undergone many speculative and verbal vicissitudes, with little experimental testing. Fundamental research remains to be done in this area.

312

It is an interesting commentary on the role of the human personality in scientific progress that two analysts of approximately the same generation, trained under the same teachers, should turn to such diametrically opposed extremes as did Klein and Horney: one seeking the explanation of psychopathology in the experiences of the first months of life, the other seeking explanations in the stressful present. In view of what we know of the identity of opposites in unconscious psychological processes, the genesis of such polarities is not hard to understand clinically, but they clutter up the pages of scientific history with needless and sterile controversies.

One can recognize in this disagreement an old scientific conflict in modern dress. The question of whether the neurotic process is "environmental" and "cultural" in origin or "biogenetic" has a nostalgic flavor. It is obvious that, whether we are discussing the facts of physical structure in the animal kingdom or the facts of psychological development in the individual, neither heredity nor environment can operate without the other. It is relevant to ask how early in life and under what circumstances conflicts can be rendered unconscious and thus become sources of neurotic difficulty; and at what stage in development hereditary or genetic influences cease to play a determining role, and how and at what point environmental forces enter the picture. In the argument about this second question one can sometimes detect the irrelevant influence of political bias (see Chapter XXI). To attribute to current economic and social stresses the power to generate that subtle, intricate, and universal problem known as the neurotic process is grinding a political axe, which should play no role in this issue. It is an attempt to say "what bad economics can cause, good economics can cure." Unfortunately, both assumptions are questionable.

Protagonists of these varying views agree at least verbally on one point—namely, that neuroses have their origin in unconscious inner conflicts. Even here, however, disagreements arise, since men use the concept "unconscious" with different connotations. Adler and Horney seem to mean thoughts and feelings of which we may be unaware but which are quite close to the surface of consciousness and which, with little difficulty, can be rendered conscious by direct confrontation. In some respects this is a return to an early analytic assumption that experience forced Freud to abandon. At the other extreme is the mystical position of Jung, or the subdepths implications of Klein and the early Rank. These respectively place the unconscious psychological organization on suprapsychological or subpsychological levels of organization.

The Freudian position stands between these extremes. It places the origins of unconscious processes in that age period during which the child slowly acquires the power of symbolic thought and expression (1974a). It recognizes that we are able to perform preconsciously, and often with greater economy, every psychological function that we can perform consciously, and that there is a continuous interaction between these two streams of psychological forces and events. The consciousness process weighs, codes, and samples the preconscious stream and subjects it to symbolic representation. This interaction is complicated by a dynamic process that prevents the emergence of unconscious processes into consciousness, except as disguised or "symbolic" acts, thoughts, images, and feelings. It is this opposing force that necessitates the use of special technical devices, such as psychoanalysis, in order to bring material from unconscious levels of the personality into consciousness, without distortion. Indeed, were it not for this active barrier, there would be no need for any such technique as psychoanalysis. Consequently no method of investigating or influencing human behavior that fails to deal with this resisting force is, in any meaningful sense of the word, "analytic." This is a dynamic and realistic concept of the nature of unconscious processes and of their relationship to preconscious and conscious processes. From this fundamental position, there are various divergences— some tacit, some explicit. Sometimes they go to the heart of the entire structure of psychoanalysis, either by denying by implication that there are such unconscious processes as psychoanalysis describes, or by regarding the unconscious processes as impotent and insignificant, or else by relegating them to a mysterious, spiritual or subpsychological world of their own. An even more fundamental problem is interwoven with the question of the age of onset of the neurotic process, to wit, whether neurotic difficulties are due to conscious disappointments, conscious frustrations, conscious deprivations, conscious impulses, and conscious conflicts, or *only* to those which are unconscious.

In summarizing these controversies over facts and theories, we can do no better than to paraphrase the late Robert Waelder: Controversies in analysis are over the biological (instinctual, "genetic") as opposed to the sociological sources of the neuroses; over the deeper or more superficial concept of the nature of the unconscious processes; over the greater or lesser importance of earlier or later ages in individual developments; over the relative importance of sexual conflicts and of conflicts over hostility and self-assertion; over whether these conflicts must be unconscious if they are to produce neuroses, or whether they can exert the same harmful influence when they are merely conscious reactions to deprivation, frustration, and disappointment.

Differences of opinion among analysts about the relation of analysis to religion and to political, social and economic change have already been discussed in Chapters XIX and XXI.

Controversies over Technique

Special advantages have been claimed for variations in psychoanalytic technique, but few of these claims have been adequately tested. Indeed, most of them have not met the most basic requirement of experimental science—namely, that when trying out the effects of any changes, only one change should be made at a time, since, if several changes are introduced simultaneously, it becomes impossible to evaluate the effects of any one of them. With other factors, this makes research in psychotherapy a laborious and time-consuming task—which is one reason why there has been so little of it.

Most of the early changes in technique were the steps in a maturing process out of which crystallized the essentials of psychoanalytic technique as we know it today. There have been several such steps.

(a) The first was the development of the use of free association as the chief technique of exploration (see Chapter VIII). Free association replaced the initial use of hypnotism and direct persuasion, which were abandoned early, leaving behind a persisting prejudice against further experiments with these techniques. This bias is being resolved as new modifications of experimental hypnosis develop.

Free association was first used chiefly in an attempt to explain symptoms. Soon it was applied to such related phenomena as slips, dreams, and fantasies, until finally it became the major instrument for the psychoanalytic investigation of the chronology of a whole life history and for the investigation of the personality as a whole.

(b) Next came the gradual recognition of the role of transference and countertransference and the consequent necessity for preserving the analytic incognito (see Chapter IX). The goal here was to clarify for the patient the role of unconscious feelings in all of his human relations by using the unconscious components in his relation to the analyst as an example, at the same time lessening his resistances and facilitating his free associations. From time to time there are analysts who seem to forget the lessons learned in the tough school of analytic frustration, and who abandon all concern with the analysis of transference processes. The fundamental principles involved have already been discussed in Chapters VIII and IX where the importance of maintaining the analytic incognito is stressed.

Some of the adherents of the environmentalist viewpoint argue for free social intercourse between analyst and patient in order to give the analyst an opportunity to observe directly the behavior of his patient in current situations. The price paid for this is exorbitant, since it makes it difficult if not impossible to analyze unconscious components of the transference, and equally difficult to analyze the unconscious components in the patient's conscience, apart from the superimposed standards of the analyst. All this limits the freedom of the patient's associations; and since free associations are our pathway to unconscious levels of psychological processes, and since informal conversation between analyst and patient requires the selective communications of ordinary speech, such informal contacts slowly but surely bring the essential analytical work to an end.

(c) The next major development was the use of interpretation as a subtle tool for the weakening of resistances, replacing the original naive use of blunt confrontations and symbolic translation.

There was, at first, no recognition of the role played by the forces that obstruct the flow of free associations in the emergence of unconscious material into conscious processing. Consequently, early psychoanalytic technique consisted of the direct confrontation of patients with blunt statements of what they were "really" thinking, feeling, or wishing. Conscious behavior, thoughts, and feelings were quickly translated into their symbolic unconscious equivalents. Experience soon demonstrated the limitations and dangers of this approach and the necessity of attacking the resisting forces before attempting to impart any direct insight. It is remarkable that from time to time some analysts will forget even this elementary forward step in the evolution of their technique. This is an issue of special significance in relation to all brief forms of psychotherapy, analytic or otherwise.

(d) There was an early broadening of the field of analysis from its original concern with symptoms alone to a reconstruction of the chronology of an entire life, and finally to a consideration of the structure of the personality as a whole, with all of its assets and liabilities (currently miscalled "ego analysis").

It may be worthwhile to keep in mind the ever-present danger of lapsing from the tough task of analyzing to the easier and more gratifying role of moralizing. The analysis of the "personality as a whole," and some of what is called "ego analysis" can be old-fashioned moralizing in newfangled, pseudo-analytic terms. This is equally true of some of the talk about "weak" and "strong" egos, which is found in current "orthodox" analytic literature. Name-calling, is still name-calling even when done in scientific jargon and by an analyst.

Over each of these natural developmental stages there have been recurring controversies because, interestingly enough, most of the lessons that have been learned have also been forgotten repeatedly and have had to be relearned. Ultimately, the effect of this on any science is salutary, since it forces the developing science constantly to re-examine its premises. It is unfortunate only that this retracing of steps and re-examination of premises has sometimes been proclaimed to the public as a great new analytic discovery or innovation, when in reality it was a return to something old. This has confused the laity, and has served only to publicize some particular dissenting group for a few brief years.

(e) Another area of controversy over technique centers around the continuity or discontinuity of treatment (see Chapter VII), i.e., whether it is better to continue an analysis indefinitely and without interruptions, or to analyze for short periods with repeated interruptions (as advocated by Alexander et al., 1946). There is a related controversy over the duration and frequency of the sessions. These variations involve no fundamental divergence from basic psychoanalytic principles, but their value and limitations have not yet been established or adequately tested.

Only in the analysis of children has the issue of continuity acquired realistic significance. Here, two quite opposite schools have developed: one advocating long and continuous analytical treatment, even at an early age; the other defending brief periods of intensive analytic work on the symptomatic upsets of childhood, then waiting for the next flurry of symptoms before carrying treatment further. On theoretical grounds there is something to say on both sides of this question; but there has as yet been no objective comparative study of the long-run results of these two approaches on comparable groups of children. Heated words are exchanged between the two sides, without producing much light.

(f) In keeping with the evolution of psychoanalytic theory and the divergences that have arisen from time to time, analysts vary in the focus of their attention. Some concentrate primarily on immediate situational problems and daily experiences, some chiefly on various stages of early life. Others deal almost exclusively with dreams or with the quality or "structure" of the personality. It is inevitable that temperamental differences among analysts will be expressed through an enthusiastic overemphasis of one or another approach. It would seem evident, however, that common sense dictates an attack on a broad front, including symptoms, symptomatic behavior of all kinds, chronology, personality, and, finally, current problems, omitting none of these components of the total picture from searching inquiry. One can only deplore the efforts of some analysts to make a public crusade for an exclusive emphasis on one or another fragment of the whole.

(g) From time to time analysts have tried to introduce artificial changes in the patient's life, in his work, in his personal habits, and the like. Such attempts deliberately to generate tension during the course of treatment have been discussed in some detail in Chapter XII. They are sometimes of considerable importance in working out the details of treatment, but they are not fundamental departures in analytic technique. There have been disagreements about the feasibility and efficacy of such attempts (notably as proposed by Ferenczi, 1919, 1921), but this has not remained a controversial issue.

(h) Finally, there is the tendency of some deviants to forget another elementary lesson: that the neurotic process makes it impossible for any neurotic patient, even with the best will in the world, to accept or follow good counsel and wise advice until the neurotic necessity to be unwise has been analyzed. Consequently, the use of guidance in an attempt to bypass the slow, hard labor of analysis usually fails.

Lurking behind some of these issues is the essential question of whether to analyze at all. Whether or not they realize and acknowledge it, those who hold that the immediate situation is the source of neurotic difficulty cannot be concerned about unconscious levels. The analysis of unconscious forces therefore seems to them relatively unnecessary. This is the tacit implication of much of Horney's position. On the other hand, for those who are convinced that repressed unconscious conflicts are at the root of the neurotic process, technical deviations that obstruct or fail to assist in the uncovering of unconscious material are unacceptable.

One must conclude that many of these particular deviations are actually not new; they are steps backward, not progress—attempts to solve the problem of the neurosis on too superficial a level and in a manner tried and found inadequate years ago.

The Frontiers of Research

Where, then, are the advancing frontiers of psychoanalysis? In relation to what analytic problems can we look for mature research? As in other scientific fields, the significant advances in psychoanalysis are usually those of which the general public hears least. Indeed, many are still blueprints for investigations being planned or undergoing preliminary trials. Few receive attention in the popular press. This, of course, has great advantages since anonymity and obscurity make it possible for the investigator to approximate a contemplative and objective spirit (1952c).

(a) Technical Research

There are researches that bear directly on techniques of treatment, all of them attempts either to shorten treatment or make it more effective. Among these are studies of various physiological and psychological procedures by which the free flow of random associative material can be accelerated and maintained. There are studies of methods of manipulating the state of consciousness during analytic sessions, and of inducing and controlling the twilight state that lies between sleep and waking when the mind tends automatically to return to its own storm centers. There are also experiments on methods of deconditioning, that is, of breaking up destructive associative links.

Some of the most important research in the area of technique centers around the problem of *insight*. In Chapter V, Section 6, we pointed out that, in essence, insight is the patient's full understanding of the meaning of his own illness, and depends upon his ability to fill in essential memory gaps for both experience and feelings, whether recent or remote. This, in turn, makes it possible to appreciate the relationship between emotionally charged experiences and the structure and derivation of the personality and the neurotic symptoms. All of which is, however, merely the statement of a working hypothesis, not of a proven fact. Many fundamental problems concerning the role and efficacy of insight remain unsolved. Certain patients are cured almost miraculously through such insight as we have described, while others, in spite of similar insight, achieve little or no therapeutic relief. The reason for the difference is not yet clear. To say that in the latter case the insight was partial is an assumption, and not always verifiable. Furthermore, there is the alternate possibility that insight may not always work the same way. There may be illnesses in which a retrospective recovery of events and feelings is not effective, and for the relief of which one must in a sense turn back the hands of the clock and relive old experiences as though they were occurring in the present. This is sometimes achieved experimentally in hypnotically induced states of regression to those earlier ages in which the distorting experiences occurred. Nothing final can be said about these problems, except to indicate that the basic hypothesis of therapy through insight is an area of utmost importance for future psychoanalytic research (1965c, 1967d).

There are other more superficial but nonetheless significant studies of the effects of variations in details of analytic technique. As we have already indicated, such studies are meaningless unless they take care to vary only one factor at a time. A few examples will suffice as illustration: the sporadic and still inconclusive tests of the effects of varying the frequency and duration of individual sessions; the conduct of analytic sessions in solitude or in the presence of more than one analyst; experimental analysis in groups; the combination of ordinary analytic techniques with analytic processes in groups.

Of basic importance to not only technical but also clinical research is the development of methods of recording and reproducing the factual and observational data of psychoanalytic psychiatry. No science can progress beyond an elementary qualitative stage until its data can be recorded without distortion, reproduced for subsequent study by more than one observer, and subjected to detailed quantitative as well as qualitative evaluation. The introduction of such methods into the analytic situation creates complex difficulties. Some analysts feel that these difficulties make it impossible to employ any methods of mechanical recording for the reproduction of analytic experience. Such an attitude would hold up the progress of psychoanalytic science indefinitely and the use of continuous tape recordings and of sound film is slowly being tried out, both for investigative and for teaching purposes. This is the first step toward a comprehensive qualitative and quantitative analysis of random associative material. The entire apparatus of modern statistical methodology and machinery will some day be brought to bear on these problems. This, however, waits upon the development of the proper type of specialized research institutes for the study of the psychological and physiological manifestations of the neurotic process (1956b, 1969).

(b) *Clinical Research*

There have been as yet no systematic comparisons of the efficacy of any forms of analysis with different neurotic constellations, none, at least, that are statistically adequate, or which have been followed over a sufficiently long period of time. As a matter of fact, in order to carry on a comparative study of therapeutic results, it will be necessary to meet certain fundamental prerequisites, none of which are available today.

(1) In the first place, psychoanalysis must no longer be confined to the field of private practice, in which it was born and nurtured. Endowments are needed to

subsidize psychoanalytic studies in hospitals and medical schools, in educational institutions from the nursery school through the university, in social agencies and courts, in industry, and in special institutes for research in psychoanalytic psychiatry (1951a). Such research institutes must be built around treatment centers where selected types of neurotic illness can be analyzed without considering the ability of any individual to pay, so that systematic cultural-anthropological, socioeconomic, and psychoanalytic studies can be made on statistically adequate samples, both random and selected, and followed up over an adequate length of time.

(2) Comparative studies of the response of different neurotic constellations to the analytic process require as a preliminary step a careful re-examination and perhaps a basic reshuffling of currently accepted nosological categories. Such studies can be made only if they are carried on conjointly with neurophysiologists, clinical psychologists, sociologists, cultural anthropologists, and social workers, because this study will require the evaluation of physiological as well as psychological forces that produce and shape the neurotic process and their quantitative estimation, and these in turn must be related to the cultural mores and the socioeconomic forces in which the neurotic process has been developed.

(3) With the aid of clinical psychology we need to develop new testing instruments designed to provide us with quantitative data on the relative roles of con-

scious, preconscious, and unconscious processes in the lives of the patients who are under investigation, before, during, and after treatment. It will not be possible to make precise studies of either the etiological or therapeutic process until such techniques as these have been developed. Current qualitative indices must be supplemented by quantitative tools, which ultimately will be usable in practical clinical work as well as in research. Such studies are needed also to provide us with a clear definition of the relation between symptomatic neuroses and characterological neuroses, with special attention to that most difficult of all challenges to the analyst, namely, the need to induce characterological changes (see Chapter XVIII).

(c) *Theoretical Research*

Priority among theoretical studies should be given to weeding and pruning the overgrown garden of analytic concepts and terms. This is important in any verbal science which, like psychoanalysis, has developed swiftly and simultaneously in scattered lands and different tongues. The multiplication of partially overlapping and redundant concepts and terms is a source of great confusion in psychoanalytic thinking and tends to obstruct its further growth.

Areas of research in theory are almost infinite in their possibilities. There is not a single aspect of psychoanalytic theory that cannot be subjected to objective tests for verification or qualification. One might give as an example the film studies by René Spitz of the effect on infants of separation from the mother for varying periods of time and at varying ages. This was a first step toward an objective study of one of the basic problems of human development. The next step is to trace in those same infants the later fate of these experiences as manifested in articulate and inarticulate play, in conscious and unconscious fantasies, in physiology, in dreams, in personality, and finally in subsequent symptomatic history.

Analytical studies of the cultural anthropology of the ·neuroses are being made. It is dismaying that the *incidence* in our own population of not a single neurotic symptom has been established, much less that of the subtler neurotic personality distortions. We do not know what that incidence is in relation to age, economic or educational group, religious affiliations, national origins, or in relation to population-density, occupations, or the like. This lack of factual data should make us skeptical when we hear positive statements about the relative roles in the evolution of neurosis of cultural and environmental factors as opposed to genetic and biological forces. Heated arguments that anticipate factual information can never be more than an expression of bias.

This, then, is an area of research into fundamental theoretical concepts and working hypotheses that demands the coordinated efforts of sociologists, cultural anthropologists, clinical psychologists, and psychoanalytic psychiatrists in the study of random samples of all elements of our population. Such a project would include, naturally, a re-examination of the entire story of psychosexual development by teams of scientists who are adequately trained and mature enough to correct the errors made by the naive methods of Kinsey and his co-workers (1948c, 1955).

We do not even know today what correlation there is, if any, between the size of families and the incidence and development of neuroses. Data are needed on the variations in psychological development that arise out of different types of family constellations: e.g., family size, age and sex differences among children, separations from one or another parent at different age periods, the effects of illness, accident, and death, and the type of early birth and early nourishment. All of these variables and many others must some day be studied in terms of their influence on ultimate psychological development.

Finally, a test of the value of preventive psychiatry remains to be made. This would involve the selection of a stable and representative community in which every facility of modern psychiatry would be made available to an adequate random sample of the young couples who were about to marry or about to have children, providing psychiatric education and psychiatric treatment for both the children and adults. After ten or fifteen years these children could then be compared to a control group from the same community with respect to their adjustments in homes, schools, playgrounds, sports, and community as a whole, and as to the morbidity and mortality rates among them.

This is by no means an exhaustive list of all possible areas of psychoanalytic research. It is merely an effort to indicate some of the frontiers in which research can and should be carried out by unfettered scientists who would owe no immediate service either to students or to patients, but who would be psychologically free to pursue uncharted courses to unexpected and unpredictable truths. This is the way of scientific progress.

The Techniques of Scientific Controversy

In Chapter XVIII we quoted Claude Bernard's astute observation that scientists, like all human beings, suffer from vulnerability to bias. In addition to this internal source of error, scientists are not infrequently subjected to social pressures that may further warp intellectual judgments. Such external pressures are particularly strong in any science that stirs popular prejudices, or whose conclusions directly influence health and welfare. There are always some scientists who find it difficult to resist such pressures and who, wittingly or unwittingly, shape their scientific convictions to curry popular favor or to win the support of foundations. If scientists are human beings, analysts are no exception.

This flaw in human nature has played a significant role in the history of science. A gross example is the Russian controversy over genetics. Subtler manifestations of the influence of external pressure are seen in certain psychoanalytic controversies. Among these is the argument over the relative influence of cultural and biogenetic factors in the development of the

331

neuroses. Another is the disagreement over the value of briefer forms of psychotherapy or of attempts to treat large groups of people simultaneously (1973c). Pressures that arise from social needs can have both good and bad effects; they prevent complacency, but they may also lead men to make incautious claims. The mere fact that work is done under pressure does not of itself invalidate the work (witness the developments of radar and of atomic energy during World War II), but it adds immensely to the necessity for caution.

To be self-critical about research in therapy is harder than in any other field, because therapeutic research generates so much wishful thinking, both in the investigator and in the public waiting impatiently for help. When to this source of error is added a vigorous demand for quick and easy cures, the dangers of quick and easy research and of exaggerated claims are multiplied many times. None of these considerations lessens the importance of the attempt to find brief and economical forms of analytical therapy. They merely place on all who may undertake to do research in this difficult field the responsibility not to make popular claims until their findings have been checked repeatedly by their scientific peers and colleagues. This means that new departures in theory and technique should not be announced to the public in popular books and magazines before they have been presented in technical journals where their validity can be tested by other scientists. So important is this principle, that it is fair to say that the human value of scientific controversy depends on the scrupulousness with which conflicting claims are tested *before* they are presented to the laity. This is an essential social responsibility science has to society.

It is well to bear in mind that, like all human activities, research is born of emotions which are partially rooted in frustration. Sometimes this frustration arises from the work itself, sometimes from unrelated aspects of the scientist's life. The research impulse may be driven by domestic unhappiness or by personal rivalry and ambition or by a need to be important or by other human foibles, as well as by larger and more generous human aspirations. If each notion is immediately proclaimed as a great new discovery which will solve all problems and cure all ills, the unconscious emotional forces that infused the research are likely to warp the intellectual processes, with the result that the research itself and the subsequent scientific controversy will become a source of popular confusion. If, on the other hand, the scientist's findings are subjected to clinical or experimental tests before they are broadcast to the public, the conscious and unconscious sources of the investigator's activities remain a matter of private concern to the investigator alone. Therefore, society should leave science alone, in the sense that it must not warp the truth either with prejudice or with undue urgency; and, in return, science must leave society undisturbed by its internal controversies, putting forth no unproven claims to a waiting and needy world. The more urgent the human need, the more silent should

333

be the scientist. Atomic energy was not released by a war of words in the popular press.

Violations of this elementary principle have marred in some measure the history of psychoanalysis. Controversy as such has not been any more frequent or more heated here than in other scientific fields. Equally violent feuds have arisen in physics and chemistry, or about so seemingly innocent a question as whether certain blood cells arise from one type of parent cell or from two. Whenever such controversies directly influence the treatment of sick people, the public follows them with an intense interest. Consequently, in matters of health, a public parade of controversy does more harm than it would over issues which are more abstract and remote. To dissent is healthy. It is not the fact of psychoanalytic controversy, but the manner and manners of it that have been deplorable; it is a sin against man and against science to parade dissension publicly and to proclaim oneself a new analytic messiah, thereby gathering proselytes who must of necessity come largely from the uncritical laity. We would do better to follow the example set by Freud who worked for ten years in almost total obscurity before the impact of his work was felt by the scientific world at large.

Chapter XXVII

THE HOMUNCULAR FALLACIES, THE REIFICATION OF ABSTRACTIONS, AND QUANTITATIVE FALLACIES

The analyst and the sophisticated layman are justified in speaking of the *processes* by which we distinguish between the "I" and the "non-I" worlds, and also of those processes by which interactions are made possible between the two, the processes by which we empathize and identify with others and by which we evaluate and criticize ourselves, whether consciously or unconsciously or both. We are not entitled to speak of abstractions called *"the ego"* or *"the id"* or *"the superego."* We can, however, speak of ego processes, of id processes, and of conscience processes, including the self-evaluating processes. All three of these have conscious, preconscious, and unconscious components. The processes of self-evaluation add up to the "superego processes," but not to *"a superego."* We make precisely the same error whenever we speak of *"the ego,"* instead of the subtle and complex constellation of processes that, together, make up a person, his individuating qualities, and especially the processes by

335

which he interacts and exchanges with the outside world—i.e., all of the processes by which he relates to the non-I world—whether by acts of cognitive symbolic communication, of affective expression, or by the interchange of the stuffs essential to the individual's survival, i.e., the interchange of body temperatures, or the interchange of cellular and chemical elements that subserve the continuation of the species. These again do not give us the right to subdivide this abstraction ("the personality" or "the ego") into fragmentary ingredients, to each of which we then attribute a variety of qualities, quantities (1947b), powers, and functions. Such a fragmentation of the personality into homunculi, into little men within the whole man, is reminiscent of the mythological bacteriology, physiology, and psychology of the seventeenth, eighteenth and even the nineteenth centuries. It is a sad error but no accident that, especially in their earlier years, psychoanalytic metaphors made use of such anthropomorphic thinking, with all of its attendant fallacies. It is also no accident that, in the same early phase of its development, psychoanalytic theory (whether orthodox or deviant) borrowed concepts of mass and energy and force from hydraulic engineering, electricity, mathematics, and physics, concepts that had been useful if sometimes misleading even in their own fields, but were wholly erroneous when misused in the effort not merely to describe human psychology but also to explain it.

The concepts of "internalization" and "incorporation" are gustatory metaphors. By such inept trans-plantations, even the most "elegant" metaphors can lead to the most inelegant, misleading, and question-begging pseudoexplanations.

This traps us in a different dilemma. It is literally impossible to think or to ruminate or to communicate about the imponderables in any such field as human psychology without using metaphors and figures of speech. As I have often said, it is relatively safe to do this if we are careful to use them only as verbal graphs, as descriptive diagrams with which to make our ab-stractions more understandable by projecting them in condensed forms, almost like the visual imagery of a dream. But this implies that we must always keep clearly in mind the fact that they are only artifices and not, strictly speaking, theories or working hypotheses at all. In short, they can be used safely as *adjectives but never as nouns.* As a matter of fact, the moment we use them as nouns (which means as objects in their own right) we land ourselves in a verbal and logical morass. Year by year psychoanalysis has been getting into deeper trouble with nouns. Adjectives are far safer. Let us stick to them.

One expression of this has been in the development of splinter groups, each consisting of pseudo hetero-doxies, but each facing exactly the same troubles as do the orthodoxies; each group tends to forget that the same dilemma applies equally to the theoretical con-structs of the heterodox group as to strictly "orthodox" Freudian psychoanalysis. To use concepts such as *"the*

libido," with the assumption that this is an independent form of energy, explaining variations in behavior,
is only saying in pseudoscientific, metaphorical language precisely what the man on the street says when
he declares that someone ran away "because" he was
afraid, or that someone committed murder "because"
he was angry, or that someone committed rape "because" he was oversexed, or that someone did something over and over again "because he had a habit,"
without realizing that in each case the argument has
become circular. No one has yet solved this dilemma,
and I do not presume to think I have been more
successful than others.

Nor must we overlook the fact that Freud's own
model of the mental apparatus was derived (as at that
time it had to be) from a misuse of the metaphors of
hydraulic and mechanical engineering describing the
new phenomenology of electricity current in his day.
This misled Freud into thinking of "instinctual" energy
and libido as if it were a fluid electrical current which
could be dammed up, diverted, and accumulated,
which could overflow its banks, break through dams,
etc. A few years later it misled Adolf Meyer into an
equally fallacious nosological system of "The Ergasias"
(i.e. "Ergs"). For Freud and Meyer these became
explanatory principles and not merely descriptive
figures of speech. Such concepts are no longer permis-
sible, nor are any of the more recent "structural"
metaphors, so popular today.

Furthermore if there is no such thing as "the ego,"

there can be no such think as *ego* psychology or *ego* analysis; and since these concepts are neither valid nor helpful as descriptive devices, I cannot use such an anthropomorphic phrase as "regression in the service of the ego" or a "conflict-free sphere of the ego," although both of these are popular clichés in the current language of psychoanalysis. Let me repeat that we must challenge ourselves to think in terms of wholes and not of parts, to think of the personality as a whole and not of *the* Ego or *the* Id, or *the* Superego. We can speak of ego processes, id processes, superego processes, if we always remember that these abstractions are useful only so long as we restrict them to characterizing and describing a sum total of those aspects of human behavior which must work harmoniously together if a man is to live at all, to interact livably with his environment, and to survive with any degree of peace and happiness. From time to time I have to allude to some of these newer verbal metaphors of psychoanalysis, but this leads me to the further hope that, although I cannot avoid dealing with some of these obscurities of analytical writing, the net effect of my critical re-evaluation of our language will be a move toward clarification and simplification not only in language, but also of our thinking.

The elimination of overlapping, redundant, and contradictory concepts is similar to pruning and weeding an overgrown jungle. It makes it possible to see the trees again, as well as the woods, and to view their sturdy trunks with all the respect and reverence due to one of the great creations of the human mind. For none of the true greatness of Freud's insights into human nature is diminished by weeding out the tangled *verbal* underbrush that hides their roots and giant trunks.

Chapter XXVIII

ERRORS IN PERCEPTIONS, IN SEQUENCES, AND IN INTERPRETATIONS

Freud was a gifted and precise clinical observer. The complex phenomena he observed and described are, in general, incontrovertible; but unless the sequences of events are accurately observed and recorded, no interpretations of their interdependence can be accurate except by accident. Accuracy about sequences does not *guarantee* the accuracy of deductions as to casual chains; but any inaccuracy about sequences certainly guarantees the inaccuracy of any efforts to establish interdependent relationships. The fact that B follows A *can* mean that A causes B, but *only if this sequence is invariable*. If B does *not* follow A, then A cannot have caused B. This is why accuracy in the perception, recall, recording, and reporting of sequences is essential if these are to provide us with the basic clinical data for interrelationships we hope to establish. Psychoanalysis itself has taught us to respect human fallibility in precisely these processes, and we have no right to expect basic new advances in psychoanalytic theory and technique until we have schooled ourselves to use new audiovisual instruments to replace and correct

341

man's fallible and unaided perceptions, recall, and reporting (1958b, 1969; Geerstma & Mackie, 1969). Even when the phenomena Freud observed are incontrovertible, the accuracy of their recording, sampling, ordering, and interpretation depends upon a precision of which the human mental apparatus is inherently incapable. Because adequate gadgetry for recording, reproducing, and sampling human perceptions was lacking in those days, what Freud observed and reported had to depend upon the selective processes of his fallible recall of his fallible perceptions; and we in turn have had to depend upon his fallible reports of these fallible recollections. Yet the essence of what he has taught us through psychoanalysis and the essence of what we have learned (or at least should have learned) is that human perceptions, human memory, the retrieval and recapture of bits of experience, and their symbolic representation and reporting are all vulnerable to error. Fallible reports of fallible, weighted samples of fallible recollections of fallible perceptions are hardly a sound foundation on which to build any science. The wonder is that we have been able to build at all. *Freud tacitly acknowledged this when he wrote down his own dreams!*

The future of psychoanalysis (and indeed of all psychologies) depends inescapably on the use of gadgets which increase the accuracy and dependability of each of these steps. Inevitably every such gadget introduces its own errors. But this is true throughout the history of all sciences. Drawing a sample of blood from a vein introduced errors we had to learn to recognize, to limit, to render constant, and then to correct. Similarly, the microscope introduced errors we had to recognize, acknowledge, standardize, and correct.

In psychoanalysis, such corrections require special precision in the use of concepts and in the use of words for the formulation of useful hypotheses concerning the interdependent relationships among the clinical phenomena which are observed. Great as Freud was as a clinician he was not always as free from confusion in his use of theoretical concepts. He was if anything too fluent, and this fluency and the fact that he rarely rewrote has often been mistaken for clarity; but there is no single paper or book of Freud's that could not benefit from condensation, pruning, editing, and reorganization. This of course is equally true for Anna Freud (and for all of us). It is about time that we paid to both of them the ultimate, high tribute of abandoning exaggeration in our evaluations of their enormous contributions.

We can confidently expect a new era in psychoanalysis (and indeed in all experimental and clinical psychologies) when we begin regularly to use audiovisual instruments to correct and supplement our fallible, unaided perceptions, our fallible memories, our fallible processes of retrieval and sampling, and our fallible reporting. We do Freud no service and we pay him no tribute when we pretend that he was immune to the psychological vulnerabilities to which all mankind is prone. His greatness does not require that we attribute to him an infallibility which no human being can claim.

Chapter XXIX
A RESUMÉ OF FALLACIES

One of the remarkable features of Freud's lifework has been the fact that his contributions to human culture in general and to our understanding of the dynamics of normal and pathological psychology have survived in spite of subtle fallacies in his language and logic. It has been our great good fortune that this happened. How it happened should someday be the target of special research by some uncompromising analyst trained in philology and dedicated to the clarification of analytic language and thought. In such an investigation, the first step will have to be a systematic recording of the fallacies themselves; a few of which I will cite here, as fragmentary examples.

(1) All considerations of human psychological phenomena deal perforce with items we cannot measure, but about the variations of which we have to think, speak, and write. Therefore, we are forced to use quantitative metaphors, analogies, and figures of speech borrowed from the so-called "hard sciences," where bits of data can be counted and measured. So in psychology, the man in the street, the experimental and clinical psychologist, the ethologist, and the analyst talk *as if* they can count and measure, and *as if*

they have measured phenomenology, which actually remains unmeasurable. As I have noted, we must thus rely upon descriptive metaphors, which renders us vulnerable to recurrent fallacies.

Furthermore, the very words we use must be carefully scrutinized because they can be used in several different senses in the same study. This lands us in additional difficulties. Such an innocent word as "balance" is an example: we speak of a "balanced" person or personality, of emotional "balance," or the "Vital Balance" (Menninger, 1963). Obviously these are only figurative. They are useful to describe the feeling they give us; but they are not explanatory. They characterize goals rather than processes. Furthermore, they tend also to obscure the fact that, although we think that we are characterizing someone *else*, what we are really saying is, "This man does not upset *me*. He does not make *me* feel unbalanced. Therefore *he* must be 'balanced.'" This is what I have in mind when I say that much of our quantitative language, as applied in psychology and especially in psychoanalysis, consists of observations interlocking with projections of *our own* inner affects.

Consider this in relation to the late Walter Cannon's sophisticated concept of homeostasis. It can be used to characterize specific clusters of biochemical processes (1948a, 1956a). On the other hand it can also be misused to explain differences in behavioral patterns. Here, the multiple dangers of metaphors become clear.

These fallacies have led to difficulties in formulations by Freud's followers and his critics. They have therefore been a source of error in Freud's own writings and also in those of many of his followers (viz. Rapaport and Hartmann), and equally in the formulations of such critics as Linus Pauling, Horney, Rado, Sullivan, etc. It has been one of the weakest points in the logic of "orthodox" Freudian psychoanalysis, and in all of the "heterodox" deviations. Of course analysts are not alone in these errors.

(2) A further confusion arises when a metaphor is misused as though it were a working hypothesis, i.e., a scientific theory that could be subjected to experimental test and verification. For example, the so-called structural "theory" is not in fact a theory or working hypothesis at all, but a metaphor, a figure of speech, an analogic image. As pointed out before, if used solely to diagram our thinking, such metaphors are relatively harmless, but the moment explanatory values are ascribed to them they become misleading verbal shortcuts.

(3) Another troublesome fallacy results when the misuse of metaphors leads directly to the reification of abstractions, to which we then and incorrectly attribute qualitative and quantitative variables. Thereupon, their use is no longer restricted to descriptive purposes, but is as though they furnished us with valid explanatory principles.

(4) Moreover, the reification of abstractions leads to anthropomorphisms to which further qualitative and quantitative variables are attributed in our attempts to

find in them explanations of variations in behavior, when at best they can furnish us only with approximate and analogic descriptions of such variations.

(5) This leads to still another misleading fallacy, which I have called the homuncular fallacy; i.e., the fragmentation of the personality into psychological units to which we attribute qualitative and quantitative variations which, insofar as they are valid at all, are valid only for the *Gesamt Personlichkeit* (Alexander, 1930). We become still more deeply mired if in our search for explanations we treat each such hypothetical fragment as an entity with an independent "power-pack" of its own.

(6) In turn, this is closely interwoven with still another confusion; i.e., the tendency to transplant from the "hard sciences" concepts of quantitative change that are only partially valid even for the hard sciences themselves. We encounter this constantly in the misuse of such pseudoexplanatory concepts as are expressed in the term "sublimation" in the "economic" principle itself, in fantasies about "strong" and "weak" egos, strong and weak libidinal cathexes and investments, etc. (1962b). These figures of speech, borrowed (or should I say stolen?) from the language and concepts of high finance, would be amusing if they did not lead us to believe that by their use we have explained changes that we have at best only described with a certain poetic feeling. We fall into the same error when we assume that such abstract descriptive

metaphors as "sadism," "masochism," and "narcissism" are *forces* that can vary quantitatively.

(7) Out of these errors grow another pair of familiar fallacies. In addition to the familiar *post-hoc-ergo-propter-hoc* fallacy, it leads to teleological fallacies in their most banal forms: to wit, if *B* follows *A*, not only must *A* have caused *B* (even if the sequence is not invariable—a gross *post-hoc* fallacy); and not only does it make the error of assuming that hypothetical variations in the *amount of B* measure hypothetical variations in *amounts of A*; but it also assumes that *A must have had the causing of B and of variations in B as its major purpose*, whether this purpose was conscious or unconscious. This teleological lapse is one of the most serious of all of Freud's conceptual and linguistic fallacies. It is what makes serious errors of the accepted misapplications of such concepts as masochism and sadism.

(8) There are also some glaring sins of omission, most notably the absence of any clear exploration of the true nature of psychological change, and the even more glaring omission of any criteria of change in the psychological sphere (1968a).

(9) Set in this jungle of verbal and logical fallacies we find just *one* recurring and serious clinical error, which we dare not pass over in silence; i.e., Freud's proneness to make extrapolations and generalizations from a single clinical example.

(10) Finally and unhappily, Freud, like Jung, often

tried to convince merely by repetition. This led him to use many redundant, and overlapping phrases and concepts. Because of these redundancies, analytical literature resembles nothing so much as a jungle in desperate need of weeding.

Finally I must return to the most tantalizing and important questions of all: to wit, how in spite of these errors has psychoanalysis been able to make such a major contribution to human culture? And how can psychoanalysis now be freed for further progress by ridding itself of these entrenched flaws?

Chapter XXX

THE ROLE OF PSYCHOANALYSIS
IN THE EVOLUTION
OF HUMAN CULTURE

We turn next to the impact of psychoanalysis on the cultural scene. Nothing man ever undertakes is more difficult than just being a human being, unless it is the struggle of the fallible human adult to bring up the vulnerable human child. Man has been at these two tasks for many eons, yet he is only beginning to perceive and to admit how difficult and how unsolved are the problems that attend them. He has learned that with every step of growth and maturation, beginning with the acquisition of the symbolic process and symbolic language, an impairment of his freedom for further change begins (1974a). This starts subtly in infancy. Life thereafter, and psychotherapy, become an unremitting struggle to recover that freedom, which is in essence the freedom to change (1968a) and to go on changing. Psychoanalysis, in spite of its many flaws, is a major effort to find out *why* this occurs, why freedom is so easy to lose and so difficult to regain. Secondarily, psychoanalysis is not only an attempt to understand this, but also to deal with it. In fact, the

351

greatest potential future contribution of psychoanalytic psychiatry to human culture may well evolve precisely out of the psychoanalytic study of this problem and of our consequent failures as human beings, parents, teachers, and therapists. Psychoanalytic psychiatry alone among our cultural instruments has set itself the task of studying this phenomenon humbly and in earnest, and without pretending to know the answers before it has studied them. In this basic sense, psychoanalysis will be to the evolution and maturation of human culture what the clinical pathological conference has been to the maturation of medicine. It is this objective that makes of modern, dynamic, and, especially, psychoanalytic psychiatry the bridge between the "hard" sciences and the humanities (1966c, 1973b).

Freud himself, when stalled, made perhaps his greatest mistake by turning to a search not for new techniques, but for new theories. Unhappily, his followers have fallen into the same trap. Yet, new theories or new metaphors will merely mask old failures and cannot help us forward. Progress will not come from new theories, even when these are sounder than the old. Instead, sounder theories should evolve from greater dependability of primary data, which, as I have written, have for too long relied upon unaided perception, sampling, recall, and report. Progress must depend also upon a more precise use of language in which to report this primary data.

Another challenging mystery is not peculiar to psychoanalysis, but has been recognized as true for all of medicine; namely, the fact that therapeutic successes or failures do not provide dependable evidence for the accuracy or inaccuracy of a theory. All applications of the biological sciences to the problems of human health and illness have to take into account so many simultaneous variables that there is no constant or easily predictable correlation between the accuracy of a theory and the therapeutic results achieved by its applications. This is true of any form of treatment. Cod-liver oil was valuable for human growth and bone metabolism, but *not* for the reasons originally adduced before the role of vitamins had been recognized.

One could cite countless other examples from somatic medicine and from every form of psychiatric therapy (e.g., electroconvulsive treatment, modern psychotropic drugs, pharmacotherapy, the older fever therapy, "Dauerschlaf," the treatments based on the conditioned reflex, on operational conditioning, etc., and especially from psychoanalysis, where success and failure of our therapeutic efforts seem at times to bear only an accidental relationship to the accuracy or inaccuracy of theoretical constructions). It is undeniable that psychoanalysis has its share of both successes and failures; but this obvious fact should lead directly not to the formulation of new theories, but to an unsparing review of the logical strengths, weaknesses, and fallacies of our modes of thought and speech and, especially, of our techniques.

Despite the criticisms I have expressed, I remain

convinced that psychoanalysis is one of man's greatest sources of hope for ultimate success in his battle to solve many of our most baffling human and cultural problems. Yet, if such answers are ever to be found, we must start by facing the fact that many profound mysteries remain unsolved.

REFERENCES

Alexander, F. (1930), *The Psychoanalysis of the Total Personality: The Application of Freud's Theory of the Ego to the Neuroses.* New York: Nervous and Mental Disease Publishing Company.

Alexander, F., et al. (1946), *Psychoanalytic Therapy.* New York: Ronald Press.

Brenman, M. & Gill, M. (1947), *Hypnotherapy.* New York: International Universities Press.

Dement, W. C. (1972), *Some Must Sleep While Some Must Watch.* Stanford, Calif.: The Portable Stanford.

Ferenczi, S. (1919), On the technique of psycho-analysis. In: *Further Contributions to Psychoanalysis.* New York: Basic Books, 1952, pp. 177-189.

———— (1921), The further development of an active therapy in psychoanalysis. In: *Further Contributions to Psychoanalysis.* New York: Basic Books, 1952, pp. 198-217.

Fisher, C. (1965), Psychoanalytic implications of recent research on sleep and dreaming. *J. Amer. Psychoanal. Assn.,* 13:197-303.

Freud, S. (1900), Interpretation of dreams. *Standard Edition,* 4 & 5. London: Hogarth Press, 1953.

———— (1927), The question of lay-analysis. *Standard Edition,* 20:179-258. London: Hogarth Press, 1959.

Geertsma, R. H. & Mackie, J. B., eds. (1969), *Studies in Self-Cognition: Techniques of Video-tape Self-Observation in the Behavioral Sciences.* Baltimore, Md.: Williams & Wilkins.

Healy, W. (1917), *Mental Conflict cnd Misconduct.* Boston: Little, Brown.

Kubie, L. (1930), A theoretical application to some neurological problems of the properties of excitation waves which move in closed circuits. *Brain,* 53:166-178.

———— (1934), Relation of the conditioned reflex to psychoanalytic technique. *Arch. Neurol. & Psychiat.,* 32:430-435.

———— (1941a), Book Review: Pavlov and His School by Y. P. Frolov. *Psychoanal. Quart.,* 10:329-339.

———— (1941b), The repetitive core of neurosis. *Psychoanal. Quart.,* 10:23-43.

———— (1942a), Review Pavlov, I.: Lectures on conditioned reflexes. Vol. 2: Conditioned reflexes and psychiatry. *Psychoanal. Quart.*, 11:565-570.

———— (1942b), The organization of a psychiatric service for a general hospital. *Psychosom. Med.*, 4:252-272.

———— (1945), The value of induced dissociated states in the therapeutic process. *Proc. Royal Soc. Med.*, 38:681-683.

———— (1947a), Elements in the medical curriculum which are essential in the training for psychotherapy. In: *Transactions of the First Conference on Training in Clinical Psychology*, ed. M. R. Harrower. New York: Josiah Macy, Jr. Foundation, pp. 46-54.

———— (1947b), The fallacious use of quantitative concepts in dynamic psychology. *Psychoanal. Quart.*, 16:507-518.

———— (1947c), The impact of modern psychiatry on medical education, medical practice and hospital organization. *Bull. Johns Hopkins Hospital*, 80:348-360.

————(1947d), Psychoanalysis—costly fad or boon to mankind: Reply to Monsignor Fulton J. Sheen. *The New York Herald Tribune*, April 20, 1947, Sect. II, p. 7.

———— (1948a), Instincts and homeostasis. *Psychosom. Med.*, 10:15-30.

———— (1948b), Medical responsibility for training in clinical psychology. *J. Clin. Psychol.*, 5:94-100.

———— (1948c), Psychiatric implications of the Kinsey Report. In: *Sexual Behavior in American Society; An Appraisal of the First Two Kinsey Reports*, ed. J. Himelhoch and S. F. Fava. New York: Norton, 1955, pp. 270-293.

———— (1950), The dilemma of the analyst in a troubled world. *Bull. Amer. Psychoanal. Assn.*, 6:1-4.

———— (1951a), Husband-wife. In: *The People in Your Life*, ed. M. M. Hughes. New York: Knopf, pp. 28-63.

———— (1951b), The neurotic potential, the neurotic process, and the neurotic state. *U.S. Armed Forces Med. J.*, 2:1-12.

———— (1951c), A reply to a reply. *Bull. Amer. Psychoanal. Assn.*, 7:146-147.

———— (1952a), The child's fifth freedom. In: *Our Children Today*, ed. S. M. Gruenberg. New York: Viking, pp. 136-146.

———— (1952b), The independent institute. *Bull. Amer. Psychoanal. Assn.*, 8:205-208.

———— (1952c), Problems and techniques of psychoanalytic validation and progress. In: *Psychoanalysis as Science*, ed. E. Pumpian-Mindlin. Stanford, Calif.: Stanford University Press, pp. 46-124.

_____ (1954a), The forgotten man of education. *Harvard Alumni Bull.*, 56:349-353.

_____ (1954b), The fundamental nature of the distinction between normality and neurosis. *Psychoanal. Quart.*, 23:167-204.

_____ (1954c), The pros and cons of a new profession: A doctorate in medical psychology. In: *Medical and Psychological Teamwork in the Care of the Chronically Ill*, ed. M. Harrower. Springfield, Ill.: Charles C Thomas, pp. 125-170.

_____ (1954d), Psychiatric and psychoanalytic considerations of the problems of consciousness. In: *Brain Mechanisms and Consciousness*. Oxford, England: Blackwell Scientific Publishers, 1954, pp. 444-469.

_____ (1955), Dr. Kinsey and the medical profession: A review of *Sexual Behavior in the Human Female*. *Psychosom. Med.*, 17:172-184.

_____ (1956a), Influence of symbolic processes on the role of instincts in human behavior. *Psychosom. Med.*, 18:189-208.

_____ (1956b), An institute for basic research in psychiatry. *Bull. Menninger Clinic*, 20:281-287.

_____ (1956c), Psychoanalysis and marriage: Practical and theoretical issues. In: *Neurotic Interaction in Marriage*, ed. V. W. Eisenstein. New York: Basic Books, pp. 10-43.

_____ (1956d), Some unsolved problems of psychoanalytic psychotherapy. In: *Progress in Psychotherapy*, Vol. 1, ed. F. Fromm-Reichmann and J. L. Moreno. New York: Grune & Stratton, pp. 87-102.

_____ (1956e), The use of psychoanalysis as a research tool. *Research Reports*, 6:112-136.

_____ (1957), The need for a new subdiscipline in the medical profession. *Arch. Neurol. & Psychiat.*, 78:283-293.

_____ (1958a), *Neurotic Distortion of the Creative Process*. New York: Noonday Press, 1969.

_____ (1958b), Research into the process of supervision in psychoanalysis. *Psychoanal. Quart.*, 27:226-236.

_____ (1958c), Some theoretical concepts underlying the relationship between individual and group psychotherapies. *International J. Group Psychother.*, 8:3-19.

_____ (1959), The relation of the conditioned reflex to the preconscious functions: *Transactions of the 84th Annual Meeting of the American Neurological Association, Atlantic City, June 15-17*, pp. 187-188.

‗‗‗‗ (1960), Psychoanalysis and scientific methods. *J. Nerv. & Ment. Dis.*, 131:495-512.

‗‗‗‗ (1962a), The concept of dream deprivation: A critical analysis. *Psychosom. Med.*, 24:62-65.

‗‗‗‗ (1962b), The fallacious misuse of the concept of sublimation. *Psychoanal. Quart.*, 16:73-79.

‗‗‗‗ (1962c), Letter to the editor: In defense of psychoprobing. *New York Herald Tribune*, July 8, 1962.

‗‗‗‗ (1963a), Medicine as a spiritual challenge. *J. Religion & Health*, 3:39-55.

‗‗‗‗ (1963b), Editorial: Missing and wanted: Heterodoxy in psychiatry and psychoanalysis. *J. Nerv. & Ment. Dis.*, 137:311.

‗‗‗‗ (1963c), Neurosis and normality. In: *The Encyclopedia of Mental Health*, Vol. 4, ed. A. Deutsch. New York: Watts, pp. 1346-1353.

‗‗‗‗ (1964a), The challenge of divorce. *J. Nerv. & Ment. Dis.*, 138:511, 512.

‗‗‗‗ (1964b), Editorial: The changing economics of psychotherapeutic practice. *J. Nerv. & Ment. Dis.*, 139:311-312.

‗‗‗‗ (1964c), Provisions for the care of children of divorced parents: A new legal instrument. *Yale Law J.*, 73:1197-1200.

‗‗‗‗ (1964d), Research in protecting preconscious functions in education; Papers and reports from the ASDC Seventh Curriculum Research Institute, held in Washington, D.C. on December 2, 1961. Transactions published by the Association in April, 1964, pp. 28-42.

‗‗‗‗ (1964e), A school of psychological medicine within the framework of a medical school and university. *J. Med. Educ.*, 39(5).

‗‗‗‗ (1965a), Critique: Eysenck, Hans, J.: The effects of psychotherapy. *Internat. J. Psychiat.*, 1:175-178.

‗‗‗‗ (1965b), The cultural significance of psychiatry: The potential contribution of psychiatry to the struggles of the human spirit. Annual meeting of the Friends Hospital. Distributed by Publication Office, Friends Hospital.

‗‗‗‗ (1965c), The struggle between preconscious insights and psychonoxious rewards in psychotherapy. *Amer. J. Psychother.*, 19:365-371.

‗‗‗‗ (1966a), Editorial book review: Percival Bailey; *Sigmund the Unserene. J. Nerv. & Mental Dis.*, 412:393-394.

REFERENCES

_____ (1966b), An example of psychotic disorganization arising in early childhood out of a prepsychotic neurosis. *Amer. J. Psychother.*, 20:615-626.

_____ (1966c), A look into the future of psychiatry. *Ment. Hygiene*, 50:611-617.

_____ (1966d), Psychosis: A logical outcome of the neurotic "chain reaction." *Frontiers of Hosp. Psychiat.*, 3:6-8.

_____ (1966e), A reconsideration of thinking, the dream process and "the dream." *Psychoanal. Quart.*, 35:191-198.

_____ (1967a), The overall manpower problem in mental health personnel. *J. Nerv. & Ment. Dis.*, 144:466-470.

_____ (1967b), The overall manpower problem and the creation of a new discipline: The nonmedical psychotherapist. In: *Mental Health Manpower*, Vol. 2. California Medical Education and Research Foundation, pp. 112-120.

_____ (1967c), The relation of psychotic disorganization to the neurotic process. *J. Amer. Psychoanal. Assn.*, 15:626-640.

_____ (1967d), The utilization of preconscious functions in education. In: *Behavioral Science Frontiers in Education*, ed. E. M. Bower and W. G. Hollister. New York: Wiley, pp. 90-109.

_____ (1968a), The nature of psychological change and its relation to cultural change. In: *Psychoanalysis and Contemporary Science*, Vol. 1, ed. R. R. Holt and E. Peterfreund. New York: Macmillan, pp. 25-37.

_____ (1968b), Pitfalls of community psychiatry. *Arch. Gen. Psychiat.*, 18:11-28.

_____ (1968c), The psychotherapeutic ingredient in the learning process. In: *The Role of Learning in Psychotherapy*, ed. R. Porter. London: Churchill, pp. 224-232.

_____ (1968d), Unsolved problems in the resolution of the transference. *Psychoanal. Quart.*, 37:331-352.

_____ (1969), Some aspects of the significance to psychoanalysis of the exposure of a patient to the televised audiovisual reproduction of his activities. *J. Nerv. & Ment. Dis.*, 148:301-309.

_____ (1970a), The psychoanalytic relationship as a corrective model for all medical relationships. *Canad. Psychiat. Assn. J.*, 15:549-555.

_____ (1970b), The retreat from patients. *Internat. J. Psychiat.*, 9:693-711.

_____ (1971a), A doctorate in psychotherapy: The reasons for a new profession. In: *New Horizon for Psychotherapy*, ed. R. R. Holt. New York: International Universities Press, pp. 11-36.

_____ (1971b), Multiple fallacies in the concept of schizophrenia. In: *Problems of Psychosis*, Part 2, ed. Doucet et al. The Hague: Excerpta Medica, pp. 301-311.

_____ (1972a), Illusion and reality in the study of sleep, hypnosis, psychosis and arousal. *Internat. J. Clin. & Exper. Hypnosis*, 20:205-223.

_____ (1972b), The nature of psychological change and its relation to cultural change. In: *Psychoanalysis and Contemporary Science*, Vol. 1, ed. R. R. Holt and E. Peterfreund. New York: Macmillan, pp. 25-37.

_____ (1973a), The process of evaluation of therapy in psychiatry: Critical influence of the timing of the assessment on its outcome. *Arch. Gen. Psychiat.*, 28:880-884.

_____ (1973b), Psychiatry as a Bridge Between the Humanities and the Hard Sciences, lecture presented to the Tudor and Stuart Club, Jan. 1973. Unpublished.

_____ (1973c), Unsolved Problems in the Use of Group Processes in Psychotherapy. *J. Nerv. Ment. Dis.*, 157:650-676.

_____ (1974a), Impairment of the freedom to change through the acquisition of the symbolic process. *The Psychoanalytic Study of the Child*, 29:257-265. New Haven: Yale University Press.

_____ (1974b), The nature of the neurotic process. In: *American Handbook of Psychiatry*, Vol. 3, ed. S. Arieti. New York: Basic Books, pp. 3-16.

_____ (in press), The language tools of psychoanalysis: A search for better tools drawn from better models. *Internat. J. Psycho-Anal.*

_____ & Kubie, R. H. (1948), Destructive personalities. *J. Appl. Anthropol.*, 7:36-40.

_____ & Margolin, S. (1944), The process of hypnotism and the nature of the hypnotic state. *Amer. J. Psychiat.*, 100:611-622.

_____ _____ (1945), The therapeutic role of drugs in the process of repression, dissociation and synthesis. *Psychosom. Med.*, 7:147-151.

Lewin, B. D. & Ross, H. (1960), *Psychoanalytic Education in the United States*. New York: Norton.

References

Menninger, K. (1963), *The Vital Balance: The Life Process in Mental Health and Illness*. New York: The Viking Press.

Szasz, T. (1961), *The Myth of Mental Illness*. New York: Dell, 1967.

Zilboorg, G. (1943), *Mind, Medicine and Man*. New York: Harcourt, Brace.